To the Students of
Concordia University
with warm regards

[signature]

I COR. 4:20

Against
the Grain

Against the Grain

Reflections of A Rebel Republican

Mark O. Hatfield

As told to Diane N. Solomon

WHITE CLOUD PRESS
Ashland, Oregon

FIRST PRINTING: 2001

Cover Design by David Ruppe
Cover photographs by Visko Hatfield and Larry Geddis

Photo credits for interior section:
Courtesy *The Oregonian*, p. 1 top; p. 4, bottom; p. 5 top; p. 6 middle and bottom;
p. 7; p. 8 top. Courtesy Willamette University–Mark O. Hatfield Library
Archives, p., 1 bottom; p. 3; p. 4, top and middle; p. 5 bottom. Mark and
Antoinette Hatfield personal collection, p. 2. Courtesy Gerry Frank, p. 6 top;
p. 8 bottom.

Printed in Canada

Library of Congress Cataloging-in-Publication Data
Hatfield, Mark O., 1922-
    Against the grain : reflections of a rebel Republican / Mark O. Hatfield, as
told to Diane N. Solomon.
        p. cm.
    Includes index.
    ISBN 1-883991-36-6
        1. Hatfield, Mark O., 1922- 2. Legislators--United States--Biography.
3. United States. Congress. Senate--Biography. 4. United States--Politics and
government--1945-1989. 5. United States--Politics and government--1989-.
I. Solomon, Diane N. II. Title.

E840.8.H3 A3 2001
327.73'092--dc21
[B]
                                                                2001017731

CONTENTS

DEDICATION

To Travis Cross.

Our lives were joined at an early age in Salem's First Baptist Church, and we rekindled our friendship at Stanford University, where we created the strategy and plan for a political career which would span almost half a century. We shared the joys and griefs of each other's lives—as well as the successes. Travis, to this day, helps shape my thinking, and his creative genius in the world of politics is unsurpassed. In honoring him, I also offer thanks to the many other faithful staff members who walked with me through joys and challenges. Together they have enriched my life and made politics both dynamic and rewarding.

AUTHORS' ACKNOWLEDGMENTS

A work such as this requires a history, a history filled with those who dedicated themselves in countless ways along the path. It would be impossible to list all the staff and volunteers who devoted themselves indefatigably to our work. May each and every one of them, past and present, know my deep gratitude.

To my colleagues as well—Wayne Morse, Bob Packwood, Wendall Wyatt, John Dellenback, Bob Duncan, Edith Green, Les AuCoin, Elizabeth Furse, Peter DeFazio, Ron Wyden, Bob Smith, Denny Smith, Mike Kopetski, to name but a few—I offer great thanks.

During the writing process, the Oregon Historical Society, the Multnomah County Central Library, and the Oregonian Library provided invaluable and tireless assistance. The Oregonian, especially, availed us of their complete collection.

I am deeply grateful to Diane Solomon for her dedication to this project. It could not have been completed without her attention to the detailed work she did and total commitment to the subject. Her ability to translate my random thoughts into words that express my spirit and memory, better than I could have hoped for, proves her skill as a writer. Thank you Diane!

Finally, I wish to thank my children and, especially, my true love, Antoinette Kuzmanich Hatfield. In politics and public service, the role of life partner is significant, yet often overlooked. Antoinette's support and contribution far exceed any of my words.

> Thank you.
> MOH

First and foremost, I wish to thank Senator Hatfield for his wisdom, humor, and brilliance—and for his trust in the task. Working together has been an honor, a privilege, and a great pleasure.

To all the colleagues, staff, and friends who allowed interviews or review of transcripts, thank you for your great gift. Al Zuckerman also gave invaluable support and expertise along the way, as did our publisher, Steven Scholl. The Oregonian library staff, particularly Sandy Macomber and John Meyers, assisted us far beyond any possible obligation. The Oregon Historical Society vailed us of their valuable collection. Marlys Pierson helped set this book in motion. Scott Smith offered valuable space and time. For all of these I am honored and grateful.

Finally, I thank my family, friends, and minyan families for their support, insight, and affection. And I thank Havah and Rivkah for Girls Club—you are the greatest and I adore you! Ultimately, this one's for Gramma Mary: a well-spring of love and light.

DNS

PROLOGUE

*T*HERE'S A MYSTIQUE ABOUT OREGON, A MYSTERY MORE breathtaking than the spray of our waters and grander than the lush verdure of our forests. An aura wider than our people and deeper than our politics.

I don't completely understand this magic, yet I've seen it reflected in the eyes of those who view us from afar—from Washington, D.C. and beyond. I've sensed it throughout my life and it's rapt within my soul.

Yes, there is a certain mystique here, and I am privileged and delighted to offer you a view. I hope it may even give you something special to take home—that is, if you're not lucky enough to already live here.

My nascent impressions of Oregon unfurled in rural Dallas, Oregon, in the late 1920s. In my mind I can still pace proudly up and down Main Street, a young boy in britches familiar with each nuance of architecture and each person that lived and worked beyond those walls. I can visualize every shop and proprieter; every name etched into my brain; every voice, every smile.

Life has become far more complex in the decades since, yet I'll start back on Main Street conjuring Chauncey L. Crider (CL) and his department store. Two departments—actually, three if you stretched.

Half groceries with a tiny hardware section, the other half, clothing. Each night, his crew cleansed that floor with sawdust. And each morning, CL's store offered a gleaming, tangy scent of oil and fresh cut fir.

Up in Mr. Crider's glass-enclosed mezzanine, perched upon a throne of a stool sat Fanny Dempsey keeping the books with her ancient adding machine and her oversized ledgers inscribed with her clean, ladylike script. I carried my grandmother's monthly grocery bill up and waited patiently while Fanny spoke on her old-fashioned stand telephone with separate mouth and earpiece. She sported bright—surely dyed—frizzy red hair, and when she put down that phone, I offered up my bill and she'd smile and stamp it as paid.

I strode downstairs and beamed, handing the stamped bill to CL. Every month we paid by the 10th so he'd hand me a bonus: a sack full of farmer's mix candy. Striped, lemon, lime, or peppermint, I can still almost roll those hard candies on my tongue. And since it was Grandmother's bill I paid, she let me abscond with all the sweets. I anticipated this monumental event each month, and as CL handed over my reward, he was as gracious as if I'd earned that money myself. He sent me off with a smile as wide as if he'd just made his biggest sale.

When Mother or Father took me to Crider's for clothes, Fred Stinnett assisted us, treating me as the honored customer even though my parents stood by with the wallet. "My goodness, Mark," Stinnett exclaimed in disbelief each time he measured me for shoes, "your foot has grown another inch!" His words reverberated such deference and wonder that I knew, at the ripe age of seven or eight, I was surely becoming a man.

I'd carry our prescriptions for compound medicines across the street to Stafron's drug store. The old gentleman pharmacist sported a toupee, and I'll tell you, I was utterly fascinated by that hairpiece. I strolled through the drug store and just stared at Mr. Stafron's head. I'd never seen a thing like it. His two maiden daughters worked right alongside him and, until the last decade or so when they died, I kept in touch. The Stafron sisters helped found the Polk County Historical Society—their sole passion.

Down the street stood Savery's drugs as well, and that was big competition. There was the Blue Garden restaurant, too, which still stands, Carl Retzer, the curly grey-haired jeweler, and a complete cast of fascinating folks. I strode up and down Main Street with no supervision, proud and confident, watching each citizen. Once, at age five, I ventured out to ride my trike a dozen blocks to my Aunt Birdie's. What a pilgrimage that was!

Dallas was a mill town where the economy survived on the lumber trade alone. At noon the fire whistle blew, and at five the mill whistle signaled the end of the work day. That last whistle was a clear warning to alert the wives their men would be home in half an hour and dinner had best be waiting.

The rhythm of life in Dallas rotated around that lumber mill. As kids, we weren't supposed to get near the place, but this was where the real men were and where I wanted to be. I'd sneak down with friends and watch the old donkey engine propel logs from the pond into the jaws of the mill itself, dragging timber with a mighty cacophany, billowing steam clouds all around us. That was high tech, all we had. And to this day, the tingly fir scent of Oregon mills reminds me of Dallas.

My friendships were central in my life too then, as they are still. I remember when Billy Walton and I strung a tin can telephone line between our houses so we could talk at all hours. And Herschel Boydston's French mother who constantly entranced me with her accent.

We had law enforcement in Dallas too, though we didn't call them cops. "Dubbs" Mulkey, the state policeman, puttered through town on his motorcycle and my buddies and I instantly froze, mesmerized by his vehicle. Dubbs explained how the bike worked and we listened, wrought with reverence. While he had us transfixed, he slipped in a few salient points about the law. The county sheriff, T. B. Hooker, stopped to talk with us as well, gifting us with little admonishments. Nothing of drugs or sex or prostitution. Oh no. He left us quaking about jaywalking and being responsible pedestrians.

Cultural sophistication was top notch in Dallas, I'll tell you that. The courthouse lawn was kept green all year, a veritable jewel on Main Street. The city band played concerts and we never missed one. Dallas was largely a German town—the only place I ever felt like an ethnic minority—with Mennonites and other families with surnames such as Hildebrand or Ediger. Because of this, one year a Madame Ernestine Schumann-Heink, a well-known German opera contralto, came to town. She had relatives in Dallas and we got lucky. Half Schumann-Heink's sons had fought for the Kaiser and half for the allies, so I suppose she figured a visit to the U.S. wouldn't hurt. Her visit was about the biggest excitement we'd ever had.

There was no television of course, and all we had at home in the way of a media center was our imposing, round-top table Philco. Radio was new, and the bugs had yet to be worked out. We suffered through static, competing stations broadcasting on the same wavelength, and plenty of eerie noises. We spent hours with one hand on the knob, adjusting, back and forth, back and forth. But regardless, we sat around that Philco like worshippers hunched intently before the altar. What a miracle of progress the radio was!

Dallas boasted a movie house as well. I'd walk with my family to the silent movies, watching as the pianist accompanied each film with her quintessential, cowboy-riding-over-the-range tunes.

And on Sunday, as I tried to sit still in church, I gazed next door to Wagner's Creamery. In summer, Wagner's gave away all the buttermilk you could drink for a nickel. I became hooked on buttermilk for life. And in the midst of that blistering heat, every once in a while the ice man anointed me with a spare, wintry chip. That ice slid so cool down my little throat, you can't imagine.

During harvest, the Stumps, a family of farmers, rode into town on their horse-drawn flatbed and blessed us with vegetables fresh from the soil. Corn, succulent tomatoes, sweet cucumbers, and other produce—as tasty and warm as if we'd grown it ourselves—were ours for a mere pittance.

For a little town, we were exposed to far more personalities and cultures than you might expect. We weren't sitting there in the plains of Kansas waiting for a hurricane to fret over. This was Oregon, and life was bursting. But there was not much competition for our attention, it's true. We had each other, and that was perhaps the greatest gift of all. I lived with my parents and my grandmother, Alice. At dinner we created our own entertainment, and it was lively. Mother was a staunch Republican from Tennessee, and Dad, a Democrat. Conversation was often political—even strident—but always respectful.

I listened to every word. I was nurtured on compassionate disagreement and consensus politics. Bipartisanship at its best. I learned all sides of Prohibition, the wets and the dries, and the slant on every current candidate. Particularly when women ran for office—and we had a few who did—they garnered plenty of attention and controversy in our home. And usually, several votes.

I suppose you could say my family was lower middle class, but I sure didn't feel poverty-stricken. My mother and grandmother canned string beans, corn, and beets from our own garden, or peaches we'd pay to pick. We laid in plenty for winter, and we reaped abundance throughout the deep, dark months. We never locked our doors, either. If we had, a neighbor might not have been able to get in and borrow that cup of sugar. Now that would have been a scandal!

Instead of locking doors, we all knew each other, we sat together over meals, and we had community. All these people and places I've described became intimate parts of our family life. There was no public assistance, only a county poorhouse where the needy were given shelter and a place to grow their own crops. We shared and provided for each other as best we could, and I wonder, how we can find that sense of community again today?

Oh, I'm not some old curmudgeon wistful over bygone days—at least not yet! And I don't expect progress to stop or my neighbors to give up locking their doors. But humans are the same as they were in the 1920s in Dallas, Oregon. We have our CL Criders and our Fanny Dempseys, our T.B. Hookers and even our famous opera singers passing through each of our lives.

But we've forgotten how to know them, especially in our cities. We've forgotten how to be with each other and how to create a community where we respect one another and truly listen, even if we disagree. Instead we have created more and more walls that divide us. I speak of every realm of our lives here, not just politics. I may be a politician, but there's one thing I've learned: Life is far more than politics alone.

Lots of small towns across the United States surely were, and are, like mine. Yet even as a child, I quickly learned the land of Oregon was different and, unique. As I labored quietly alongside my family in our garden—the garden that nourished us with its abundance—how deeply I understood the interdependence between ourselves and the earth.

When we planted a seed, it produced.

So many fled to Oregon from the dustbowl, astounded that this fact was true, awed that we could actually grow corn, beans, berries, squash, and so much more. Dallas held annual state picnics for immigrants who had moved west from Tennessee, Arkansas, Oklahoma, and Minnesota. Picnickers chatted over who had died and who'd had a new baby. I heard stories of horrid deprivation due to poor soil and bad weather, and here, all I'd known was this marvelous combination of soil and climate that offered more food from the earth than we could imagine. (And yes, a mind-boggling amount of rain as well, it's true.)

Many times, as my father came home from blacksmithing on the railroad, his face widened into a grin. "Guess what I have in my pocket?" he'd beam. I knew immediately. He emptied pockets teeming with wild hazelnuts, and we sat on the porch carving into the sweet meat, just the two of us in the quiet, freesia-pink dusk. Or, he'd arrive with a tin lunch bucket. "Guess what's in my bucket?" he'd tease. I knew that, too: wild, sweet blackberries. We ran into the kitchen, pulled down a cereal bowl and washed the berries. Then Dad skimmed the cream off the top of the milk bottle and splattered it on. We'd feast, laughing at how purple our tongues and mouths became. This was all I'd known, yet other children marveled, "Gee, we never had a blackberry before we came to Oregon. . . ."

We enjoyed our seasons, and the foods that accompanied each one. Today we can run to Zupan's—or Zabar's—and purchase berries or beans throughout the year. But these foods light up the palate so much more if we await them in their time; if we enjoy them in their season.

As a child, my father and I fished the bounty of Oregon streams. And long before the intestinal bug Giardia, we slaked our thirst on cool, clear water straight from the brook. Or I'd venture into the woods, reaching to stretch my arms around trees I couldn't possibly grasp—what we now know as old growth. We'd visit relatives near the old Grand Ronde Reservation, where Native American children taught us to spot edible mushrooms and wild licorice. Each time we foraged in the wild and I discovered something I could eat, a frisson of excitement sped up my spine. We swam the rivers and gave no thought to pollution. We used outside privies and pee-pots at night so we needn't venture outside, and we loved life.

We never managed a long vacation, just a three-day weekend here or there. We went with Aunt Birdie and Uncle Van in their big ol' Hudson and plodded up the Butler Hill Highway to the Oregon coast, carrying water because the Hudson duly overheated—at least twice. We stopped on the road, waiting for the radiator cap to cool so it wouldn't burn our fingers, then tanked up the water and headed on to the Pacific. Never have I been to that ocean without a running contest: "Who can see the ocean first?" someone yells, enthusiasm pouring off us all like sweat. We sighted that Pacific blue and clapped and cheered as though we'd just won a million dollars. Other children I knew rarely saw the ocean. "Well, I have," I'd boast, "many times."

Wildlife was a basic part of growing up, too. Cougars ate sheep then, in a day when the survival of humanity had a higher priority than the survival of a four-legged feline. Bounty hunters shot cougars for a pelt price. Raccoons and skunks were part of our culture as well, and gratefully, I was forbidden to ever shoot anything, even a bird with a BB gun. Dad went through the encyclopedia with me as I grew, drilling me to discern a weasel from a ferret, but I certainly never wanted to kill one. Once, I crafted a string-and-box contraption to trap a squirrel. Luckily it never worked. If it had, I'd have been at a total loss for what to do next.

These animals provided us with a better life, and I appreciated them as much as every natural resource we had. That was what made Oregon unique, though I didn't quite know it. Later Navy buddies would brag about other states. "We have a 50-story building!" some mate would crow. Well, I hope Oregon still can't boast that. But Oregonians raved about how unique our state was—our mountains, ocean, waters, deserts, gorges, and forests. And our natural wonders like Crater Lake, the Oregon Caves, Mt. Hood, and Mt. Jefferson. If there were no Washington staters nearby, we always claimed Mt. Hood was higher than Mt. Rainier. I hope that was as close as I ever came to telling a bold-faced lie.

When those tinted color photos hit the scene, Oregonians carried postcards or picturebooks everywhere, as if to say, "Can you believe this is what we have?" We showed off our palate of vibrant colors: the emerald greens, the azures, and the pinks, oranges, and reds of a clear dawn against Mt. Hood. And we told about the high surf pounding against arch rocks, sentinels standing beyond the shore or the huge salmon and steelhead; the bounty of our waters.

But I would be remiss in talking about the wonders and mystiques of Oregon without mentioning our iconoclastic politics. After all, that's probably why you picked up this book. It's in politics, perhaps, that Oregon is most unique. Our political history is as unusual and stunning as our Haystack Rock on the Oregon coast; as vital as the beefsteak tomatoes I bit into, warm and fresh, from my childhood garden. Yet I never wanted to author a memoir that rewrites history in my own image. So I'll try to be as objective as I can.

As a high school senior in Salem, Oregon—our state capital—I had never seen a person of color in our school. Then suddenly, in 1939, twins Leonard and Leland Williams walked into my class. I believe the only other African American I knew growing up was the man who shined shoes in Salem. He was highly respected, it's true, but I'd heard the whispers that everyone liked him "because he kept his place." I didn't know what that meant exactly, but one day Leland and Leonard were my classmates, both absolutely charismatic, great students. They brought honor to our school, plain and simple. We were at the age where we knew discrimination raged in other parts of the country— let alone in our own town—and this was a personal, life experience that expanded my horizons. I was so proud to have those twins in my class.

At the same time, Leland and Leonard's parents couldn't even book a hotel room in Salem, and that stuck with me. Clearly, it was wrong. Later, once I'd entered politics in the 50s, Oregon became one of the first states to pass a bill of public accomodations, and also one of the first to put fair employment and housing practices into law. We alternated with Wisconsin then, jockeying to offer the most progressive politics. But Oregon had already adopted the direct legislative process—the initiative, referendum, and recall process—at the turn of the century. We were one of the firsts to demand senatorial candidates be elected by the people and not by the state legislature. We were in the lead with women's suffrage, child labor, unemployment compensation, industrial accident legislation, and a progressive income tax. Louis

Brandeis himself, early in the 20th century, traveled here twice from Massachusetts as a young lawyer, impassioned to argue for our cutting-edge labor legislation.

In my life I've been honored to note that Oregon's politics fascinate people across this country. There is a national focus on our progressive legislation and innovation; on our Oregon Health Plan, our environmental consciousness, our land use planning, and on our willingness to admit past wrongs of bigotry and put them right. We had the benefit of seeing how the forest industry raped and pillaged Midwestern lands, so we got ready ahead of time. We try to preserve the bounty here, the access to education for all our people, and the health of our citizens. Even though I vehemently oppose our assisted suicide legislation—frankly, I think it's murder—I have to admit it created a groundswell of attention to wonderfully humane, end-of-life care. Our health teams are on the cutting edge of compassionate care for the dying, offering personalized services, pain relief, and state-of-the-art geriatric care in homes, hospitals, and nursing homes. People travel across the country just to see what we've done. And though we never had slaves here, our first state laws prohibited African Americans from residing here at all. We have a history of discrimination against Native Americans, Japanese, Latinos, Jews, Catholics, and others as well. Recently, we celebrated a Day of Acknowledgment in the State Capitol, resolving to work together to make sure bigotry remains only a shard of our past, never a splinter into our future.

Perhaps most of all, Oregonians are bipartisan. We're independent. I always say there are more "Is" here than "Rs" or "Ds," though not by registered political affiliation. For example, my first Democratic opponent for national office, Bob Duncan, was the honorary chairman of my last senate campaign. A prominent Democratic Oregon congresswoman, Edith Green, became the honorary chairwoman of my 1984 campaign as well.

And in 1956, when I ran for secretary of state, I learned a great lesson about bipartisanship and professional respect from Bob Holmes, a friend and Democrat from our days together in the state legislature. Bob ran for governor to fill an unexpired term at the same time I ran for secretary of state. We both won our races. But two years later I became the Republican candidate for the governorship, and I challenged Holmes and won.

Yet we were still friends. In fact, Holmes came to Portland weekly to appear in "Let's Face It," a political TV commentary. In all eight years I was governor of Oregon, Bob never second-guessed me. He even had me on his show a few times. That was a remarkable model. I knew it would have been infinitely easy for him to pop off at me time after time. After all, he had a perfect forum for it, with a huge audience! But his professionalism struck and enamored me. I tried to follow his pattern throughout my career. Even when my most vigorous opponents attacked, Bob would loom in my mind and I'd keep my mouth shut, tight. I wasn't always successful, but Bob gave me a standard I knew was the right one.

Oregonians have this kind of independent flair for life, an attitude of openness to change and innovation, a willingness to hear all sides. We share power here among the many, and I love that too. (I become gravely concerned whenever I see any power—religious, economic, or political—in the hands of the centralized few.) I suppose you could say Oregonians are non-conformists, but personally I love it that we confound the pundits and political polls alike. We pride ourselves on being entertainers of change, friendly to new ideas, and willing to experiment. We make mistakes, but we learn as well.

Yet partisanship, misuse of power, and the marketing of politics are a few of the problems that currently challenge our freedoms in this nation. They abuse and deny us—the people—the standard and quality of government we deserve.

And that, perhaps, is what makes Oregon most unique, and one of the best reasons I have to embark on this book. Here in Oregon we work at independence and freedom. But it's not disorder and lawlessness. It's not the wild west. It's community, civility, and respect. It's an old, yet new perspective of listening and honoring that I hope—just hope—might offer one key to revitalizing our entire political and social culture in this country.

That's why, finally, I sat down to write these reflections. I can't offer everything, yet I can offer my personal perspective. First, I wanted to be clear about where I'm coming from. It's Oregon, and I want to thank you, so much, for paying a visit.

Prologue

I hope something I say sparks a resonance deep in the hearts and minds of you, the people who create this great, wide land. Because that's where I've sought to aim each thing I've done. For the people of Oregon and the nation we all call home.

Mark O. Hatfield
Portland, Oregon

Section One:
Family

CHAPTER ONE

The Early Years

*I*T HAS TO BE STATED AS A FACT: MY MOTHER, DOVIE, AND HER mother, Mary Alice, were pretty unusual characters.

Don't misunderstand, I use these labels in the most endearing possible sense. But these two women were bred of the Victorian era, with long skirts and plenty of cultural inhibitions. Their job was to breed, to nurse, and to provide comfort—period. Gratefully though, that mold broke wide open when it came time for Mary Alice and Dovie to come of age.

My grandmother married at 16, in East Tennessee. She, her new husband Thomas Austin Odom, and both sets of parents were strong Unionists and Republicans, very anti-slave. But they lived in what was still the old South; war wounds were fresh and the South hadn't found a way to heal and move on. I wouldn't exactly call Grandmother and her husband landowners, though I suppose they were. They had a bit of land—just enough to feed their family. Even though that sparse parcel gave them a speck of status, life still proved plenty difficult, both politically and otherwise. So at the turn of the 20th century when the air itself was aflutter with tales of western migration, they listened. There stood hope and opportunity in the West, just waiting to be plucked. And my ancestors were nothing if not plucky.

Mary Alice, Thomas, and her father, Wesley Trent, followed their dream and migrated west in 1909. After settling in, Grandpa Odom became the constable of Dallas, Oregon, and our family's first politician. He and Mary Alice had five children—my mother being the oldest—and all seemed well until one day, when Grandfather Odom's wagon tongue came loose while he rode. The tongue hit the curb, jolting the wagon, and catapulted my grandfather to an awful, premature death.

My grandmother was young, in her early-30s, and suddenly a new widow with five children to feed. My mother was 19. And all this in a setting without support, without insurance or social services. Mary Alice was uneducated, though literate, and her trouble had just begun. Soon Carl, her 10-year-old, contracted polio, and the next and only male in line, Carson, had to report to work at the sawmill. Luckily Grandmother had a large house and she did what she could. She transformed her home into a boarding house and took in sewing. All three daughters—Dovie, Birdie, and Margaret—helped with tailoring and creating new clothes. Somehow, the family survived, perhaps on sheer will.

Theirs wasn't survival based on economy alone, but survival based on readjustment and endurance; on the ability to adapt and live. The only alternative was not to adapt, and to swiftly wither away. Losing a partner is a serious, traumatic devastation, but how much more so when the wife was so totally dependent upon the husband. Grandfather Odom had controlled everything in their household. Mary Alice had never paid a bill or written a check, nor known how. Now she had no choice but to adapt; her life and the life of her children depended on her ability to do so.

To complicate everything, Grandmother had hearing loss and couldn't handle the telephone. So Mother, as the oldest—with an independent personality to match—was not only willing but anxious to take over a leadership role. Essentially, she co-led that family with her mother. I'm sure that was why she didn't marry until she was 28. Oh, she wasn't an old maid, she had plenty of suitors. But she had her own life to live. There were many strong personalities in that household. I'm sure there was a sense of competitiveness in the air too, a need to prove as a female, she was queen. Amongst her siblings, there was no question Mother won that competition.

Meanwhile, my father, Dolen, had grown up in Roseburg, Oregon, and suffered his own grave loss. At age four or five, his mother died of an illness. What a stark age to lose a mother: old enough to understand she is gone forever, but far too young to comprehend why she had been taken her away from him. On top of that, my paternal grandfather remarried shortly after, and it was immediately clear that Dad and his sister, Sadie, would not experience a happy childhood within the bosom of this new "family." Dolie and Annie Hughes, favored maternal uncle and aunt, graciously gave them a true home, a loving relationship, and a warm family life.

In his teens, Dad's father wanted him to return to the farm where a strong farmhand was needed. I'm sure Dad was resistant, but he did his duty and went home. After a year, he escaped to college at Oregon State, then soon left school to join the Navy during World War I. Discharged as the war ended, Dad was in no hurry to get back to his father's house. Instead, he secured a job on the Virginia railroad. Soon though, he missed the smell and feel of Oregon soil. When he learned of a job on the Southern Pacific Railroad near Dallas, Oregon, he bought a ticket home. He worked for that railroad for 42 years straight. His father, I'm sure, was none too happy at losing his free source of labor. But Dad was exactly like Mother in that way: he tread his own path, though perhaps more quietly.

Mother, at this point, was off to the teacher's college, Oregon Normal School (now Western Oregon State College), determined to blaze her career. She completed a two-year degree and landed her first job up on the Siletz river at a tiny, rural one-room schoolhouse. She boarded with a family several miles away, and rode her horse to work each morning. She carried a pistol, too. There were cougars in those woods—not marauders—and she knew she could defend herself. She never had to use that pistol on a cougar, but much later I would ask, wide-eyed, what she would have done if she'd found herself face to face with a cougar. "I would have shot it!" she exclaimed, no thread of worry or fear lining her voice—just sheer indignation. That was my mother.

Living on the sleepy Siletz was not exciting enough, and the only recreation at all was in Taft, downriver quite a few miles. Mother had to get to Taft by boat and travel during the day. She rode downriver with a couple friends on Saturday afternoon. Saturday night they all had dinner, then sauntered over to the dance hall for square dancing. They literally danced all night, ate breakfast at daybreak, then traveled back upriver. After a few years, Mother had had enough of the Siletz. She returned to Dallas to teach and to help at home.

Mother always said she knew she would marry my father the first time she saw him, and I learned early never to doubt her will. Dad was handsome, there was no question about it. She met him at the Methodist church in Dallas where he sang in the choir, and though they never shared with me the details of their courtship, knowing the two of them, I imagine it might have been quite fiery.

They married when she was a ripe 28, and he a mature 34. And just as Mother would have it, they eloped. They never shared with me why they did that, either, but I can certainly speculate. Mother was so independent she had no use of tradition for tradition's sake. Besides, her mother couldn't afford to put on a wedding. There wasn't a particularly cordial relationship between my mother and my father's stepmother, either. The older woman had a grating way of introducing my mother that permanently set Mom's teeth on edge. "I want you to meet Dolen's woman," Dad's stepmother would emphasize, as if my mother was an object, a mere possession of my father's. The woman obviously didn't know who she was dealing with. Mother was a feminist before feminism. Her wedding was no exception, and I imagine Dad was so enchanted he had no objections to anything she wished.

A couple years later Mother gave birth to me, yet I certainly wasn't easy to come by. I had to be delivered via cesarean, and somehow my father was allowed to support and watch throughout the ordeal. I wish I knew what went through his head at my arrival, but I don't. I couldn't hear what he said at that moment—too much water in my ears, I guess. After me though, my parents were instructed by ol' Doc Bollman not to have any more children, and they followed his advice. Forever I was destined to be an only child.

The first home I knew was at 814 Hayter Street in Dallas. Grandmother lived kitty-corner from an open field, in the house where she still took in boarders. There was a well-worn path across the field between our homes as we tread back and forth. Our garden lay blooming in that field, a jewel to us all.

When we finally bought our first car I must have been around seven. I remember my parents finding a used Chrysler in The Oregonian for $600. We took a little train to Derry, the nearest stop, where the Red Electric mainline escorted us up through McMinnville and finally into Portland.

What excitement! We bought that car, and Dad wasn't the only one driving us home, are you kidding? I sat in the back, beaming, as he alternated with my mother in the driver's seat.

Mother was as wonderful as a mother could be, but it's true she didn't exactly settle down to motherhood like all my schoolmates' mothers had. Dad didn't have a business I could go into, and he didn't farm prunes. Most of my friends ended up working in the mill or on the farms like their fathers before them. There certainly wasn't anything wrong with that, but Mother was determined that I would have absolutely any opportunity I chose. She wanted to move us all to Salem, the big city, and figured she better return to school so she could get a job good enough to move us.

By now we were on the cusp of the Great Depression. You didn't pick up and move—even I knew that. I mentioned how we knew the seasons by the foods we ate. Well, life had other rhythms as well. In winter you got out your long johns, your raincoat, your boots. In summer you had the exhilaration of throwing them all off and going barefoot. You had to watch where you walked; cement was far too hot for bare feet. Wood walkways were fine, as long as you avoided slivers and red hot nails in each plank. Fall meant ordering a cord of wood for the sawyer to cut. Dad and I piled the fresh cut fir in the shed; the best insurance we had against winter. We put up pickles and sauerkraut in huge crocks, stringed and broke beans and canned them ourselves.

Double boilers roiled while the old wood stove crackled, interminably hot. The entire kitchen grew moist and warm with benevolent, nourishing smells.

But when I did get to throw off my shoes, I noticed some children had thrown theirs off much earlier. It wasn't a choice—that pair of shoes was the only pair they had, and they needed to preserve it as long as possible. Dallas held canned food drives through schools or churches, and we handed out food on our own as well. I was aware of the financial plight so many faced.

All year around, hoboes were a vivid part of our lives, too. I was struck by their patched pants and scruffy clothes. Each wore a pack on his back with a rolled up blanket attached. Sometimes they could afford a raincoat, more often not. These men were polite, some obviously educated, and they spoke of their families back East to anyone who would listen. Reverently they shared their most recent letter from their wives, found, like a gem, at General Delivery. They had traveled all this way because of the promise of work here, the dream of opportunity. Yet too many left disappointed, never able to send for their families, and often unable to get back home.

When they knocked at our door, we gave hoboes food and a chance at dignity. Give them bread, give them whatever we had, I learned, but let them have a chance to earn it if they wished. Dad left wood outside our woodshed primarily for that purpose. If they wanted to chop wood, we wanted them to have the opportunity. If they wanted only food, that was fine with us as well. Many families, even in winter, had hoboes sit out on their back steps. In our house, if it was a cold day they were invited straight into our kitchen and welcomed at the table. Life was inutterably hard for these men and I knew it. Both my parents had work and we were lucky to be solvent. So many had fallen on desperate times.

This was the beginning of my lifelong lesson in inclusiveness, pluralism, and aiding the less fortunate—three virtues well practiced in my home. I learned there were all kinds of people that make up our world, and that was wonderful. I learned to respect the downtrodden. We were all the same, after all, and each one of us deserved honor and dignity. We had no words like inclusiveness or pluralism then. My parents simply lived them.

Against this backdrop, Mother was steadfast in her determination that I have real opportunity, not just some fragile dream that might never grow wings. And she was tenacious in bringing this about. Yet going back to school was no easy proposition. From the time I was six until I was eight, she left home each week for Oregon State College. She drove our Chrysler (Dad walked to and from work in Dallas) to Corvallis. She knew she had to qualify for a job in Salem if she was to move us all there, and she needed a baccalaureate to justify her plan. So she left each Monday morning and didn't return home until Friday night. For two years.

Some might think this was a scandal, a travesty for a mother to leave her only child. But I loved every moment and never once felt deprived. My father and I rented our house out and moved in with my grandmother. She had only one roomer at this point, and that left plenty of space for us. I started school while living with her, at six years old. It was 1928, the year one of my great heroes, Herbert Hoover, was elected.

I loved my mother, but I didn't miss her. Like my ancestors, I adapted. Grandmother looked after us and that was even better. She was far less strict! I could stay up late or not brush my teeth every night, and each time I wanted to go play I needn't ask. "I'm going over to see Billy," I'd announce. That was fine by Grandma.

I also assumed responsibilities while Mother was at school that I'm sure I otherwise wouldn't have taken on until much later. Nothing death defying, just simple tasks. I ordered groceries by phone as Grandma couldn't use the contraption. I lifted up that receiver and called Central. Mrs. Hull was Central to me, and she was from church. "Where's the fire, Mrs. Hull?" I'd call when the fire whistle blew. "Where's Doc Bollman, Mrs. Hull?" Or, "Mrs. Hull, I need the store," I'd speak for my grandmother. Mrs. Hull knew every number, I never had to give her one.

Dad made Mom's absence easy too. He played father and mother, though Grandmother did everything she could in the maternal role as well. I was fortunate Dad was different. He didn't go out to evening meetings like many other fathers, instead he stayed home with me. I knew the stability, the confidence, the security of his strong presence. We listened to the radio, and I'd try to get my hand on that knob first as designated dial flipper. We read together—Tom Swift and his air rifle, the Bobbsey Twins, or Huck Finn. Dad loved to pore over maps, and we would gaze at National Geographics, just the two of us. Someone once told me safe sex in our day meant reading National Geographic, and perhaps that's true. But primarily we loved those maps. "Here are the Himalayas, the Rockies, the Alps, the great seas," I can hear Dad intone, rapt with the wonders of geography.

Mother came home every weekend, and that was probably more of a treat than if she lived with us week round. I'd run out to the car into her open arms, giving and receiving a generous hug and a big smooch. We were affectionate and warm, all of us. We kissed everyone. Then I'd cut right to the chase. "Where's my candy bar?" I asked, and she offered up a Mountain Bar. Nuts, chocolate, cream, and a cherry hidden deep inside. I savored that candy every Friday.

I knew Mother was different from other mothers, but I felt my life was completely standard. It was simply our life. Perhaps it was a bit unusual, but I certainly didn't know it. I just knew how to be flexible, and that was a greater gift than even a mountain of Mountain Bars.

On those weekends all together, the evening meal grew into much more than its weekday fracas. Dinnertime proved the zenith of our day. Sure we ate well, but that wasn't the highlight. First, we all sat down and listened to Father say grace. By the time I went to school, Dad taught me to say grace in his place. Everyone else was silent for that one solemn moment. And that was the only quiet moment we enjoyed. As soon as we breathed "Amen," conversation broke out like some virulent, happy virus. And it was lively.

Dinnertime conversations were particularly lively later, after Franklin D. Roosevelt was elected President and we moved to Salem. We could have had a hurricane in Florida to mull over, or a storm in New England, but Roosevelt always dominated the conversation. And my folks were not fond of him, to be sure. Grandmother couldn't even hear the radio, but she forbade the instrument to be used in her house to listen to FDR. He was a "wet" and my parents were religiously "dry" prohibitionists. This was a moral issue, and Roosevelt embodied evil incarnate.

This was true even though Dad was a Democrat, grumbling over the paucity of Democratic nominees every time he received a sample ballot. Marion County was Republican—it still is—and Mother never gave up trying to persuade him to vote her way.

Meanwhile, we're all trying to eat dinner, and Grandma can't hear, so if the conversation was of interest to her, I translated in loud tones. "Grandma, they're talking about President Roosevelt!"

She'd scowl. But just as I was her communicator, she proved to be a great advocate and defender. All these roles were gifts, invaluable ever after. She was my third adult, and what an advantage I had by knowing her love. It's a tragedy that every child growing up today doesn't have a third, beloved and caring adult. It was essential to me, and to my wife Antoinette and our children as well. And certainly in my case it offered a happier, healthier childhood.

But back to dinner. I remember Hannah Martin, a woman, a Republican, and a lawyer, running for state legislature. Father wasn't happy about voting for a woman for anything. "Why should a woman run when there are plenty of men out there?" he'd boom over the potatoes. "Well, sure," Mother would retort, "if you want to vote for a dumb man running against a smart woman, go ahead." Of course to her, every woman running for anything had to be smarter than her male opponent. Dad would come back with, "Well, I'm voting for one Democrat, at least. And the only one running is running against her."

Obviously, Mother believed women ought to be anything they chose. She had lived her own life, breaking ground way back as a single woman on the Siletz. Some men fear strong women, and some men even dislike them. I grew up knowing strong was simply the way women were meant to be.

By now Mother had finished school, received her degree, and landed a job at a middle school in Salem teaching Home Economics. She had created her wish, and had actually moved us all to the city at the peak of the Depression. Grandma sold her house and moved too. This was a time of unparalleled economic turmoil, and every house we rented was eventually put on the market by the owner. We lived in four rentals before we could possibly afford to buy. Some call this hardship, but I saw it as sheer benefit. Again, everything was in change and flux, and I learned once more to adjust and adapt to a changing world.

When you live through cataclysmic shifts like the Depression and World War II, you inevitably become conscious of change and get comfortable with it. There is no choice, nor did I want one. Adaptability was part of me, as comfortable as my well-worn long johns.

A final note about those early years. Dad always worked on the railroad as a blacksmith, but if he could have, he would have been an artist. During lunch or any down time, he took up scrap iron and crafted creative wheelbarrows that ended up too heavy to even lift, or hewed whatever else he could in massive proportions. Once, he brought home two pizza-size steel rings with a loop flourish attached to each one. He hung those loops on ropes and swung both rings from a tree.

I learned to swing on those rings. I'd pull up to sit in one and pump until I could drop my torso down and swing from the bottom of the ring. I'd stand on the lower edge of one, swinging, or put my feet in one ring and my hands in the other, arching my back and swaying away.

I suppose I could have joined the circus, and many would probably say I did just that. But that's not what we called it back then. It was politics, pure and simple that my parents had taught me to love, and it was politics—circus or not—I inevitably swung toward.

CHAPTER TWO

Forging the Young Politician

With milkshake bets, Spin the Bottle, and Boy Scouting, my adolescence was pretty standard. But several events changed my life forever, the first when I was only 13 and excited as I'd ever been. I was a Boy Scout and about to fulfill a huge dream of attending an international Boy Scout Jamboree. Not only that, I was going to Washington, D.C. to do it—a place so far away as to be almost unimaginable. Mom and Dad had scrimped enough to barely send me; an incredible feat in 1935.

I was about to meet boys my age from all over the globe! The world suddenly reeled, kaleidoscoping incomprehensibly beyond Salem, Oregon.

But abruptly, tragedy struck. We received word of the polio epidemic that was devastating D.C., and the Jamboree was swiftly canceled. I was crestfallen. At the same time, I realized sickness could strike anyone, anywhere. Moreover, it could be so virulent as to change the plans of those the world over. What a defining moment. Sickness and disease were enemies to be fought ever after.

But the story wasn't over. Scouts from China and the Philippines were already aboard ship, well on their way to the U.S. They re-routed to our shores, and the Northwest Scouts convened at Camp Parsons on Washington State's Hood Canal. Woe to all those Eastern boys who completely lost out.

Now our proportions were altered. Instead of so many Americans minimizing the number of Asians in our midst, our numbers were balanced. And the Chinese (unlike the Filipinos) did not speak English. I had never met a human soul that didn't speak "my" language. But at the Jamboree, we communicated regardless. We used sign language, facial expressions, and every unique gift kids have to reach across cultural lines. We taught these Scouts a few words of English, and I can still proudly count to five in Chinese. Fifty years later, I would be back in the Phillippines, and one of those scouts met my plane displaying the autograph book I'd signed half a century before, allowing us to renew our friendship.

Children have no artifice, no preconceived impediments to meeting and making friends with those unlike them. In Sunday school we had always sung, "Red and yellow, black and white/They are all precious in His sight," but those were lofty words, not experience. My parents taught we were one human family and one people—we were to treat all alike with kindness, honoring the Golden Rule. They absolutely recoiled from news of Hitler's rise. "Look what can happen when you're not involved in your politics," they warned. But here at my Jamboree, these values suddenly flourished to life. I learned to appreciate those not of my culture, to find common humanity well beyond words. And I never forgot it.

Much later, my own four children would attend public school in Bethesda, Maryland, which constituted a slim, 10 percent WASP minority. Surrounded by children of embassy staff from the world over, they came home saying, "Daddy, a girl from Japan joined our class today and she didn't know English. We taught her how to count, and we learned some Japanese, too." I smiled, knowing a circle had been completed. Eisenhower knew this well: "One day, these politicians are going to have to step aside and let the people have peace."

That Boy Scout Jamboree pulled a screen aside in my life, shedding bright light, relevance, and meaning on the precepts of diversity and inclusiveness I had always learned. Suddenly, those beliefs became vital parts of my very fabric. Around this time, in 1935, the State Capitol in Salem burst into flames. There were murmurs of arson. After all, the state had talked for years of building a new Capitol. And it was rather curious that the fire trucks, a few blocks from the Capitol, took 20 minutes to arrive after the fire began. Eventually, firefighters sped from Portland, Albany, and Oregon City to help, even stretching hoses across Willamette University next door to pump water from the mill stream. Tragically, a corner of the building collapsed, killing a volunteer firefighter, a Willamette student.

Yet the blaze kept hold and people scurried in and out once or twice, desperate to save relics—their desk ornaments and hand held, precious mementos. No one thought to salvage the artistic portraits of past statesmen, a legacy in the Capitol and a great loss. And still the fire glared inexorably on. We watched from a safe distance until the final crescendo, the copper dome lighting the sky aflame and plunging to the ground in a thunderous crash, all spectacular color and light.

Immediately, the call went out for a national architectural contest to design the new building. Francis Keally, a New York architect, won in New York and when that Capitol was constructed and dedicated, all Salem knew. I played my clarinet and marched in the band at the dedication, strutting proudly each step.

The following year, 1936, I reeled over another issue. WPA (Works Progress Administration) workers at our school sported FDR bumper stickers on their trucks and—following my indignant queries—informed me they were required to display them. That wasn't fair, and besides, it was free advertising! I'm sure all those workers were staunch FDR supporters. After all, he'd put them back to work. But they humored me nonetheless when I'd start spirited discussions on the legality of coercion and free publicity.

Besides, I knew Alf Landon would beat FDR by a long shot. Why? *Literary Digest* told us he would, and they even predicted a landslide. No wonder to this day I abhor polls! I bet seven milkshakes that Landon would win, and when he didn't, I took it personally. I moped for days, sure it was completely my fault. My parents bucked me up, assuring me I'd done all I could. After all, I'd passed out yellow felt, sunflowery

Landon buttons, and every time the polls looked better I'd ante up another milkshake and argue my cause to anyone who would listen.

My teachers consoled me in my grief, too. I suppose they were Democrats, but this was Oregon and that didn't make a bit of difference. They encouraged me to give reports on Landon or on Republican rallies I'd attend every chance I could; they welcomed my questions and political interests.

It took me about a year to pay back those shakes, and I learned my lesson. It was my first and last entrée into gambling.

Still, politics electrified me. There was a sense of excitement, a thrill in learning about the personalities and stands of each candidate. Personally, being a weakling surely helped. Scrawny Hatfield, never once made the cut for sports. I was like that kid who got sand kicked in his face in the Charles Atlas ads. Instead, politics gave me a sense of purpose and self-esteem. I knew the political scene, and I set out to prove it every year at the State Fair.

The fair was big each summer in Salem, and the most glorious part was watching the hawkers. I'd listen to women on the soapbox, selling perfect, forever-sharp knives, and I stood transfixed. I knew this was the best attraction of the entire fair. These women and men were gifted, capturing the full attention of their audience. I analyzed their words even then, thinking this wouldn't be much of a political speech. It was persuasive—those were darn good knives!— and that was important, but too commercial, and too intense.

Dad dragged me away to inspect the farm animals, which was fine, but I skipped out as soon as possible and made my way to the Republican campaign booth. Each year I'd chat with the people behind the booth, and it wasn't long before I was manning the booth myself. When Willkie ran in 1940, Oregon was alive. Here was the second vice presidential candidate ever to run from Oregon—McNary. It was Salem's centennial year as well. What a state fair that was. I helped create the Willkie/McNary float, and only afterwards did I realize we'd spelled Willkie with one l. I should have caught that. It wasn't even my responsibility, but I should have caught it—and I didn't. Of course, that dropped l gained us plenty of attention and publicity. It just wasn't exactly the type of publicity I thought helpful.

I graduated in 1940 and matriculated into Willamette University—

the oldest university west of Missouri—that same fall. Sunday after-
noons I worked as a guide in the Capitol. The maintenance crew provided me with a big brass ring holding a master key to every room, and
I offered visitors quite the grand tour. On slow days I quietly let myself
into the Governor's suite. More than once, I deferentially pulled out
Governor Charles Sprague's stately chair, sat down, and irreverently
laid my feet upon his desk. I'd like to sit in this chair someday, I'd
smile to myself, simply daydreaming.

Decades later, while serving in the U.S. Senate, my experience in
historical tours came in handy. I revered our national Capitol and
learned all I could of its history. Senators from other states approached
asking, "I have a group coming up from Oklahoma, will you give them
a tour?" I always tried to oblige. Aside from constituent groups, students visited as well. I'd take them all on the Capitol subway and revealed secrets few who walked the halls of the U.S. Capitol ever knew.

In the mid-1800s, for instance, long before air conditioning or
even deodorant, Washington, D.C. was as meltingly hot and humid as
it can be today. Many, if not most senators resided in boarding houses
lacking bathing facilities, and finally passed a resolution to buy and
install four to six bathtubs in the Capitol itself. These were no ordi-
nary clawfoot tubs. They were crafted from Italian Carrera marble—
the same marble Michelangelo used to sculpt his David. And they were
long tubs, plenty lengthy for these tall men to stretch out in. They
were finally shipped over from Italy and installed in the Capitol basement so senators could bathe at their leisure.

During a remodel before the Bicentennial a few of the baths were
discovered behind walls. Afterwards, I took visitors through byzantine
heating and cooling ducts and showed them the huge marble baths
surrounded by the exact tiles still installed on the floor of the Capitol.

I'd also take visitors to the Senate Appropriations quarters. Magnificent as they were, when I took over the chairmanship after Senator
Warren Magnuson's (the Democrat from Washington state) long and
successful tenure, there was work to do. He never wanted to vacate the
quarters for refurbishing. Old bookshelves full of junk lined the walls,
installed simply to cover heating ducts and covered with ghastly green
curtains. A ratty sink sat in one corner, threadbare carpeting barely
covered the floor, and chewing tobacco stains spotted it completely,

courtesy of former spitting senators. Jerry-rigged phone booths stood in one corner, and incredible Constantine Brumidi artwork lay on the walls and ceilings, so covered with residue you could not make out the colors. We restored all the artwork until it gleamed, removed the bookshelves, replaced the carpets, and put in glass doors—an idea my wonderful friend Senator Danny Inouye (Democrat from Hawaii) had. "We should make this door glass so the public can watch our proceedings," he said. Thus came the Daniel Inouye memorial window.

Next, I'd take visitors up to the "Ladies Gallery" of the old senate. I led them up narrow stairs to the gallery in the old senate chamber, where a sign still plainly reads: "Gentlemen will please refrain from putting their boots on the railing because mud from those boots falls on senators' heads." In those days, wives often came to Congress with their husbands and, being gentlemen, the men always vacated their senate seats for their wives. Not only did we have no air conditioning, but we had poor heating in winter, and all the men filed off to the cloakroom fireplace to prevent shivering. As a solution, they built the Ladies Gallery, so wives would kindly remove themselves from the Senate floor and men could proceed with their business.

Finally, I took guests down to the bowels of the Capitol, to the rotunda. Right below the dome a hole in the floor was originally built so visitors could view the sarcophagi of George and Martha Washington. Rather macabre, certainly, and the families agreed. They laid their loved ones to rest at Mt. Vernon instead. The hole in the floor was duly filled, but still lay excavated beneath. There to this day lays the catafalque of Abraham Lincoln. That catafalque is used to carry the caskets of our fallen presidents and heroes, John F. Kennedy, Herbert Hoover, and General MacArthur among them. Right beside the catafalque is a tiny room that served as a jail for a charming and beautiful grand dame of D.C. during the Civil War. She lavishly entertained, yet soon found herself guilty of entrancing secrets out of Union personnel and divulging them to the Confederate military. Until a proper jail was built for her outside the Capitol, she was jailed next to where the catafalque now rests. Of course by the time the jail was completed the war was over. Besides, she had been so charming and well behaved they set her free.

But way back on December 7, 1941, I was on duty at the Oregon State Capitol. It was just a lazy December day at that—few visitors came through. Suddenly someone yelled that Pearl Harbor had been attacked. We all startled, the janitor immediately running to his office to flip on the radio. Every few minutes he ran back to give us an anxious update. The Oregon Coast was surely the next target and the Capitol building must be the greatest treasure the Japanese could ever desire. Wide-eyed, we peered out into the street gazing westward, literally scouting for foreign soldiers. Finally, assured there weren't any in sight, we locked up the Capitol and went home. Like every other American, I was an unnerving jumble of anxiety and fear.

I headed straight to my parents' house. We huddled around the radio for news, any news at all, completely stunned. There was such a scarcity of information coming through that we gathered for hours, anxious for every little word. Thank goodness FDR himself didn't speak that night, as Grandma probably wouldn't have let us listen to him, even then. With pure conviction, I announced I would be going to war. Like all my able-bodied friends, I would be reporting for war service as soon as possible. I chose the Navy, and Dad, a Navy man, proudly agreed. "Son, that's the right branch." I can only imagine the worry and fear wrenching inside the heart of my father, mother and grandmother. Their only child was surely going off to war. But they simply nodded assent, keeping their nightmarish thoughts to themselves.

Out of fear, we pasted colored cellophane across our headlights with tiny slits to see the road, and covered windows with blackout shades. Neon lights and street lights were shut off for months. We prepared for war immediately, and as soon as I could I reported directly to the Naval Reserve. There was a crowd of us, of course, all earnest young men ready to fight. Tragically, one of our classmates had already been lost. A victim of polio, he had chosen suicide rather than being labeled a "slacker." At my age I couldn't quite grasp that, feeling only confusion and grief for the poor family.

At the recruiting station our personnel data was recorded, then we stripped down into those infamous lines of naked, timid, blustery almost-men. Here I was, ol' scrawny Hatfield, 130 pounds at almost six feet tall. Completely surrounded by beefy athletes flexing their muscles, I thought surely there was no way I could possibly make the cut. What utter ignominy that would bring upon myself and my ancestors!

The doctors drew closer and closer down the line, and my anxiety blossomed. I knew in my gut I was about to be humiliated in front of each and every one of my peers. And it was my turn next! No turning back. The physician finally reached me while I held my breath, offering only a strangled, cracked grin.

He paused beside my light human specimen, an indecipherable expression on his face. I still wasn't breathing. "We're going to have to fatten you up a little, aren't we?" was all he said, moving on down the line. I was sure he must have made a mistake, but I slipped through. And here were these other huge guys getting nixed for their flat feet or the color blindness or what have you. What a boost for my ego!

Immediately on the heels of Pearl Harbor came suspicious whispers about the Japanese neighbors we had lived with all our lives. "How loyal are they?" people questioned, even making false, spurious distinctions: "Well, it's the older ones who we have to worry about. They don't even speak English," and on and on. Soon, Roosevelt ordered all Japanese interned, and it wouldn't be until 1988 that restitution would finally come for this hateful act.

For me, internment became a ghastly reality as my own classmates were pulled away. We knew Anna Takiyama and Henry Tanaka. We went to school with them. They were great students and great people, certainly as American as we were. One by one, though, these friends were scooped up. I walked to the train depot to wave goodbye, my mind completely befuddled. What was happening to us? Why were we being divided from our friends, from other Americans?

As I slowly left the station I felt intimidated by older men there observing our goodbyes and taking down names. I had absolutely no context for thinking about this whole garish, racist twist. Except I knew setting one people against another was categorically wrong.

I was ready to go straight into service, but the Navy indicated they would call when they wanted me. Meanwhile, they recommended I finish as much schooling as I could—at my expense. I studied straight through summers and took 18 credit hours a term to be prepared when that fateful order to report showed up in the mail. I graduated a year early—1943—just in time.

Yet I had no idea what was to befall me.

CHAPTER THREE

An Only Child in War

A S A TEEN, I WAS A RIGID ISOLATIONIST. THINGS WERE BEYOND BAD in Europe, definitely. After all, we listened in Social Studies as Hitler's voice piped through the public address system, shrill and raspy, screaming with agitation. His voice alone gave us the creeps. And in translation, we were appalled by Hitler's violation of his neighboring countries, by the Anschluss of Austria and the Munich Pact partitioning Sudetenland, part of Czechoslovakia, to Germany. But we were 18; inviolable, protected by vast oceans from these horrific events. Besides, Europe hadn't yet paid back war debts from World War I. What was the point of becoming involved in another of their battles?

In a shocking flash, Pearl Harbor changed all that. Bidden or not, we were drawn in and World War II became our concern. The Axis might even broach our own shores next. Isolationism was over.

One day I blithely played—well, attempted to play—golf on a beautiful, crisp March day in Salem (yes, every once in a while Oregon snatches sun in March). And soon after I found myself riding away on a train to Plattsburg, New York—located right on Lake Champlain—

reporting for duty. The lake was frozen so solid that cars easily drove across to Vermont. Frigid temperatures were shocking enough, but that empty, bitter cold was but a harbinger. I was in the Navy now, a war dumped unceremoniously in my lap, and I had to prove myself in order to earn my officer's commission. Thoughts of actual warfare were still unreal, yet creeping with alarming speed into my consciousness.

There were 2000 of us at Lake Champlain in midshipman training, and one by one, each of us was interviewed as to what advanced training we preferred. Inexplicably many of us had a sudden, unstoppable passion for public relations training, a noble, completely out-of-the-field post. Somehow our training officers managed straight faces. They knew what we soon discovered: we were training for amphibious warfare.

Once on liberty leave, I took a train for New York City. Compared to Salem, New York was mindboggling. What were those buildings doing there, too tall to reveal the sky? We didn't have those in Salem! And what of all the people, so frenzied? I was happy enough to reboard my train, full of men in uniform like myself, mostly returning to training. Right away someone mentioned Eleanor Roosevelt was on board and I perked up. I wasn't fond of the Roosevelts, but I was immediately curious and determined to see her. Not because she was the ugliest, homeliest woman ever created (to my young mind), but because she was a great first lady and I would not let the opportunity pass. I paced up and down the aisles until I spied a woman quietly reading a book, unmistakably Eleanor.

"Excuse me," I said, "My name is Mark Hatfield."

"Have a seat," she gestured.

I sat and spoke my true colors. "I was president of the Young Republicans at Willamette University," I stressed, as though she'd be interested. She didn't bat an eye. We began to chat—nothing political or profound—and I immediately became conscious of her hands. In gestures, in speaking, those hands were magnificent, dancing to accentuate every word she uttered. I was so impressed with Eleanor's presence, graciousness, and charisma that any impression I had of her homely looks immediately disappeared. I had been carried away by first appearance, and ever after I realized true beauty of spirit and personality are never captured by photographs. I also became an observer of hands, a habit that has given me pleasure and pause ever since. And I was imprinted with a deep respect for this remarkable woman.

After training I was so green as a new ensign—a "90-day wonder"—it was unbelievable. As soon as they shipped me to Coronado Beach, California, they informed me I was to serve as a wave commander. I was delighted. I'd get a class of Navy women—the WAVES, they were called—to drill into obedience with a simple hup, two, three, four. What could be better!

I soon learned a wave commander commanded a line of 10 small, 25-foot, LCVP (Landing Craft Vehicle Personnel) boats. We would carry Marines diligently from ship to shore, then return to ship and unload warfare gear and equipment for troops. Simple.

I traveled to Long Beach to ship out, reporting to the newly christened USS Whiteside (AKA-90), along with 360 sailors and 38 fellow officers. My folks met me to offer their goodbyes and I was still upbeat, having only a remote sense of what was before me. My parents knew more than I and among other things, they knew I'd have plenty of time to read at sea. They gifted me with an inscribed, 1944, six-volume set of Carl Sandburg's biography of Lincoln. Lincoln was already a hero of mine, and my parents were right. I was to get through the entire set during the war, and I still have that edition. Mom and Dad offered their best wishes. I can only guess at the turmoil bubbling inside them.

finally we were off, sailing in the direction of Pearl Harbor. first we gathered with a group of ships on Maui to stage simulated invasion activities. Where we were actually headed in the Pacific was so top secret that every map we consulted had the name of our island destination excised from the map itself, a neat hole. On liberty in Honolulu, when we mentioned we were with the USS Whiteside, every cab driver knew exactly what island would be ours to invade. To the last one they bettered the U.S. military's less-than-stellar attempt to keep us clueless.

"Why, Iwo Jima," the cab drivers spouted. "Anyone knows that. You guys are headed straight for Iwo Jima."

We sailed on and soon I received notice the executive officer wished to see me in his office.

"Hatfield, I've gone over your Navy jacket—your personnel file—and I see you have some public speaking experience."

"Yes, sir."

"There's a tradition in the Navy, you know. Divine services have to be held each Sunday, and we don't have a chaplain in the ship's complement." I could not imagine, in any way, what this possibly had to do with me. I stood stock still. "On shore leave in Hawaii," he went on, "we picked up this box." My gaze followed his pointing finger, reaching a crisp box of newly minted hymnals and bibles. "I've decided you're the one responsible for divine services on this ship."

"Sir?"

"You heard me."

"I've never led a service before in my life. Sir."

"I gave the order, and you'll do it," he commanded me with a wave, then pivoting back to his work.

I headed straight for my quarters, knowing it was now I who was in dire need of divine service. I spilled my plight to my three bunkmates, one a Protestant like me, the other two, Catholic.

"Well, you're certainly not going to have Catholics participating in a Protestant service," balked Tom McCoy. "I'll read the rosary!" He marched right back to the executive officer, offering to lead a Catholic service.

Meanwhile, word got around. Two enlisted men approached me on deck. "We hear you're leading divine services," they said.

I nodded, chagrined.

"We obtained something during shore leave, Sir. For services."

Darned if they didn't bring out a knee-high pump organ—God only knows from where. Then another bunkmate, Ken Likes, a wonderful graphic artist, mimeographed the order of service. He also did a great job of playing that organ while frantically pumping away.

Lo and behold—presto—we had a sanctuary at sea.

Somehow, I lived through my own three-or-four-minute homilies every week, usually droning on about loving God and fellow human beings; a strange topic, looking back, when we had just been trained to vociferously despise "the enemy." On Christmas we even held midnight services with the Catholics and a joint choir.

Though I only played chaplain one day a week, people soon identified "Hatfield" with that role. They gravitated toward me as someone who might listen. "Can I talk to you sometime?" they asked.

I was no counselor, and frankly, I felt pretty uncomfortable. What could I possibly have to say that might help? Soon though, I realized a good listener was mostly what these men needed. They came to me with their fears about war, or with letters from wives detailing the awful struggles kids had at home without a father. They brought Dear John letters from girlfriends—or worse, wives—writing of the loneliness they felt at home and how they solved their problem by taking up with other men, to the utter anguish of the men pouring their souls out before me. These men would talk—sometimes weep—and clear their hearts.

Often, I didn't say much of anything. They needed to talk and I wanted to listen. Somehow, sometimes, I hope healing took place. I was honored to be there, to be trusted, and did all I could to honor that sacred trust.

Soon we reached our destination, and Iwo Jima became my first battleground. We hit that beach on Monday, February 18, 1944 and immediately on this godforsaken strip of sand, all our meticulously staged invasion plans crumbled to dust.

I thought we would walk ashore free. After all, B-17s had bombed the hell out of this place for 75 straight days—what could be left? How could there possibly be enemy troops alive on this narrow, two-mile-wide and four-mile-long slip of land?

But just as we reached shore, we were completely fouled up. first, as vessels or troops hit land, it wasn't land at all we struck but volcanic beach more like quicksand. A coffee-ground shore that stalled our tanks and mired the Marines over their boots. In Maui I'd staged stoic attacks as we hit the gently sloping beach, ground ashore, and swiftly dropped our ramp to release our cargo. No one happened to mention Iwo Jima didn't have a gently sloping beach. In fact, it had a sharp edge. Shore hit water and abruptly turned south, creating a deep and severe drop off. All the boats bumped ashore time after time, unable to stabilize no matter how hard we tried. Larger vessels began taking in water each time they opened their ramps. Many smaller LCVP boats actually sank.

I had my own three crew members with me and 25 Marines who had just come aboard. I'd never met them before in my life, and here they were, standing in full battle gear shoulder to shoulder, filling our boat, ready to meet their fate. My responsibility? Deliver them safely and return for more Marines, time after time after time. Well I certainly hadn't trained for this kind of landing and my coxswain, Elvis, couldn't beach the craft.

Elvis was the best coxswain in the entire boat division. And back in Hawaii I'd defended him in a court martial. At the gate of Pearl Harbor he'd gotten drunk and beat up some Marines, then was summarily called to court martial. Every accused was allowed to choose someone to defend him, and Elvis chose me. I queried him at great length, and his friends as well. I brought in witnesses and showed exact events hadn't transpired as they had been recorded at the gate. He was found innocent and from then on the two of us were bonded. We had trained together, meticulously executing battle plans. Now we both knew those plans were in vain but our lives still depended on each other, on getting more Marines in and winning this island. He and I were on the line with everyone else, and we both knew it. All we wanted was to get out alive. Beyond that, I had no thoughts, no feelings. Nothing but sheer instinct.

Finally, Elvis shouldered our LCVP in between other vessels to stabilize and discharge our personnel. Somehow, our Marines disembarked.

I thought the worst must be over, but I wasn't even close. Like every other man, I knew fear and terror on a level I couldn't even fathom. As soon as the Marines disembarked, my tiny boat all but drowned. We took on water and my crew bailed as fast as they could, frantic, under fire every minute, deafening artillery right over our heads. My two Navymen were petrified. Without a thought, and at the same time, they threw their bailing buckets into the open sea with the bailed water, losing the only tool they had to save us. "Take off your helmets and bail!" I yelled over the cacophany of gunfire.

They stood silent, frozen.

"Remove your helmets and bail!" I ordered, this time louder.

Numbing silence. Not a twitch of a muscle.

I slapped my hand on my sidearm and repeated the command.

Suddenly, they jerked from their war-induced stupor, removed their helmets, and saved our lives.

I had to isolate myself in this inhuman, shock-ridden environment. I couldn't choose between escorting troops in under tremendous attack or sitting in the water until things calmed down. I had to move, and now. I focused on my one command, my next goal, my next troop of Marines to help ashore. My only questions became: How do I get from here out of danger? How do I do my duty? How do I live to bring another boatload in? And I knew, in each and every moment—in virtually every nanosecond—that in fact if it had my name on it, it would be mine. I thought of my parents, my grandmother, and how hard it would be for them to lose their only offspring. I didn't want that, I wanted to survive. So it wasn't out of bravery or strategy that I ordered my men to bail with their helmets, it was pure and instantaneous reaction. It was innovation, survival.

Next, that dead volcano, Mt. Surabachi, snafu'd us. Hot Rocks, we called it. Inside were tunnels, like veins running throughout a body. And inside those tunnels, burrowed deep like blood cells, were Japanese troops quietly waiting to attack.

They used our fouled up landing to their best advantage. As we diligently worked our way from our quagmire, they constantly fired from Mt. Surabachi while more troops lobbed mortar shells from the opposite side of the island. Our troops were under fire virtually every moment and men were losing their lives already, littered across the beach in anguished poses of death.

In and out, in and out, four days and five nights we struggled in our small boat, eating sea rations. We bobbed at sea at night while ships sent up starshells, lighting the sky on targets so that motherships could fire. Each dusk I awaited dawn's breaking so we could begin again. And as dawn broke I went ashore, leading Marine troops and cargo in and shuttling wounded out of that blood-besotted beach. Some Marines simply froze as they saw that mess of tangled bodies filling the beach. Somehow I kept on, one foot in front of the next.

The noise alone was phenomenal. This was one of the last major battles utilizing battleships, with 16-inch guns shooting 16-inch projectiles. On the beach, I ran beneath whizzing projectiles, mortals squealing, orders, commands, redirections shouted from every direction, the sound of the sea intensifying it all. I felt an utter, nightmarish chaos. Except for the fact that I had the misfortune of being starkly awake.

Quickly, hospital ships began overflowing with wounded, and we needed to take injured onto our own mothership, the Whiteside. My mates and I conveyed troops into our tiny infirmary but that too rapidly overflowed. Next, I helped ferry the wounded on stretchers to fill our decks. Still there wasn't room. I filled in as a pharmacist mate, holding IV bottles as our vessel bobbed vigorously up and down at sea. With others, I sent stretchers down from ship to shore to load and bring up ever-more wounded. I carried young strong bodies onto the beach, only to bring back the wounded and the dead. These were some of the men we had just landed on the beach, now returning, their human faces twisting in anguish, their gaping, unfathomably bloody wounds spilling over. I listened to the inhuman sounds of their moaning, pure hell. Why were my comrades fallen while I was spared, I ceaselessly wondered. Yet automated in the action of war, there was no time to ruminate. Each moment I fought violent currents and the ship's motion while aiming to hoist up a steady target—a wounded mate on a stretcher. If I moved an inch in the wrong direction, I might lose the man. I wanted desperately to help him, but knew he could fall any second. And it was my responsibility.

Fear was as ever present as breathing. I knew our intelligence was incomplete, and I had no idea what would befall us next. It was inevitable I'd find out.

A day or two later on the beach one of our men yelled, "Look!" pointing to the flag raising on southern Mt. Surabachi—that famous moment immortalized in statue. We were winning, yes, but had not yet won. Our troops had to venture into every cave and tunnel to torch out each last enemy. finally, I heard word we'd captured the airstrip, yet the battle was far from over.

By now our ships were teeming with wounded to the point that, as I toiled on the beach, endlessly discharging men and cargo, the USS Whiteside received orders to leave battle and sail for Saipan where the nearest Naval hospital awaited our wounded. The ship set sail and my crew and I, stunned, were left ashore on the beach with one day's K rations. What an empty, groundless feeling, staring as my mothership took off without us.

We continued our work and I spent that night bobbing in our small craft, gazing at starlight and sleeping little. By daybreak I received orders to take off with the next ship and catch up with the Whiteside in Saipan. As I reached our new destination though, my crew and I learned our ship had left the previous day. We chased the Whiteside across the length of the Pacific to the New Hebrides—off New Zealand. I read and tried to enjoy this brief respite from war, but Iwo Jima was never far from my mind. The bloodiest battle in the Pacific, we ultimately lost over 6,820 troops—with over 19,000 wounded—on that tiny island alone.

Eventually, at Espirito Santos off New Zealand I caught up with the Whiteside. I headed right back out with a convoy of LSTs, smaller, slower ships, this time headed for Okinawa.

I've often been asked what it was actually like, what I felt, face to face with war and inhumanity; the dying and the dead. I have to answer that I adopted a fatalistic attitude. As I said, "If it has my name on it, it has my name on it, and there's nothing I can do," was the lingo we all spoke, empty bravura meant to aid each other through the overwhelming pain and suffering humans inflicted upon humans.

By the time I reached Okinawa though, most soldiers simply walked ashore. There was no fire on the beach, nothing but a plethora of burial caves. Curious, I strode inside with others to witness the ground filled with shelves of bones; the most recent skeletons pushed toward the back to make room for the latest burial. Easily there could have been enemy troops inside the caves, and just as easily we could have been picked off like so many flies.

My respite was brief. There may not have been enemy fire ashore, but the Navy took a severe beating, nonetheless. We were close enough to Japan to be bombed from the mainland, and Kamikaze planes and swimmers intractably attacked American forces. Each night, two of our boats left the ship to move in opposite directions, churning up smoke from our smokemakers as we circled the Whiteside which set off her own smoke to help hide our whereabouts. But Kamikazes flew in low and crashed directly into Navy ships regardless. And mine was a cargo vessel, not a warship. We had only one five-inch mount and 40 and 20 millimeters to defend us. The Navy ships shot down as many Kamikaze planes as they could, but our vessels took many direct hits as well.

We took shifts on nighttime duty. If I sighted a Kamikaze swimmer, we were to throw a cable out to a partner boat and detonate the Kamikaze before he could detonate us. It was absurd—the cable connecting two boats with the deadly swimmer would likely detonate both our boats as well.

I often had this night smoke duty, manning the smokemaker and peering into the inky sea, searching for stealthy Kamikaze swimmers. In that darkness, sleep deprived, blind, you can imagine you see phantoms approaching in the water when nothing is there but the roiling sea. We shot off pistols when we feared a Kamikaze was in sight, and each man in his bed knew terror if he heard that sound. One day, tension exploded. A Kamikaze plane appeared to be flying directly toward our ship. Stunned, we all watched its approach—several men running about yelling and wreaking chaos. Swiftly, the pilot crashed directly into the ship behind ours. Death had been merely missed, but right beside us, it hit its ill-destined target.

During one point, as we loaded healthy men down all-too-mobile webs of rope, I was so intent, sweaty, focused in each second on this death-defying job that nothing distracted me. Suddenly, a mate yelled down from the ship, "President Roosevelt is dead!"

That went completely over our heads. One of my boat crew yelled back, "So what!" I was so focused on loading each man that this news did not even register—until much later.

After Okinawa, we sailed for Batangas, in the Philippines, to stage an invasion of Japan. We were in the midst of staging when word came of the bombing at Hiroshima. Who ever heard of Hiroshima? And bombing was commonplace, what was the big news? But then the rumors flew. The land was decimated and would be unable to foster crops for years; the water, poisoned for decades. I had no idea what a nuclear bomb was, absolutely no conception. And still, the stoic Japanese did not surrender. It took the second bomb, at Nagasaki, to convince them all was lost. The Japanese government sued for an armistice.

We received orders into Manila to pick up MacArthur's troops so they could begin the occupation of Japan. On September 2, 1945, I sailed toward Tokyo Harbor crossing the bow of the anchored USS Missouri. I watched Japanese diplomats board the Missouri as MacArthur received them, and thus, witnessed the ceremony of the signing of the Armistice, an incredible moment in history. Fifty years later, in 1991, I was invited as part of the delegation to attend the 50th anniversary sevices memorializing Pearl harbor. We were entertained on the battle ship Missouri.

As I sighted Tokyo Harbor, the surrounding hills were checkered with white sheets, as MacArthur had ordered, to disclose every last gun emplacement. Clearly, if we'd invaded we would have been caught in a murderous crossfire.

Instead, MacArthur staged a pageant. He flew in a military band and lined up thousands of small boats like ours, circling each other and flying an American flag, waiting for their call into the beach to discharge occupation troops. The band broke out in "The Ol' Gray Mare She Ain't what She Used to Be." Here we watched, alive, sure we'd averted what would have been the ghastliest, bloodiest battle in the Pacific. The water glittered and gleamed with thousands of our flags, accompanied by our own music. We were safe. Deeply moved, our troops disembarked one by one. The band lightened each step— we had somehow been spared. Jubilant, I thought I was through with this war.

In our second trip to Japan, our ship was sent to Kure Harbor to discharge additional American occupation forces. I witnessed the last of the Japanese Navy who had retreated into that harbor; all their war-ships, cruisers, and aircraft carriers anchored in row upon row, pulled in tight to defend the homeland. We respected the Japanese Navy from major battles they had fought so valiantly, including Midway. Now I saw these forces and knew we barely missed an unspeakable massacre.

And as Kure sat close to Hiroshima, I soon found myself with several others, sent on to "observe" Hiroshima, that shattered city, just one month after the bomb. The destruction I saw in Tokyo couldn't compare here. The devastation lay indiscriminate and the people cowered at our arrival, garbed in patchwork clothes. Well over 100,000 of their neighbors had been incinerated by one bomb.

As we arrived, people on shore hid their young protectively behind their backs, obviously hungry. On impulse, one crew member brought out his sack lunch and broke off pieces of sandwich, sharing it with those who were the "enemy" just a few short weeks before. Gradually each of us followed, eager to give away our own food to the stunned survivors of this destoyed city.

I had been trained to hate these Japanese. I would have almost relished killing them in battle. War creates such a raw, stripped-down human being, if someone at Hiroshima would have made one ill-timed move, I suspect we would have shot them.

Instead, I lifted up a small, Japanese child and was purged, spiritually renewed as hate flowed from my system. I had been a victim of this, my own hate. Here were people I dehumanized in my mind throughout the war, thinking of them as one vast, massive enemy, not human, not like any of us. Now on their shore I knew the brilliant truth. They were exactly like us, suffering, afraid—human. Oh, so human. As the adults relaxed and smiled, as my lunch was completely given to the children, my loathing vanished. I stood awash, clean in an epiphany which has never deserted me. Hatred had gushed out, transmuted into the powerful balm of compassion.

While ashore, two curious young Japanese men invited us on their bikes, peddling us through narrow trails cleared of rubble—no streets remained. We spied glass, fused together by sheer heat, and scorched, bar-like markings on a bridge indicating the direction the miles-away nuclear heat had seared. Buildings were in ruins, patches of the city still smelled of dead bodies, and rubble revealed bones and household implements. The few people left dug for possessions, aimlessly wandering Hiroshima looking for any remnant of a former abode, an identity, a relative, neighbor, or friend. The entire city lay silent but for their muffled voices.

As we left, I thought of my father who had fought in the war to end all wars. We, too, hoped our war could end this madness. Yet we felt uneasy, concerned we wouldn't be able to control this awesome, nuclear power. Our world was, frighteningly, one world in a way we had never recognized. There were no barriers left; not even oceans provided safety.

Some wished their loved ones could have seen the indescribable wasteland we witnessed at Hiroshima. But I never did. The sights of war haunted me and all I wanted was to get home.

Nor did I ever wish that catastrophe, that infinite amount of suffering, on any people. I even feared for my unborn children. Was this the type of warfare they might be forced to fight?

Hiroshima would forever mark my deepest thinking. I had seen the unbelievably destructive power in our possession: nuclear attack. And it was not good.

Yet still I was not destined for home. Instead, our ship sailed to Haiphong to pick up Chiang Kai-shek's newly arrived troops. We were then to bring them back to China so they could fight for the nationalist regime against the communists. In Haiphong, I wrote my parents.

October 26, 1945

Haiphong, Indo-China

Dear Folks,

Here we are in Indo-China adding another spot on the globe to my world travels. We anchored about 1000 (10 o'clock) in the muddy water off Dason Point. Very shortly our ship was surrounded with native boats begging for food and clothes. It was sickening to see the absolute poverty and the rags these people are in. We thought the Philippines were in a bad way, but they are wealthy compared to these exploited people.... the people here have never known anything but squalor since the French heel has been on them. They are wonderful seamen and handle their odd junk-like fishing craft perfectly whether they be 6 yrs. old or 60 yrs. old. One of the mess cooks brought the garbage cans out and dumped them overboard, and before you knew it the natives had fished every peeling and scrap out of the water....

On the beach we were sickened by the sight of the poverty of the natives. It is just like Willkie said in his One World—you see the mansion on top of the hill with the many shacks surrounding it. I tell you, it is a crime the way we occidentals have enslaved these people in our mad desire for money.... I can certainly see why these people don't want us to return and continue to spit upon them. There is so much

constructive work that could be done here in the Orient and sometimes I get the urge to come out here and do something. . . .

All my love,
Mark

I was a Navy lieutenant at the "ripe age" of 23 then, little realizing
I would face war again and rely on this heartfelt letter which expressed
it all.

In what is now Vietnam, I witnessed women desperately seeking
food to feed those they loved. While the Chinese loaded burlap sacks
of rice on our ship for their own provisions, Vietnamese women rushed
each sack one by one. They poised a flat basket in one hand, using the
other hand frantically as a trowel. They called out in their native tongue,
scooping dirt and debris into their baskets, hoping to sift out a few
stray grains of rice that slipped through. With these spare grains, they
would feed their families.

The Vietnamese had been poor to begin with. But when they were
occupied by the French and the Japanese, they had lost most of their
crops. They didn't know if, when, or where they might find their next
meal. They were clearly starving, yet as we peered up and above them
all, atop the hill the French blithely gambled in their plush casino.

And rather than helping, within two decades we Americans would
give them more suffering than they had ever known.

From Haiphong we sailed for Qinhuangdao, where the Great Wall
comes down to the sea. In the early morning our convoy approached,
warships firing onto the beach, pushing Chinese Communist forces
back so Nationalist troops could land. Instead of an amphibious landing, we were able to discharge troops onto a modern wharf constructed
by a young American engineer at the turn of the century—Herbert
Hoover.

It was now my time though and, ultimately, I did sail home.

Disembarking in San Francisco, bands welcomed each of our ships
and every man on board with a lively "Open Your Golden Gate." My
mates and I sped to the nearest restaurant and ordered nothing but
lettuce after lettuce after lettuce salad, chased down with cold, fresh
milk.

I was not destined for Oregon yet. Instead, I received assignment to the Shore Patrol in San Francisco as my final duty, rotating through some of the toughest neighborhoods in town. The Tenderloin District, with its 5,000 bars, and the area south of Market Street, an even grizzlier scene, to name two. I had two enlisted assistants with billy clubs, but I patrolled with no sidearm or weapon of any kind.

One night we were called into the Fairmont Hotel, where military personnel had taken over a party and grown increasingly raucous. Men shouted, throwing drinks over the mezzanine rails, busting things up. If you've ever visited the Fairmont, you know well this is not how they prefer to do business.

Here we entered, my two assistants and I, walking straight into the commotion. "All military personnel are to disperse immediately out of this room and out of this hotel," I proclaimed loudly. "And we're here to ensure you do so." The men listened, waiting, gauging whether I meant business. I stood my ground and they soon began funneling out. Those that couldn't or wouldn't leave (most incapacitated by alcohol) were removed bodily by my assistants. My voice must have sounded rather daunting, and that's a good thing. If the party hadn't dispersed, I have no idea what I would have done next. The hotel, to say the least, was quite grateful for our success.

Many of our actions on Shore Patrol were judged risky or courageous. Today, with the drug culture, they would be deemed utterly foolhardy. We didn't think of drugs then—alcohol was plenty bad enough. And I didn't consider my acts courageous; I had a job to perform and I found it much less demanding than hitting the beach at Iwo Jima or Okinawa. At least here we drew no enemy fire.

Our team patrolled the streets, emptied bars during brawls, helped sailors attacked by hoodlums. Our office sat right across the alley from the coroner's, where bodies were ferried after uprisings at Alcatraz; fresh cadavers with bullet holes piercing their bodies.

Yet I was home, free, alive. And after several months I finally rode back to Oregon in uniform, equipped with one duffel bag and not much else.

To this day I cannot watch a war movie. If I do, memories blossom fresh in my mind and just as swiftly, my eyes fill with tears.

Section Two:
Political Life

CHAPTER FOUR

Entering the Arena

*A*FTER THE WAR, I ENTERED LAW SCHOOL AT WILLAMETTE AND spent a dismal year—I didn't like law and law didn't appreciate my finer points either. I was far more interested in my current girlfriend than my studies, and eventually I did my professors a great favor. I left before being asked to leave.

I took off immediately for graduate school at Stanford University, heading straight for political science, my true obsession. I studied year-round on the GI bill, finished my master's and completed a year of doctoral work. Then all plans changed.

At Stanford, I found Travis Cross, a friend from Salem days. We'd go out for a bite to eat, scheming about politics in Oregon and what we could do to enter the scene. Travis wanted to stay in the background, to be the one to send a candidate into orbit. I was crazy enough to dream of being projected into flight. We jotted down post-doctoral plans, then in 1947 tragedy hit. A plane crash left Oregon's Governor Earl Snell, President of the Senate Marshall Cornett, and Secretary of

State Robert Farrell all dead. Travis and I decided I best get home.

Later, just before fall term, G. Herbert Smith, president of Willamette, offered me a political science instructorship and offered Travis a post as director of information and alumni affairs. My job paid a modest $300 a month, just enough to get by with my parents subsidizing room and board. The next year, 1950, I went back to G. Herbert Smith and asked to continue teaching while I ran in the primaries for state representative. By then I was involved in the local Cancer Society chapter, the local Radio Free Europe, and the Citizens Committee for the Hoover Report. I was vice chair of the local Republican Central Committee as well, and Travis had booked me with a radio commentary of my own we called "The Political Pulse." By this time, people had often asked, "Hatfield, why don't you run yourself instead of just talking about politics all the time?"

The Willamette president granted his approval for my campaign and asked that I also take on the job of dean of students. I learned a style in that post that would serve forever. Instead of calling students into my office to grill or scold, I called them in and quietly asked, "Do you have anything you need to tell me?" My questions came bolstered by a handy box of waiting Kleenex. Students seemed far more eager to pour forth their woes—and we got a lot more accomplished—than if I had taken the standard attack approach.

When the day came, I marched across State Street from Willamette to the Capitol to file my papers for candidacy. I say "march" because a group of faculty and students at Willamette, led by Bill Bissell, put together a ragtag "Oom-Pah-Pah" band from the Phi Delta Theta fraternity to accompany me into the Capitol. During the campaign, two Willamette co-eds—Margie Powell and Jackie Chute—received permission to use "Dear Hearts and Gentle People," just once in Marion County, and gave the words a facelift. "We love those dear hearts and gentle people," it began, including the names of as many Marion County towns as possible,

> Who live in Marion County....
> We hear a new name is on the ballot
> Mark Hatfield soon will run....
> From the banks of the Santiam to the Waldo Hills

We know Hatfield's name will be a topic of renown
He'll represent you in the legislature and never ever let you down....

The band proved so great that most in the Capitol turned out just to see what the racket was about, and the support became a good way to achieve name recognition. The next day a photo of us showed up in the newspaper in living black and white. I publically announced the campaign in Silverton, where I would announce every candidacy to come ever after. It was superstitious, I guess, like the guy who swears by lucky socks. Silverton never let me down.

Travis helped run my first campaign, and he proved brilliant both as a strategist and an analyst. His plans fit my style, and he was to play a unique part in my future success. He, and later Gerry Frank and others like them, were critical keys to my entire political career.

In this first race, I ran against 11 Republican candidates in the primary and seven others (four Democrats and three Republicans), in the general election. Whoever won the top four places on the ballot— all hailing from Marion County, not districts—would take the race. We didn't run from districts back then.

Travis and I both knew attorneys and businessmen seemed to dominate the political field in Oregon, and I was neither. Instead, I was a professor, and this was the '50s. Joseph McCarthy was afoot and people like me were considered soft on communism, as ridiculous as that now sounds. A student of mine had even been quizzed by a fellow passenger on a bus. "Why are you reading the Communist Manifesto?" came the query. "My instructor requires it," the student answered. "Who's your instructor?" the passenger shot back. "Mark Hatfield," came the reply.

My course was Soviet government and politics, and I couldn't have gotten far without my students reading the Manifesto, but that's not how some saw it. Thus, in my campaign, Travis and I both knew we had to do things differently. We determined to mobilize people instead of money—to know citizens and let them know me. Then they'd make informed choices, the best kind.

Traditionally, Republican candidates visited only the local banker, newspaper editor, and so on. But to me, social activity, grassroots advocacy, and classic liberalism were nothing if not emblematic of

Abraham Lincoln's Republican Party. I was a Populist, shaking hands and listening to as many people as I could rather than relying on campaign literature or distant handbills. We piggybacked onto several respected—and respectable—citizens in each community, and those folks walked the streets with me, a great entrée to people on the ground. I had sponsor groups in Hubbard, Woodburn, Mt. Angel, Jefferson, and Salem, and wanted to hear from each and every citizen, not just local leadership. I believed in the people and wanted to work with them. It was my job to introduce myself before they wrote me off as simply another candidate.

I was booked at lunch and evening meetings—every Kiwanis, Rotary, grange, union hall, or PTA, I was there. I listened, considering carefully what people said rather than spinning back what they wanted to hear. I knew they may well disagree, but I hoped to gain their respect for my forthrightness. My parents had drilled that into me: seek respect first, not popularity.

In a later campaign, I once showed up at a grade school commencement in the small town of Shaw to address eight graduates. That same night I had been invited to speak to several thousand people at the Portland Coliseum. Yet I honored my commitments in the order I received them, and even though Travis urged me to take advantage of the Coliseum opportunity, I refused. The grade school was where I had promised I would be. As a consequence, every television station in Portland came to watch and film that tiny commencement, and I'm sure we ended up with more publicity than we ever would have had if I'd cancelled the graduation appearance for the Coliseum.

Once I made it to Salem, many legislators wondered why I was wasting so much time and energy, still speaking. Why go off and speak so much and so often? But that's how I stayed in touch, maintained contact with those who supported me, and stayed accessible. It worked in the first campaign, and I depended on that approach right thought to the end—whether in the midst of a campaign or not.

If citizens expressed support in my first race, Travis or I took down their names on cards. Or folks came up and gave us cards on their own, offered support, told us they wanted to help. Our files were filling. After every coffee klatsch I'd come back to my secretary and say, "there was so-and-so there, and she does this and her husband does that and they have kids ages such and such...." Somehow, I tried to remember each individual and we took notes so I'd recall them all when we sat down to write thank-yous.

We never asked political affiliation—even then, bipartisanship was the point. I dreamed of representing all my constituents, not just Republicans. What an absurd form of representation that would be, listening only to those in your party. People aren't Democrats or Republicans, they're people. Party affiliation of my constituent is so far down my list of priorities it is almost invisible.

During that first primary, Mr. Miller, a Silverton high school teacher, asked me to speak on ballot issues to his senior social studies class. His students weren't voters, and wouldn't be for several years. But that was beside the point. Many students who visited my office year after year wouldn't be voters for even longer. But they were people I represented as much as their parents—perhaps even more so, as they didn't yet have a voice of their own. Besides, I got as much of a kick from their sitting in my chair as they did from sitting there. My staff continually stared at their watches during these visits. After an hour (when the students had been scheduled for 15 minutes), the staff shooed them out because I couldn't do it myself. And back in Silverton, Mr. Miller was so grateful I visited his students that he went out and delivered literature, stumping speeches for me himself.

We visited women's groups and retirement centers. I squatted at wheelchair level and listened to the concerns of the over-70 set (I can say that now, since I'm a card-carrying member). I even gave a talk at the Labor Temple, earning the endorsement of the Teamsters themselves. Now that was a news item: Republican receives labor endorsement! Their's was the sole endorsement I earned in that first campaign. And the Teamsters have stuck with me for the rest of my career.

In the end, of the 12 nominees for that first primary, three of them were incumbents. I joked with my father that if I lost by one vote in the primary, it would be his fault. He marched straight down to the courthouse and changed his affiliation to the Republican Party.

Our system worked. I came in first in the primary, then first in the general election. I would be making $600 a year. Soon, I was offered an insurance job that made $10,000 a year. Wow, too bad I didn't want to do that—I could have been a "millionaire!"

Soon, I was teaching 8 and 9 o'clock classes at Willamette and dashing over to the State Capitol for the 10 o'clock session.

During that first term I would reaffirm the strength of my convictions. It began with colored oleo, a hot Oregon dairy issue. During the war, most people couldn't afford or get butter, using oleo margarine instead. But oleo was simply a thick white slab with a little yellow coloring vial attached. Every housewife had to mix the coloring into the oleo, then remold the margarine before placing it on the table. What a waste of time. My fellow representative, Maurine Neuberger, knew it too. She wanted to repeal the ban on pre-colored oleo, and went so far as to don an apron on the House floor, taking a mixing bowl in hand and making all of us watch as she took the time to stir the golden coloring into the oleo itself. I was all for her repeal—why should some have to go to all this trouble just because they couldn't afford butter? After all, we even had pre-colored butter out of season, there was nothing unusual about that. But Marion County dairy farmers in Mt. Angel and elsewhere—my constituents—were vehemently opposed to pre-coloring oleo. That would prove awful for competition. I voted for colored oleo anyway, and every expert announced I had just committed political suicide (believe me, that may have been the first time, but it was far from the last time I heard that death knell).

After my oleo vote, I went right into the meat grinder, so to speak, and offered my opinion to local dairy farmers. "Look," I said, "you don't have to agree with me, but at least listen to what I have to say." They did, and they still didn't agree, but they must have respected my honesty.

It was so simple to express honest convictions and keep the record straight and consistent. How difficult it must be to remember what you say to whom if you're changing positions to suit whatever forum you find yourself in. And I dare say, telling the truth causes a lot less trouble.

While running from classrooms to the Legislature, I still kept up on all the bills at hand. Except once. These were the days when a representative's sole staff was one secretary. No research assistant, no support staff, nothing. And we had no office, either. Nothing but my desk on the floor of the House. Secretaries and representatives sat side by side in the House and literally worked from their small space. If someone came to speak with me, my secretary had to get up and leave to vacate a chair, and everyone in earshot was privy to the conversation. We packed our office in our arms every day. Files lay at our feet, stationery and correspondence stuffed and grew inside those old, brown expandable folders. And when needed, 60 secretaries down the hall vied for 30 old manual typewriters in a sterile, institutional room.

I rushed in one day during my second session and began chatting with someone over an issue. Before I knew it they were calling the roll and I needed to vote on a measure I was unfamiliar with. The bill would open adoption court records to anyone who chose to see them. My secretary, Lois Siegmund, and her husband had just adopted a daughter and I knew she followed this bill closely. "How do I vote?" I asked as the roll drew near. "Nay," she said.

"Nay," I called when they spoke my name. Well, turns out there were 59 ayes against my nay. Everyone else in the room turned my way as if to say "What happened to you?"

Quietly I asked, "What did you tell me to do that for?"

Lois explained she didn't believe court records should be wide open to anyone. Not that no one should have access to them, but certainly not everyone. I listened. "I guess you're right," I assured her.

And ever since, standing as the lone voice in opposition—which has happened more times than I care to remember—is quite comfortable when I have my convictions standing strong beside me.

I was re-elected in 1952. During that session I helped pass one of the bills I was to remain most proud of throughout almost 50 years of public service—and well beyond.

My interest in this issue began when I was a student at Willamette and the Columbia Broadcasting Company sponsored concerts bringing cultural benefits to small communities like Salem. I was a student representative on the concert series board. Customarily our artists performed in Salem, stayed the night in a hotel, then boarded the train or plane to their subsequent destination (Salem was no much more than a way station between San Francisco and Seattle). We had two hotels in town, the Senator and the Marion, both owned by the same man and neither very fancy. Yet the hotels saw fit to maintain a straight "No Coloreds" policy.

I confronted this racist rule when I'd invited Paul Robeson to dinner at our fraternity after his scheduled recital. Robeson, 6'4," had broken the color barrier with the Metropolitan Opera as he performed beside a white female soprano. Known so well for his voice and rendition of "Old Man River," he was also an advocate for human rights. His speaking voice, his frame, his hands, all outsized, were so impressive in this visionary man. After our visit however, I had to drive him all the way to Portland for lodging.

One year, the concert series had enough capital to invite Marian Anderson to be our star attraction. She blessed us with her performance at the community concert and I found in her a gracious manner and charisma. Listening to Anderson sing I grew entranced. She closed with her customary encore, "Ave Maria"—completely accapella. I walked out of the auditorium almost ecstatic, in awe of her tremendous personality, her talent, her beauty. Yet again, I had to drive our famous performer up to Portland for a night's rest. (I'm sure she had to pick up the entire conversation during our trip. I was still in a sheer trance.)

So years later, during my second legislative term, I knew many representatives had tried to pass a public accomodations act before me, attempting vigorously to bring Oregon into the 20th century. They had failed more than once. But I co-sponsored a new bill along with Senator Phil Hitchcock, with one of our greatest opponents being the Salem hotelier, a veteran House member himself. This act was contrary to the policy of the beverage industry, the hotels and motels across the state. They all stood united against it, he told me.

"Not all of them," I replied. "Prestigious hotels in Portland graciously honor everyone."

In the session just prior, a fair housing act passed. Additionally, the present Speaker of the House, Rudy Wilhelm, was a friend of mine and referred any hot items to the State and Federal Affairs Committee. Nothing could be hotter than civil rights, and Rudy sent it straight to State and Federal Affairs. I chaired this committee. We weren't certain we could win, but we moved that bill out of committee and it became the spotlight of the entire session. Few others expected us to win either. Why should we? The bill had failed several times before.

Desperate for votes, we even approached the wife and secretary of one House member. She supported our measure but her husband stood undecided. "We've done our best with him, now you've got to convince him," we told her. "We need his vote badly." One by one we earnestly canvassed allies and opponents alike, and when the vote came, we actually won.

And me? I gained arguably one of the greatest victories of my entire career. Anyone could get a room in any Oregon hotel now, and I knew justice had been served.

During my second legislative term in 1952, I was destined to meet Antoinette Kuzmanich, the greatest person in my life. In 1954 as I went on to the State Senate, Antoinette campaigned down one side of the street for me while I campaigned down the other. She was a sheer natural, and our story will wait, just a bit.

After that senate term in 1956, I finally knew politics had to play a greater role in my life than academia. I enjoyed teaching, and I'd gladly go back if ever I faltered in public life. But I had a passion for politics that would fire me for nearly 50 years. I retired from duties at Willamette and ran for my first full-time, statewide political post: secretary of state.

These were Democratic days and I became the sole Republican to win statewide office that year. We had a budding team now: Warne Nunn, my administrative assistant, Travis, my press secretary, and two secretaries: Lois, my personal secretary, and another wonderful woman, Leolyn Barnett, who became appointments secretary. We kept busy with state business and one of our many responsibilities included state grounds. Travis was so detail oriented that, among other things, he decided we had to have a way to contact the maintenance crew because there was no phone line to their shed. Issues like this would bother him until solved. Of course, Travis figured it out. He put a flashing red light outside his office, facing the maintenance quarters. And when the light flashed, the crew was to report to duty. Travis's light worked.

Until the superintendent of state police, General HG (FOD)

Maison, came by. "If you want to have a light, fine," he said, "but I don't think either of the two women working here are quite fit for the job Travis is advertising with his red light." Needless to say, Travis changed it right away.

Two years later, the incumbent Democratic Governor Robert Holmes, was completing his two-year, unexpired term and faced re-election. On the Republican side, Sigfried Unander, the state treasurer, was the favored son and heir apparent of the party, and had been all but anointed as Republican candidate for governor. He would run against Holmes. At the time of this race, well-heeled clubs still existed that were in the business of choosing and financing their choice of candidate for office. From the time of my first race, I'm sure they wondered who I was, this kid who came out of nowhere and was trying to run their business. They won just about every race, too.

Political friends, though, soon found Unander could never beat Holmes. Their polls showed he would clearly lose. The same friends tracked me down in my office, enthusiastically mentioning they'd discovered I had a good chance against the governor. I entered the five-way primary against the establishment's favored Unander, among others, and came away with over 50 percent of the vote. I won the general election for that four-year term as well. I somehow garnered over a third of voting Democrats, and even came away with a campaign surplus. I gave back to big donors ($5,000 at that point was about as major a contribution as you might get) and set a $1,000 limit on contributions. Then I became Oregon's governor at age 36 and never lost an election thereafter. (I had actually lost two before—senior class president in Salem High School to Elvin Holman, my cousin, and student body president of Willamette University, to John Macy. Both posts went to very well qualified men.)

But my success wasn't about me. It was about style, about my need to be in touch with those I served, and my insistence on staying in touch long after I won office. I visited every county in Oregon at least once a year, and my volunteers all competed as to who could keep me busiest. I was a baton passed energetically from county to county. I must have dedicated more sewage disposal plants, more schools, more parks, and broken more ground in every part of the state than anyone in history.

One time a representative grew incensed that I had a speaker installed in my office so I could listen in on the proceedings from the legislature. I'd inherited the speaker from my predecessor and didn't think much about it. All proceedings were completely public anyway. But she marched into the office and let me know.

"Here," I said simply, ripping the speaker from the wall and offering it into her care. She marched straight back to the legislature with her victory trophy.

If there was a natural disaster in Oregon, like the Columbus Day storm of 1962 or the Christmas flood of 1964, I was right on the phone to the mayors. "What can I do to help?" I'd ask. During the flood, when Oregon sustained over $224 million in damages, I lived in our emergency control post in the Capitol basement for nigh on 48 hours, missing Christmas with my own family. Some had criticized me for wasting money to create the emergency center shortly prior—what would we ever need that for? But it proved invaluable. Previously, my secretary had to type proclamations of disaster by candlelight on an old manual typewriter. Now, we were prepared. I asked officials to call me personally at any hour at emergency central, spoke on the radio four times to reassure citizens throughout the flood, and worked constantly to help every person in any corner of the state who phoned with a problem. I sat in that folding chair without sleep for two days. Simply, that was my job.

When I finally reached the U.S. Senate, I came home every month and got out the maps again. My staff and I pored over them and published my schedule in the papers. In every part of the state we held "Meet Mark" meetings, open to anyone who wanted to show up or ask a question. I wanted to hear and, more critically, I needed to listen.

People power; that's what elected me and kept me focused throughout political life. I couldn't have done it without the people of Oregon, nor would I have wanted to. There wouldn't have been any point.

CHAPTER FIVE

Growing a Family

W HEN I BEGAN TEACHING POLITICAL SCIENCE, THE CLASSROOM was totally different than classrooms today. Not due to fashion trends, though those were markedly different as well. Nor was it the tone of then current advertising, with housewives in head scarves, or men in evening wear chivalrously smoking cigarettes.

All these differences were true, certainly, but the striking difference was the sheer number of students older than I. The war was brutally fresh in all our minds, and the majority of students had served as I had. They were catching up with education thanks to the GI bill, and more often than not, I lectured men who were my seniors.

Other pursuits had also fallen by the wayside during the war, not only education. Certainly the most prominent of these was women. I was one of the youngest bachelors in my classroom; there were many older men who hadn't yet married. "Weekend weddings" before men embarked for war duty had been common, but many of those men were ones I counseled aboard ship as they inevitably received Dear

John letters. As for me, I had dated plenty before the war but hadn't fallen in love. And I certainly hadn't been ready to marry.

So as I became an instructor at Willamette, I held several passions on my plate at once. One was teaching, the other, politics. And last but certainly never least, was women. I dated women who were attractive, yes, but intelligence was tantamount. I most enjoyed women who carried on intellectual conversations, who liked politics. I knew where I was headed and had seen how unfair it was for politicians to drag spouses into political lives when the spouse was uninclined. How selfish to let myself be swept away by emotion alone and marry a woman who hated entertaining countless surprise guests, wished to stay home at night, or grew bashful in the public eye. No matter how much I might like her, I couldn't bring myself to drag any woman into a political life she might not fully understand—and even may abhor. Politics awaited and I wanted a willing partner.

Harley Hoppe, a fraternity friend at Willamette, changed my history forever. He was a natural-born promoter, bringing Stan Kenton and other big name bands to campus. He sponsored events and made pocket cash in the process. Perhaps he even placed a bet on me. "Hey," he called on campus one day, "I know this young school teacher at Parrish Junior High, and you should meet her. She's very," his eyes widened, "attractive. And personable too, Mark." He went on and on about this young woman, and I knew he must be promoting me to her in the same diligent manner. He tended to exaggerate, but something he said intrigued me. "I'm taking her to a school dance," he went on. "Why don't you just show up and meet her?"

Well, I was dean of students, you know, and it came within my official purview to drop in on dances now and then to make sure all ran smoothly. I took my responsibilities seriously, and for some reason, that dance became utterly essential to the completion of my duties.

I showed up at the event and it may sound corny, but it's true and I'll say it regardless: I was stricken. Stricken by her flashing, fiery brown eyes, her poise, her ease at meeting a new person. I was impressed, and yes, quite attracted. I liked this girl.

And that was the first time I met Antoinette Kuzmanich.

I always initiated calls for first dates with some expectation I wouldn't be rejected. I never wanted to bluster in, instead developing a well-honed strategy. (I suppose that echoes straight into my political life as well.) In any case, often a third party reassured me because they knew us both. Antoinette was no exception. I was friends with a local district judge, Val Sloper from high school, and his wife, Chris. She ran a beauty shop and we would all pal around together, playing bridge. Pretty soon I uncovered a secret: Chris cut Antoinette's hair.

"Why don't you take her out?" Chris chided, Val providing her cheering section.

"Maybe I will," I waffled.

I finally got up the gumption to call, and when I did, Antoinette at first mistook me for someone else. That was fine. She began telling me, or ostensibly this other man, she'd just gone to a political lecture on ballot issues. Even better she didn't know my identity—she was making points and wasn't even aware of it.

She finally figured out who I was and accepted my offer. We took the Slopers with us on that first date. How well I remember Antoinette's beautiful black velvet suit. With her dark eyes and hair, she simply sparkled with class. We ordered roast beef au jus and as the waitress lowered our meal to the table, the plates swam with meat juice. And swim they did. That waitress poured the au jus directly down Antoinette's new suit. It completely ruined her outfit. The waitress flustered while the Slopers blurted out, "Oh my goodness, your new suit!"

Yet Antoinette was cool under fire and I watched each move. "That's all right," she reassured as the devastated waitress wiped furiously at the stain, working it deeper and deeper into the fabric. "Accidents happen," Antoinette said, never flinching a muscle. She knew how to keep calm in any crisis, and I was impressed.

Antoinette pursued her own career at that time, as she always has, and I pursued mine. She had no need to curry her status by way of me, she had plenty of her own. After graduating with her master's in educating from Stanford, she took a job as counselor for girls and teacher of social studies at Grant High School in Portland.

Besides the sheer pleasure I felt in Antoinette's company, I also felt right at home. I gave her my complete attention and my heart lept ahead, urging me on.

I often parked at the curb at Grant High after her classes, striding in to escort her to the car. High school students waved and ogled as we got back in the car and pulled off. By the time I became secretary of state, Antoinette worked at Portland State—28 years old and chief counselor for women. Both of us loved our work, encouraging each other ahead. Already, we made a great team.

We courted for years, but there lay a grave problem between us as thorny and unwieldy as a kept secret, and that problem was religion. I had been raised Baptist and she, Catholic. In those days, long before Vatican II, marriage between Catholics and other Christians simply wasn't tolerated.

In my heart I knew Antoinette was the woman I wanted to marry— the only one for me. Yet I also knew it was fundamental to share faith in marriage. I knew faith would ever contribute to our happiness, our common bond, our future parenting. Antoinette was certainly as Christian as I, but if I went to her church, I couldn't take communion. She could take communion in my church, but it wouldn't be looked on with approval by her own. If we married, strictures would be placed on me to raise our children as Catholics, a huge commitment I didn't feel able to fulfill. We dated for years and knew exactly what we wanted—each other—but neither expected nor could possibly ask the other to change in such a fundamental way.

When Antoinette left for Stanford to complete her master's (and probably to leave me so she could think), the two of us corresponded. In those days, Catholics weren't urged to read the Bible but the Missal instead—the Catholic liturgy. So that Christmas I gifted my love with a bona fide Catholic Bible, translated directly from the Latin, complete with the pope adorning the frontispiece. When she returned to Stanford, I sometimes cited biblical verses in my letters. Then, Antoinette analyzed the passages. We both believed love imbued our respective faiths, and she grew to know faith could be based in love, not fear (the latter is naught but "fire insurance" against the ravages of hell). She still attended mass each morning but began to know a freedom she hadn't before, a sense of direct contact with the divine, without need of an intermediary. As for my upbringing, instead of pope or priests and a divine chain of command to one's God, each Baptist church was totally controlled by congregational will, free to innovate, and thereby freeing parishioners to find their own way to the divine.

One Sunday afternoon the two of us were invited to dinner at Doug Coe's, an instrumental friend who had helped me transform my religious beliefs into action. He and his wife Jan welcomed us, and Doug pointed out the common religious ground we were already on. "You two are talking the same language," he insisted. "There's no problem here. Keep your focus on the love for the Lord your faiths both teach, and you'll be fine."

He was absolutely right. Let's not let institutions become an impediment to our common faith in marriage, we both thought. And that was it. A major obstacle had been cleared with love, and there was nothing in the way of intertwining our lives.

(As epilogue, on our recent 41st wedding anniversary Antoinette and I repeated our vows at St. Anthony's Parish with our good friend Father Mike Maslowsky presiding. There a sacred circle was completed.)

I'm embarrassed to admit I don't remember how I proposed, but somehow I did. I do remember we announced our engagement in 1958 amongst a close group of staff at Warne Nunn's house—it was all in the family. Our staff was that tight. Travis and Warne even had what they called "the oath of duplicity." They worked so well together that they swore if I fired one of them, the other would resign. Of course they knew they never had to worry. I depended on them both so much. Besides, I couldn't quite bear to fire anyone—that was Warne's job!

Everything felt right during our engagement. Chemistry, companionship, and oh, how I loved that woman. I knew she was the one. She still is to this day—we recently celebrated our 42nd anniversary and I feel exactly the same way. When she leaves town,I miss her before she reaches Chicago.

The engagement, though, was nothing if not public. The Oregonian found us at a football game and snapped an engagement photo for the paper. I ran in the May 1958 primaries for governor and we set our wedding date for her parents' 30th anniversary. We campaigned together and at events, women offered corsages to Antoinette and made sure to seat us together. We quickly learned, while approaching any head table, to gauge the length of the table cloth hanging down facing the room. We wanted to sneak our hands together underneath without being found out.

On July 8, 1958, at Hinson Memorial Baptist Church in Southeast Portland, we were wed. It was a hot, hot, hot summer night, and one of my ushers, Don Robinson, a 6'3" hulk of a man, stood next to a stunning bank of blazing candles. He leaned so close to the flames that the oxygen around him expired and he fainted dead away. We heard a rustle behind us but were oblivious as they laid Don out in the first pew. The poor guy was completely mortified—even to this day.

We spent our first night at the Multnomah Hotel (now Embassy Suites) then drove down to Pebble Beach to a house owned by friends of Antoinette. I never give details on our honeymoon or anything about our love life—that's private and there's precious little that can be kept private in public life—but suffice it to say we had a great time in every way.

By the time we made the trip back up the coast, the general election campaign for governor was on. First stop, we pulled into Brookings for our potluck dinner in the park and our inaugural wedded appearance. Antoinette nudged me. "Mark, take a little bit of each dish," she whispered as we approached the tables where women plied their treats. Moments later she advised, "Take some of those beans, too."

"I've already had the other ones," I protested.

"Yes, but all the ladies are watching, and you haven't had hers!"

She took to the public role with grace and sensitivity, even though debacles like that black suit fiasco were far from over. At one church event, a young woman with an infant sweetly asked Antoinette, "Would you like to hold my baby?"

"Oh yes!" Antoinette glowed, taking the infant right away. Well, you know what happened next. This time it was a bright blue suit, and that child blithely let loose, wetting the entire front of the outfit. By now I'm sure Antoinette thought this was simply some kind of political hazing. She gently handed the baby back to its mother, smiling all the while, and went on with her business.

Soon, our own babies began nonchalantly anointing us with bodily effluvia. Unfortunately, as you enter politics your family becomes a target to get to you, and they're all too easy to attack. That's perennially the way of politics, and it's small minded and hurtful. It's also hell when you and your family are under attack and you can do nothing but watch the effect it has on your spouse and children. And recently in politics, it only seems to be getting far worse.

But innocent of all this, our daughter Elizabeth joined us in 1959 and I couldn't believe her arrival. Here she was, so much black hair, pink skin, simply beautiful. Just gorgeous. She was flesh and blood of Antoinette and me; new life. I was stunned with her living, breathing example of the cycle of the universe. She looked up and I'm sure she couldn't focus a foot in front of her face, but I knew she was looking at me and smiling. I projected all sorts of lofty interpretations on how wonderfully she was responding to her new father. I felt that exact wonder each time Antoinette birthed a baby, but Elizabeth was our introduction. We each woke nights, checking her breathing, and probably re-sterilized her bottle each time it fell. The last child was lucky if we wiped his bottle nonchalantly on our sleeve.

After Elizabeth and Antoinette's normal birth and 12-day hospital stay (can you imagine, 12 days!) MarkO arrived 11 1/2 months later. The doctor invited me into the delivery this time, so I gowned and scrubbed and pushed through the swinging doors of the inner sanctum. I'm sure Antoinette had no awareness of my presence—she was focused on her task. MarkO was born just after midnight on Father's Day, amidst jocular accusations by Democrats that the timing of the birth had been rigged for my political gain!

Antoinette wanted our first son named after me. But to give him his own distinctive name, we contracted the first initial of his and my middle name, Odom, and Mark Jr. became MarkO.

Witnessing that birth was like no other experience and I was glad to have been there. Yet I had no desire for a repeat performance. MarkO's birth made me stop and think about putting Antoinette through all that—ever again. Luckily, memory mercifully fades. We soon had two more children, Theresa and Visko—that made four in six years. In the meantime, our doctor was actually reprimanded for letting me defile the sterility of the birth chamber.

They were all so different, our children. Theresa displayed the utmost in dainty hands and features—her entire manner danced, so petite. A blithe spirit, life flowed for her in spite of any rain. She's still that way. Every season is spring, and she's a sprite. Theresa was the least vocal of all our children. In fact, she had no reason to speak. She had the total attention of her older sister, brother, parents, and grandparents. All she need do was point, and any of us would do her bidding.

Finally came Charles Vincent, with no hair and a scrunched up smile exactly like Dwight Eisenhower's. He was named for his two grandfathers, my father Charles, and Antoinette's father Vincent. We call him Visko—Serbo-Croatian for Vincent, in honor of Antoinette's father's heritage. But I soon put those lofty reasons aside and dubbed my second son Viskoroni. I always marvel at how nicknames evolve, or better yet, how they just pop up. I don't know why I called him that, but he was Viskoroni to me.

Ours were all good-sized babies too; no little runts, all healthy and husky. We gave them family names and offered the girls no middle names. We wanted them to be able to keep Hatfield as they later married, if they chose.

We planned on having six children, even though Antoinette and I were lonely onlys. And after Theresa, the third, we never could figure out what to do with that extra half grapefruit at breakfast each morning. Luckily for Visko, he embodied the solution to that dilemma. Yet neither Antoinette nor I had any idea that sibling rivalry existed and all the itinerant troubles of multiple children. Once we had Visko, we decided we'd best stop while we were proverbially ahead. We've been blessed with four wonderful children, and to this day I feel sorry for those who have difficulty conceiving or finding children of their own. It's impossible to describe parenthood, even on days when you're about ready to bail out of the entire proposition. There is just nothing like it in human experience.

Antoinette was ever the mother bear, carefully keeping our children from the public eye. She vigilantly nurtured a normal life for them, not one spattered with autographs and security officers, photos and media paraphernalia. But despite her, we received threats on the childrens' lives.

We lived in a small corner house at 883 South High Street, across from Salem's Bush's Park. The second oldest house in Salem, we had added on to it ourselves. As governor, I still loved to garden, and soon I was bringing the kids along. We dug 90 holes for 90 rose bushes in the parking strip beside our house, and I mowed and kept my own lawn. Friends and strangers drove by, waving to me and the children.

One Saturday, diligently working the lawn, we discovered we were short of fertilizer. Antoinette and I piled all four kids into the car—in the days when you couldn't see out the back window for their heads. We didn't yet know how critical child safety seats and seat belts were. We drove six blocks to the feed store, then stopped at the drugstore. There I ran into a neighbor, Bruce VanWyngarden.

"You had quite a bit of excitement over at your house today!" he remarked.

"Huh?" I answered, my most intelligent. "None I know of, unless you mean mowing the lawn."

"My son drove by," my friend added. "He saw a fellow shooting straight into your house. Our boy came right home and phoned the police."

"I sure didn't know!" I said, speeding my family off to see what had transpired. As it turned out, the man was a welfare applicant who had been denied benefits and grew desperate. He spewed 10 rounds of ammo towards the front of our house, then ended up in the state mental hospital. And that could have been us, I thought, right there in the front yard, our children included.

Protesters came up our porch steps, too, often demanding to see me or Antoinette. She would tell them the governor wasn't there and they'd come back with, "Then we want to speak with you."

"I'm not the governor," Antoinette retorted just as quickly. Convicts came wanting to discuss parole cases. Everyone knew where the governor lived because the address had been sprinkled all over the papers. Unlike my predecessors, I often walked or drove a Rambler sedan to work instead of using the state-driven limousine, saving the fancy car for travel or state affairs. But for safety, the legislature decided they'd best increase security at our home, and soon a security kiosk stood in our driveway. Away from home, anonymous calls threatening to gun me down still came in, especially since my itinerary was published in every paper. If I was going to be in Hood River, I was an easy target. All you had to do was read my calendar in the *Hood River News*. Travis Cross and Loren Hicks protected me from more threats than I ever knew of. Within hours of JFK's assassination, for instance, my security had been increased.

Regardless, we did everything we could to make our children believe I was like any other father. We didn't want them spoiled nor exposed to threats. Antoinette was a veritable mother bear defending her cubs—if you fooled with her, you'd better be prepared because you'd be fooling with mother nature. Once I took two-year-old Elizabeth to the state fair and some photographer snapped her photo, placing it on the front page. Antoinette was so mad she could have strangled the editors. She let them know, in no uncertain terms, our children were not to be photographed. That time, I was only too glad to be out of the line of fire.

And as I opposed Vietnam, animosity increased. Here I was, desperate to stop senseless killing, and others wished to swap my life in payment for my "evil" deed. The irony would have been funny if not tragic. My secretaries intercepted all the mean-spirited letters I received. They would hold them in their hands and weep. Simply weep. I could barely coax the missives out of their protective clutches.

Turmoil affects anyone in political life to some degree, and I suppose if you supported the Vietnam war, you had flower children opposing you. But I suspect peaceniks were much less likely to threaten bloodshed than their opponents. I kept getting re-elected, but it sure didn't mean I was universally liked—or voted for—by all. This was the '60s. There were rampant protests, awful assassinations—John and Bobby Kennedy and Martin Luther King, Jr.—and ROTC buildings burning to the ground. Everyone was affected.

All the turmoil made Antoinette that much more vigilant. We feared for the kids' lives, but at the same time I was reminded of World War II. I was wary of all possibilities, always watching my family's back, yet I did feel a bit fatalistic. We couldn't fret away our lives hiding around in the basement, we had to live the life we had chosen, even if it meant hypervigilance. Every Tuesday, Antoinette even offered an open house, a tea for anyone who would choose to come. Occasionally, buses full of touring women pulled up at the house, hundreds of them lining around the block in umbrellas, waiting to crowd into our living room.

Antoinette did this all on her own. She just made it up. Perhaps she didn't need to, but we both felt the entire state was our community. There had been so much attrition and death in the governor's chair I was actually to be Oregon's first governor to complete a second term in the twentieth century. We craved more than a relationship with "our" party, or "our" community. We wanted to know everyone, and did our best to live up to our values.

I chose to be the people's governor, and I didn't wait for people to come to me. I went to them. It was a busy time in Oregon, diversifying our economy beyond timber, breaking ground for new industries compatible with our enviromental mission, luring in new work. "Payrolls and Playgrounds" was our motto. I'm a visual learner, needing to meet people involved in projects I'd read or heard about, and I was often out in the field. Once, I made a surprise visit to a school for delinquent girls because we heard there were problems there. I spied a light fixture with metal rings encircling and filtering the light. There were sharp metal pieces scattered about the floor, terribly sharp and dangerous. Visions of violent possibilities in my mind, I put a stop to using those lights immediately. It may sound like a small gesture, but getting out there allowed me to do a better job.

I'm an activist, too. My activism often turned up in small ways as well, no big splash across the papers but true life stories that gave me great gratification. A woman in the Columbia Gorge, for instance, recently reminded me she had been a young woman in beauty school when her mother died, and besides her awful grief she had no money to finish her studies. Her teacher phoned me during my first senate term and I scoured for funds to help. I found some, but getting them would take too much bureaucratic red tape and time. Instead, frustrated by this unmet need, I offered to loan the woman money out of my own pocket to complete her schooling. She found a life insurance policy of her mother's to cover her tuition, but she called recently to thank me. I thank her, and all those like her across this state and land who trusted me and allowed me to take a small part in their lives.

Moving to the Senate would prove a great challenge in ways like this—it became harder to move things along as I had been used to in Oregon. I had a great team during the governor years, and I could never have done any of it without my staff or the local committees across the state. Each city or hamlet was a key partner, diversifying their economy on a town-by-town basis. Getting out there to see them brought my job to life. It kept me focused on what I was there to do.

My family kept me focused as well. There aren't many perks you actually receive as a United States senator. Parking is still horrendous, haircuts aren't free, and we all pay for our own houses, clothes, food, cars, and so on. Sometimes my kids' friends thought, because of my job, unlimited bounty miraculously appeared if ever we asked—free vehicles, La Coste shirts, or homes in Georgetown. Of course it doesn't work that way, and certainly shouldn't. Even senate pay raises were something I consistently voted against. But there are perks, truly wonderful ones, which come to those serving in the Senate including your family having access to the Capitol when accompanied by a member. During the Panama Canal filibuster, when I fought diligently to hand the Canal back to the Panamanians who it rightly belonged to, (while others like Senator Aiken, Republican from Vermont, boldly announced, "I've come to the conclusion that we stole the Canal fair and square, and I'm not about to give it back!") Antoinette and the children often visited and ate dinner with me in the Senate Dining Room when sessions ran late or speech-writing required long hours. We won that fight over the Canal. And my children were able to see me at work, to walk the senate halls, to visit the inner dome of the Capitol, or the rotunda and dome of the Library of Congress, and to breathe in the same scent of awe I held for our mighty institutions of freedom.

Looking back though, I'm not sure how Antoinette and I did it all. Countless activities and four children to raise. I can proudly say I did my share of night feedings, teacher meetings, and school plays. Interrupted nights and full-to-busting days. All I can say is, thank God for grandparents. Our parents were, and are, the greatest.

Lest it be misinterpreted that our children were perfect, I'll recount a couple of typical—well, perhaps not so typical—childhood foibles. As backdrop, we always had a veritable menagerie in our home. Larry the lizard (an iguana), cats, dogs, birds, what have you.

But the boa took the cake. MarkO loved reptiles, claiming he wanted to study the species when he grew up. Just as much as he loved them, Antoinette despised them. She was absolutely petrified. She couldn't stand the idea of a boa, but MarkO wore her down. He got his first baby boa, also named Larry, at the Multnomah County Fair. Yet finally, Antoinette overruled her previous decision. She insisted he give the snake away and MarkO chose Michael Aldrin—moonwalking astronaut Buzz Aldrin's son—as the noble recipient. MarkO never even spoke to Michael. I had to arrange the whole thing with NASA.

Next, somehow, MarkO finagled himself another boa and fed it live mice. Pretty awful, truth be told, but I guess that's nature at work.

Soon we began coming home nights from events to a house as steamy as an oven. "Those kids!" I would say. "What are they doing keeping the heat so high—it's nearly 80 degrees in here!" It's true, sometimes my voice became more than elevated. Night after night this scene repeated itself and we had no idea that the boa had escaped its box. Not only that, the kids had the smarts to call the National Zoo and ask how to find an escaped boa. "Turn the heat up," they'd advised. "The boa will get hot and thirsty and come out for water."

Unbeknownst to me, I kept turning down the thermostat every night and grumbling. One night, Elizabeth awoke to a clattering in her bathroom. A glass tumbler had fallen into the sink with a racket. She ran and got MarkO up, and together they found that snake decorously draped over the shower rod. A team, they secured the slithering boa back into its box.

At breakfast, I noticed the boa caged up. I hadn't noticed it was gone, to tell the truth, but seeing the reptile fired me on. "Son," I decreed, "it's either your mother or the boa, and you have to make a choice." MarkO puzzled over that a long time, having trouble determining which of those two family members were preferable. I guess it came pretty close. I interrupted his reverie, counseling him that, in fact, his mother had to come first. He sullenly accepted the final verdict and promised he'd give the boa away. In the meantime he secreted the boa's box down into the daylight basement, the kids' playroom.

I started down there one evening and lo!, there was the innocent boa, escaped yet again, slithering back and forth up the stairs. Just around the corner from the top stair—drumroll please—sat unknowing Antoinette in the library, chatting on the phone. She may not have minded au jus or wet diaper unceremoniously dumped all over her, but snakes she could not abide. I was panicked and knew I had to move fast.

I darted into the closest room, Theresa's, the boa gaining fast upon my heels. Theresa startled, practically cutting loose with a scream, but I slammed my finger to my mouth. "Shhh!" I whisper-yelled, "We've got to get this boa caged before your mother sees it!" Theresa jumped up and snatched a gym bag while I grabbed a broom and gently pushed the snake toward its lair. All the while the boa slithered and squirmed back and forth, back and forth, just as snakes so deftly do. We caught the boa, I zipped up the bag and carried that thing to the garage. Finally, I took a breath. National outcries I could handle, but a meeting between the snake and my wife was something to be avoided at all cost. The next morning, I announced to MarkO, "I've given you your chance, now I'm getting rid of that snake!" Okay, yes, my voice was pretty elevated.

"No, no, I'll do it tonight, dad, I promise!" MarkO came back.

But I didn't want MarkO out at night. Still somehow, he begged to take responsibility and I deferred. But we moved shortly thereafter and I spied that snake once again in our new basement. The second I saw it I asked Steve Crow, one of my staff, to take it on a pilgrimage straight to the pet shop. Those weren't tax dollars at work here, don't worry. Steve graciously did it on his own time.

MarkO noticed his snake had disappeared, but was far too frightened to ask where it was. He knew he had failed in his promise. And I certainly wasn't offering him the satisfaction of knowing I'd donated his friend to a healthy home. Let him think it's been cut up for dog food, I grumbled to myself.

At some point, our children went beyond animals to keener interests. The oldest kids were always responsible for the littler ones; Elizabeth for Visko, MarkO for Theresa. When Theresa had a boy pick her up for a date, I remember MarkO telling the young man, "I want to talk to you." MarkO took him aside and I have no idea what he said. He clearly stated his expectations of how his sister was to be treated, I'm sure. And I felt plenty sorry for the poor guy.

MarkO took excellent care of Theresa, but he was excellent at stretching our patience as well. For a time we had him in a private boys school. He never wanted to go there in the first place, and tried desperately to fail his entrance exams. He was shocked when his acceptance letter arrived, despite his best sabotage efforts. Once he started classes, uniforms were mandatory. But he was western, not one of these eastern preppies, and he researched school regulations to the letter. Soon, instead of flannel slacks, Oxford shirts, and a jacket, he began showing up in cords, plaid Pendleton shirts, and some godawful ties. But he still hated that school.

At the barbershop he'd make a huge scene, too, complaining that his haircut was way too short. Finally we had to coax an unknowing barber into providing housecalls.

Hair and all, MarkO knew he was conservative. In high school he came home utterly disgusted with one teacher, an FDR Democrat with a big poster of Roosevelt in the classroom. "That teacher's so hot on FDR, I expect to see candles burned before the poster as if it were an altar," he spat, asking me for reading material in line with his beliefs. I didn't agree with his politics but I gave him titles just the same.

But MarkO was so repulsed by his school, just getting him to go each day increasingly became a test of wills. Every year we told him "just one more year," yet somehow, by the beginning of the next year we reneged and MarkO was back at the boys' school. He hung tough, but inside he must have felt betrayed and completely unrespected. By ninth grade his resentment grew to blazing and neither we nor he made any progress. Looking back, I can't really blame him for letting us know in such a big way.

Now MarkO admits it's actually a beautiful campus and an excellent school. The fact is, he'd send his own sons there if he lived in the vicinity. Today he's so conservative that when he sees a photo of himself with long hair, he immediately wants to destroy it, righteously indignant we didn't force him to cut it shorter.

God knows I tried. But one day Antoinette came to me. "You're going to have to start majoring in the majors and stop majoring in the minors," she said. "Or you're going to lose any hope of a relationship with your oldest son." She was right. It was a sheer power struggle between MarkO and me, and it wasn't about hair length or school or any other issue at all. I was intent on being the boss, pure and simple.

I finally yielded and MarkO grew his hair to his shoulders immediately. Meanwhile, Antoinette had taught me one of my most important lessons in parenting.

A few years later, I liked to think it was adolescent rebellion when MarkO went to work for President Reagan, but I'm afraid it wasn't. He became Reagan's advance man for trips all over the world; Japan, Europe, South America, and elsewhere. And in the White House itself he was so well liked by Reagan's White House staff, including Meese, Dever, and Baker, that I suppose they figured since he was okay, his reactionary senator father must be alright as well. MarkO's sheer presence helped create a bridge for me to the White House that otherwise might not have existed during the Reagan era. Likewise on our end, when friends complained about Reagan or supported me in controversy with the president, Antoinette always piped up. "All I can say is he's nice to my boy and therefore he can't be all that bad!"

MarkO wasn't our only child to rebel—far from it. Because both Antoinette and I had served as veteran educators and counselors, I suppose we expected no problems from our children. And perhaps others assumed our progeny would turn out perfectly. Both predictions failed, however. Abysmally.

In fact, only one of our four children actually attended their graduation from high school. Elizabeth made it clear in her senior year that she'd become bored with her studies and wanted nothing to do with them. She simply wasn't challenged. When we asked how do you plan to get admitted to college?—which she definitely intended to do—she announced she would take the equivalency exam. She followed through, scored extremely high and attended the University of Oregon in Eugene to pursue her interest in health care. During school she volunteered in a drug crisis center, became an Emergency Medical Technician (EMT), and worked part time in an ambulance. She then became an emergency room nurse at Providence Hospital in Portland and, after nine years, decided she wanted to improve her credentials so as to be continually challenged. At age 30, with the support of her husband, Greg Keller (head of the arson investigation team for the Portland Fire Department), Elizabeth attended Oregon Health Sciences University (OHSU) medical school and completed her residency in emergency medicine with awards. She serves now in the OHSU Emergency Department and teaches emergency medicine to medical students there.

Strangers and friends often approach us to share how Elizabeth has touched their lives. Once, for instance, Antoinette and I strolled in downtown Portland and Antoinette paused to window shop. A stranger came by. "I just want you to know your daughter saved my husband's life," she said, explaining how Elizabeth resuscitated the man after a heart attack. Elizabeth herself doesn't tell us her stories, so when others do, it's a great thrill for us.

As for our second child, MarkO wouldn't be caught dead or alive at some silly high school graduation, so he simply picked up his diploma at the school office. After the White House, he worked with the Bonneville Power Administration, the Commerce Department, and then became spokesperson for the Port of New York/New Jersey—a gubernatorial appointment. Now he's working for a high-tech company. He produced our first grandson, Mark III, whom we call Markus. We've conjugated each generation of Marks to offer a distinctive, individual name to each. MarkO also gifted us with a second son, Hunter, and a daughter, Sasha.

Of all our children, MarkO has pursued politics further than the others, and I hope it's satisfied him. Unfortunately, because of the loss of private life, the perpetual fund raising and the special interests that seem to consume politics today, I can't say I would like to see him—or any of my children—run for public office. MarkO is gifted as a crises manager, walking into any chaos and creating order. He has a remarkable way of getting people to work together, and his gifts are just as valuable well outside the political realm.

After MarkO's high school non-graduation, TT came next: Terrific Theresa. But Theresa's grades were, shall we say, less than satisfactory. I personally went to more teacher meetings regarding Theresa's performance than I care to count. In fact, we had a battery of exams conducted to discover why she had so much difficulty in high school. Everything came out great—except her grades! They were so poor she was not allowed to attend her own graduation. I pled with her to prepare for college, where she had every desire to go. Finally, she struck a deal with Emerson College on Beacon Hill in Boston, a school particularly strong in communications. If she attended summer school, took three courses and passed with at least a B average, she would be admitted on probation. That summer Theresa gifted us with three As and became admitted on the Dean's list.

She graduated, attended law school at Catholic University and—through his sister, Kathleen—met Manus Cooney, her husband. She went to work for the Federal Energy Regulatory Commission writing oil and gas regulations, and later worked in the anti-trust division of the Attorney General's office. Now on maternity leave, she's the proud mother of three little girls, Caitlin, Claire, and Tara. And as to her husband, let's just say I couldn't have picked better sons-in-law for my daughters than they picked for themselves. Both Greg and Manus are princes.

Visko was perhaps the calmest of our kids. Having seen what went before him, maybe he didn't want us to suffer anymore! Besides solitaire I love jigsaw puzzles, and Visko became my loyal jigsaw puzzle partner and "MFV"—My Friend Visko. I have a habit of rearranging all my treasured books, including my presidential biographies, so they all sit just right on the shelf. Teasing me, Visko would call at work and let me know he had just finished rearranging them all by color! My heart leapt but soon I was on to him—he never touched my books.

He was also my faithful gardener. In our first home in Bethesda we had nine-tenths of an acre of garden and lawn. I felt all the children should do their part so I assigned mowing, weeding, and raking among them. One child soon wandered off to the bathroom while another announced they had to make a phone call, and so on. But Visko always stuck with me to the bitter end.

Last but not least, he did attend his high school graduation! Yet at the final moment we were sure he had chickened out. There came each boy/girl pair, solemnly making their way down the aisle, one after another after another, ad infinitum. Finally Antoinette and I began asking, "Where's Visko? Where's Visko?" almost certain he had disappeared.

But no. Visko, our athlete, the one who majored in soccer and girls, ended the line. Evidently one girl was not sufficient. Instead he escorted two, each flanking him on one arm, as he strutted up the aisle to finish the class line.

Visko is a precise planner and totally organized, like his sister Elizabeth. After graduating from the University of South Carolina in photo arts, he knew he wanted to strike out in New York City as a photograper. He reduced his target of apprentices to Albert Watson, the famous fashion and personality photographer, and one or two others. But Visko wasn't idealistic. He knew he might not be accepted immediately. So he came home to Washington to live rent-free and eat for free with us, all the while waiting tables in The Occidental, a fine restaurant on Pennsylvania Avenue. He saved his pennies until he had enough to live for an entire year in New York without taking a job. He concentrated totally on getting onto Albert Watson's staff, and he did. He also met the love of his life, Sharron, an administrator in the fashion business. The two of them make a terrific team and Sharron is just wonderful. She is a very special person.

Visko apprenticed with Watson for five years, then became fashion director at Macy's. Very frugal, he determined that by saving money he could go off on his own and enjoy his living more as a freelance photographer in New York, which he's done successfully for several years now. Recently, he opened his first photographic show at Antoinette's art gallery, a huge thrill for the family.

Looking back, as parents I know we tried to be reasonable with all our children, never setting curfews, letting the children's behavior fall on their own consciences.

But of course all our children had their antics. They were children, after all.

And all four have made us terribly proud.

A friend once told me there's a Yiddish word, *nachas*, for what every parent hopes for from their children. Pride, joy, a sense of accomplishment and grace. That's what our children still give us. Plenty of nachas.

I hope they all sensed early the value of family. They had two sets of grandparents and, in spite of all my responsibilities, they had a mother always available and a father who dropped everything when needed. I missed a lot of landmarks, soccer games, recitals, and so on. But whenever I got a call saying I needed to be there, even if Portland was on fire, my children got priority and I sped off. I also put time with family on the calendar because I knew who came first. And long before research "proved" it valuable, one of our cardinal rules was to eat breakfast together—all together—every chance we could. We never discussed politics at the table, either. I needed a chance to hear about my family's world with no politics at all. We had family friends like Gerry Frank. "Uncle Gerry" was a wonderful third adult, and still is. Our kids were raised in community, and I hope we gave them a sense of security as well.

It's family values I speak of, I suppose, though I hate bringing up that term which means so many different things to just as many different people. To me, it means recognizing an interrelationship with others based on pure love. It's being accountable, one to another, responsible, one to another, and sensitive enough to reach out when needs arise. Family is the top priority—dropping everything else to meet the needs of your loved ones. And children only learn this by the loving examples of their parents, not by virtue of any gene, nor any lesson taught in school, church, synagogue, or mosque. Not in words, but in sincere deeds.

Family is another word for love, and if there's any legacy I've left my children, I hope it's just that; a legacy of faith and love. Above all things, I strive to love family most. Every day.

CHAPTER SIX

Inheriting the Doomed

*A*s I became Oregon's newest governor I inherited a handful of convicts on death row. And almost immediately, I was
thrown into one of the toughest quandaries in my career.

Inheriting the convicts alone was nightmare aplenty. But even
worse, during my election I'd locked myself into an ideological box
and soon found myself utterly unable to escape.

In my first race for governor against Bob Holmes, the incumbent,
he and I co-chaired a repeal of the death penalty. Both of us felt the
people should reassess this grave issue, and we fought side by side to
prove the death penalty morally wrong.

During the campaign, he and I stood on a joint platform at the old
Washington Hotel, debating before the League of Women Voters. It
was known we both opposed capital punishment, so naturally our
questioners asked us each about our position. They tried to pit us against
one another. In their view, I'm sure, they were unsuccessful. In my
view, it was deadly.

Bob was clear. "I'll tell you today," he said, "If I'm re-elected governor, I'll commute every single death sentence."

He spoke first, I was next, and the audience hushed, tense to hear my words. I wanted to distinguish myself from Holmes, though our views were so similar. Yet there was indeed one point on which I felt quite a variance. "I'm just as opposed to capital punishment as Bob Holmes," I began, explaining how strongly I opposed the taking of any human life. "But any authority and power an elected representative exercises is subject to the will of the people, as well as to legal and judicial measurement," I expounded, completely unaware of the conundrum I would soon face. "If I'm elected, I swear to uphold the constitutional laws of this state. And that includes all laws, not only those I agree with, not only laws which support my personal view, but every law. I'll look at each death case one by one. I'll exercise my right of commutation to the fullest extent of my ability on a case-by-case basis. I'll search for mistrials, for new evidence, for a miscarriage of justice every which way I can. I'll find legal criteria for commutation— not just personal opinion."

I won that election against Bob, but both of us lost our repeal. The people spoke overwhelmingly: they chose me as governor but dismissed out-of-hand my passion to uphold life.

And that's how I inherited death row.

There was quite an assortment in this bunch of doomed inmates. One was a woman, 20-year-old Jeannace Freeman, a victim of child-hood sexual abuse. In love with another woman—an unfortunate mother of a son and daughter—Freeman convinced this mother her four- and six-year-old children were in the way of their relationship. In 1961, as grisly a crime as ever was, the two women used lug wrenches to beat, strangle, abuse, and mutilate the bodies of the innocents— supposedly to make it appear as if they'd been sexually abused by some-one else. Finally, they threw both youngsters over the Crooked River Gorge near Bend. That canyon must be over 300 feet deep—equal to 27 stories—with jagged rocks punctuating each inch. John Newell, a policeman and my state driver's brother, had the bloody task of snak-ing down a gaping cavern to retrieve the bodies of those children. It was so incomprehensibly ugly, so abhorrent, he couldn't even begin to describe it. Except to tell me he vomited, continually, the entire way up the sides of the gorge.

The children's mother gave the state evidence and confessed her involvement in the murders. Though her act was certainly montrous, she was a weak character completely dominated by her lover. She received life in prison (and was paroled after seven years) while Freeman was sentenced to death. Freeman became such a hazard—even in the state penitentiary—that she disrupted all the other women with her sheer screaming and constant havoc. It grew so dire she was transferred out of state. We'd never seen anything like that in Oregon and we simply couldn't handle her in our system.

Freeman, however, was not the first death case whose execution reached my desk. Leeroy Sanford McGahuey was a 40-year-old logger and convicted murderer. He had stabbed, shot, and bludgeoned a young mother (his girlfriend), then given the same treatment to her 23-month-old son.

Meanwhile, I was becoming grimly aware I'd created my own bind, having already promised Oregonians I would uphold the law on this issue. I suppose I'd thought they'd see my way and vote down capital punishment. Obviously, they hadn't. And it was my job to uphold their will, as well as my word.

I traveled to annual governor's conferences, earnestly querying chief executives on how their states handled the death penalty. Averill Harriman, then governor of New York, had a piece in the Saturday Evening Post on opposing capital punishment and I eagerly read it. Some states didn't even have capital punishment, but many did. One governor at the conference told me he shared decisions with one or two other senior servants—the secretary of state and attorney general, I believe. Whatever they decided in a given case, it had to be unanimous. Thus, the full burden of a decision no human should ever have to make was shared by others.

That would have been great in Oregon, but it wasn't the law of this state. McGahuey's execution date approached and I found myself extremely stressed. I called Loren Hicks—my legal counsel—into the office. He advised me on legislation and legal matters and was a wonderful lawyer and friend.

I gave him a strong directive. "Loren," I said, "please find me a hook for a commutation. Anything. Just give me something so I can commute this man's death sentence."

Loren nodded solemnly, striding off to carry out his duty. Days later, he returned with his full report. "There's no new evidence, no possibility of a mistrial, and no question whatsoever as to the man's guilt. The guy even confessed in gruesome detail," Loren added tersely. "I don't think there's anything legal we can do. I looked everywhere," he confessed. "There isn't a single point we can possibly dispute. The case is airtight."

I knew he had done everything in his power, and I trusted Loren implicitly. Meanwhile, I stated clearly to the public any power I exercised had to be judged on the basis of legal criteria, not personal opinion.

I'm sure my hand muzzled my chin and lips when I answered Loren. I invariably move into that gesture in times of sadness or conflict. "Well," I quietly told him, "we'll have to go through due process. We have no choice," I paused. "This man will have to be executed."

I went home that night, and I must've played more games of solitaire than I can count. It seems so mundane, solitaire, yet this was my release. A lonely game, I took it up under stress. I'd sit at the desk in the far corner of the library while Antoinette and the children played amongst themselves. One by one, I laid out those cards, and one by one, I challenged myself. Usually it wiped clean the cobwebs of my mind and calmed all stressors away. Not this night. Oh no.

I was miserable, in absolute agony. Soon, delegations, clergy groups, and anti-capital punishment organizations all came for meetings, pleading with me. "But you oppose the death penalty," they insisted.

"Yes, I do," I completely agreed.

"Then why don't you do something?" they implored.

"I can't," I confessed. "I have no legal justification." I said I would do anything—anything at all—if I could. I had prayed and agonized over this more than any decision I ever made. But there was no legal justification to grant commutation.

Clearly, I was alone with my decision. I entertained all viewpoints in my office. I needed to hear them, welcomed them in fact. My staff knew they were to tell me the truth, always, and I wanted to listen. They never gave me what they thought I wanted to hear and they all shouldered plenty of responsibility. But the final decision was mine alone.

Now to this point in McGahuey's case, we'd received delegations but scarcely any other public response at all—less than 50 letters, perhaps the majority for clemency, but still very few.

So I went to Travis. "I want this publicized in every possible way," I emphasized. "I want the public to have the full impact of this brutality committed by the state in the name of capital punishment. No holds barred, Travis. Every gory, scurrilous detail, fully reported." He knew I meant business.

And when the night of the execution came—one of the most miserable nights of my life—Travis was there. Loren too.

Why must they always execute the doomed at midnight? Tradition, I suppose. And it's probably easier to control sleeping prisoners during such a tortured time than wide-awake ones. But I think, more likely, capital punishment is such an inhumane act that those committing it want the entire world asleep and ignorant at the moment of their deed. They have no choice but to shelter their consciences behind the night and the neatness of the law. It's macabre, simply put, and that night was the most macabre I had known.

Antoinette and I, now married for several years, had no governor's residence, but a private home. The state had strung a telephone line into our den, a red telephone with one connection: the death chamber of the state penitentiary. Travis had arranged key code phrases for the warden and me to exchange to be sure no one interfered. The warden would await a possible commutation call until one minute before midnight. Then, McGahuey's execution would become Oregon's 58th since the death penalty was used in 1904. Forty citizens had been hanged and 17 gassed to death in our state. Yes, cyanide gas was used in executions then, even a more beastly tool than lethal injection which we now use—as if you can neatly quantify the evil of state-imposed execution.

All of us paced through the living room, the den, the kitchen, complete zombies. Antoinette and I had two children then, and both slept. I remember no chitchat. We stewed in our own thoughts as the clock ticked intractably on. It's all a nightmare in my mind, figures moving hauntingly throughout the room in gray memory.

Suddenly, as in a movie, there came a knock at the door. Antoinette opened it, finding the Pastor Paul Polling, of Salem's First Presbyterian Church, waiting quietly to enter. We welcomed his calm presence. He, too, opposed capital punishment and simply came to offer support, to help us think spiritually, to expand the limited little picture we all held at that moment. Polling said a prayer for the soul of the prisoner, and his caring and concern never left me.

We all stared down the clock, wanting to end this gruesome vigil, and the minutes—inevitably—struck midnight.

At that moment another day began, the spheres surely unaware a human life had been quietly snuffed. Several minutes later the red phone rang once more, startling us all.

I answered. "The deed is done," the warden informed me.

Our vigil had ended, but would never be forgotten.

On McGahuey's end, a completely different drama had transpired. Under 150 pounds, the man stood 5'7" tall, brown-eyed and black-haired. Dressed in a bathrobe, shorts, and slippers, he smiled at the two officers arriving to escort him to the gas chamber. On his brief and final walk, McGahuey bent, picked stray blades of grass and held them to his nose. "That's the last I'll sniff of those," he said.

The officers left his robe and slippers outside the door and led him inside the chamber—a sterile silver room with several windows. They strapped his body to the fatal black chair with a perforated seat and left, locking the door behind them.

Then, placing cyanide pellets into deadly solution, the wardens and others—16 witnesses in all—watched as a cloud of gray smoke rose from beneath the fatal seat. McGahuey breathed deeply, just as he had inhaled the living grass. He glanced to the chaplain, nodded, then passed out. His entire body seized violently, his head flinging back, then forward.

Forty-year-old Leroy McGahuey was dead.

The next day, Travis utilized the facts surrounding the execution. The ugliness of this death penalty was publicized and seared into public consciousness. Before the November 1964 election, I strongly urged capital punishment show its face on the ballot once more. At the polls the people spoke again. Successfully, the Oregon death penalty was repealed with 60 percent of the vote. I was awash with palpable, deep relief.

I now had a legal basis for issuing commutation. I commuted the sentence of every prisoner on death row, though they'd been sentenced long before the repeal. Even the first woman who would have been executed in Oregon: Jeannace Freeman.

Last I heard, she was out on parole. If ever there was a case I might have thought deserved the death penalty, she was it. Still, my convictions prevailed: it was not ours to take life, and I swiftly commuted her sentence.

After my watch, the death penalty was reinstated once more in Oregon. And presently, I'm still working toward yet another death penalty repeal.

I've had plenty of second thoughts over time regarding McGahuey's case. I had to follow the legalities of my state, yet I forever ruminate. Did I have an even higher responsibility? A responsibility transcending legalities? A greater, spiritual obligation? When I ask these questions, I never get a completely satisfactory answer. I'm uneasy, still. My dilemma means nothing, of course, compared to the wasted life of the victim, but it haunts me nevertheless. I could have commuted, based on my convictions alone. Yet somehow, I couldn't bring myself to go against the law without legal justification. But I'll never completely rest with my decision.

If we're truly serious about saving human life, we should be working together, much harder, on repealing the death penalty. In the Senate, Paul Simon, the Democrat from Illinois, and I fought diligently against it. Every time others tried to extend the death penalty, even as far as to the mentally retarded, we struck back. The argument was always thrown at us that capital punishment was a powerful deterrent to murder. Research, in fact, proves it is not. It's not unusual for more murders to occur in states which uphold capital punishment than in those which don't. Besides, the majority of murders are instantaneous acts of passion, not cold, premeditated attacks where a perpetrator carefully weighs his options—or his punishment.

And even though we knew state-imposed execution was no deterrent, Paul Simon and I pressed the point. If capital punishment was such a great deterrent, I said, "we should offer the next logical step: bringing executions to every home in this country by broadcasting the executions live on television and radio. We support executions as deterrent," I added, "but require them to be conducted in cloak-and-dagger secrecy." I introduced an amendment to do just that—to broadcast executions. Perhaps Congress would realize the repulsiveness of their acts if countered with absurdity. I also knew if people witnessed execution, they would demand an end to it.

Well, our opponents went apart—it was as if we'd just dropped a stink bomb in the middle of a church service, they were so appalled. "Oh, that's gruesome!" they'd counter. No more gruesome—not even close!—than the reality of state-sanctioned death.

Much later, in the classrooms where I still teach, any discussion of abortion—which inevitably arises—leads to the question of capital punishment, gun use, and then war. I add to this list the vulnerability of those living in poverty—a grievous form of violence against humanity as well. I'm strongly against all these brutalities. We should wield no power to destroy human life in any way. I believe the hand of God is present in creation of life, and humankind cannot take that divine power into our own hands. Ever.

Abortion is perhaps the hardest of these issues to confront. It's such an irrational lightning rod in our country that I hesitate to bring it up. But it's true, I despair over abortion, believing it constitutes the taking of human life.

But for all those who would claim me as yet another missile in their anti-abortion arsenal, let it be known I don't stop there. I've struggled with this issue mightily, and I've come to unique conclusions. But they are only my conclusions, my beliefs, not to be used as ammunition in anyone's ideological warfare. Yet humbly, here they are.

I believe life begins at implantation, not conception. Thus, couples who conceive have a window before implantation to deal with their situation. I believe strongly in morning after contraception, and in all forms of contraception. I have always supported Planned Parenthood and school-based clinics, and am very proud to say so. I think sex education should be taught in our schools, and birth control should be available to all. We should get it out there for easy access by those in need. People will forever choose to have sex, but let's give them every opportunity to be responsible for their acts.

How much better, after all, to prevent a mistake than choose to take what I feel is a life. And of course, when there is a threat to the life of the mother, I certainly believe in exceptions. But I'm opposed to abortion as an easy-out prophylactic.

But like any issue, it's not black or white. In the early '80s I fought against stripping federal employees of access to federal health insurance dollars for abortion. Just as I don't believe in abortion, I also don't believe the government has any right to dictate how people spend the money they earn. And in the mid-80s, I joined my Oregon colleague, Senator Bob Packwood and others in co-sponsoring a resolution condemning violence against abortion clinics and their personnel. Violence is never a solution. To anything.

The anti-abortion lobby was never particularly fond of me, to say the least. I would ask for their help with population-control or family-planning issues, and their feeling about the sanctity of life seemed to disappear. Or I'd ask about prenatal care and women and children's nutrition programs and receive the same response. Often I'd say, "I wish you'd be as concerned about sanctity of life after birth as you are about it in the womb."

I even fought Jesse Helms on abortion, in my way. He constantly tacked abortion riders onto appropriation bills when I was chair of Appropriations. Thus, passing these otherwise non-politicized bills became all but impossible. I strode with him into his office, chatting over the entire business of riders. "I'll get you hearings or whatever you want," I told him. "Instead of tacking on a rider with no hearing, let's use authorization committees and force them to take action. We have to show as Republicans we can make the machinery of government work, instead of creating more gridlock amongst ourselves, missing bill deadlines, orchestrating a circus. Everybody in the party wins if we demonstrate our ability to make things move." Helms listened carefully and we arrived at an understanding—or so I assumed. Soon thereafter though, up popped another abortion rider on an appropriation bill. My mouth must have dropped several inches in utter amazement. I pivoted on the floor and walked straight back to Helms' desk.

He didn't believe we had any understanding at all, he said politely. And there we were, in the same old soup.

I've been asked whether or not, following my beliefs, I would deny a woman's right to choose. Frankly, I don't consider it exclusively a woman's right. It takes a male and a female to become pregnant in most cases, and the man has plenty of responsibility—and some rights— as well. Both should be held accountable. I hate being pushed into an ideological box like this, as I learned with capital punishment how simple it is to take an inflexible position and suffer unendingly the consequences. Let's just say I've stated how I feel on abortion, and I know others on both sides strongly oppose me. That's okay. We will become nothing if we cannot learn, one from the other, to find our way together.

A brief comment on gun control is deserved here as well. This is an issue I've come a long way on in the course of my career. I hail from a state full of hunters, and I support the Second Amendment right to bear arms. Yet as our proliferation and acceptance of violence has in- creased, arms have moved from their legitimate, historic role of hunt- ing game for food to a play thing in the hands of the irresponsible, the untrained, or the tormented. Saturday night specials, machine guns, bazookas, and automatic weaponry are not primarily designed for hunt- ing. We need look no further than our current epidemic of school vio- lence to see this as true. Yet as technology has become available it can help us keep guns from the hands of dangerous souls. Thus, registra- tion and licensing of firearms should always be used to separate the responsible from the irresponsible in our midst. We must control the sale of dangerous weapons so they never again land in the possession of those who would abuse them.

Poverty, though, is arguably the most prevalent violence in our society. When people are limited from access to nourishing food, de- cent housing, or health care, they are denied the ability to contribute their fullest to their society and to hold dreams and visions of a better life. We all deserve a full life, not a life cut short by hunger and homelessness. I can't think of a more pernicious violence we face to- day on our body politic, nor a more just cause we should all work to correct.

And finally, as to the most common and volitional way our country destroys human life—war—it's quite clear how I feel.

That, too, is something which will perpetually haunt me.

And nowhere more grippingly than the fatal war in Vietnam.

CHAPTER SEVEN

Standing Alone Against the War in Vietnam

*H*AIPHONG'S GRAPHIC SUFFERING STILL STOOD EMBLAZONED IN MY mind from 1945—a slow-moving, technicolor torment.

And by the early '60s, I knew we had no business there. I voiced opposition to getting embroiled in the civil war in Vietnam right away. This time, it wasn't the French being foolish or selfish—they had tried and failed. Now it was us, with some divine right to combat atheistic communism with our God-given democracy. We picked up the French marbles and began to build the game again, only this time for real, with bright red American blood.

The moment President Kennedy put his Vietnam policy into place, with thousands of combat troops reporting to Indochina, a growing unease pervaded my mind.

At San Francisco's 1964 Republican National Convention, my opposition flared. Antoinette, almost too pregnant with our third child Theresa to even make the trip, joined me nevertheless, leaving our two eldest children with their grandparents. Our general physician, Dr.

Ralph Purvine, demanded that Antoinette only travel if he escorted us. Now this was not Dr. Charles Mills, the obstetrician who allowed me entrance into MarkO's birth and would welcome all four of our children into the world. This was our GP, who loved politics and insisted he be at her elbow. What if Antoinette delivered on the plane, he argued? What if this child claimed San Francisco instead of Salem as it's place of birth—or somewhere at 30,000 feet altitude? We humored him and thus, the good doctor became ex officio member of our party.

In San Francisco, Antoinette rarely ventured beyond the hotel. She sat in the family boxes in the Cow Palace, watching as I presided over party business—marvelous entertainment, I'm sure. I served as temporary chair of the convention and held the gavel down on the floor, trying to keep order. One moment I glanced up though, and Antoinette was gone! She was there a minute before, where was she now? Was this it? Why didn't she flag me down? Her way wasn't to be shy, no matter what state she found herself in. I tried to keep calm, continued wielding the gavel and went on with my business. But I kept glancing up to the family boxes. Unbeknownst to me, she had gone to the hotel to rest—probably a far more exciting venue than our proceedings—and was watching our work on television. Theresa gracefully waited until our return to Oregon to make her first appearance.

Soon I offered the keynote in San Francisco, speaking for human rights and equal opportunity for education, employment, and housing. I attacked those who spewed forth their "venom of hate," such as the Communists, the Ku Klux Klan, the John Birch Society, and any like them. "They must be overcome and the Republican Party will lead the quest for victory in the struggle to change the minds and hearts of men because it is only by such a victory that human dignity will be won and preserved," I intoned.

Smack in the center of the Cow Palace sparkled the California delegation, many spangled John Birchers among them sporting gold lamé vests in support of Goldwater. Their leader, Senator Bill Knowland, puffed up his chest, his vest growing tight to bursting, his face florid, exploding in a baritone, "Boooooooo!"

That moment marked the first time in history any keynoter was booed by their own convention, and that anyone was me.

The Oregon delegation cheered as magnanimously as they could.

Many certainly didn't share my view—not even close! But I suppose they felt protective, and I appreciated it. A few others offered agreement. Senator John Sherman Cooper of Kentucky swung his kerchief in support, as did Senator Jack Javits of New York. I simply smiled and waited. It was an historic moment and I wasn't about to miss it. Besides, I knew our party was, and still is, plenty big enough for diversity.

This was my Republican party alright. I went on, speaking in favor of a progressive agenda, quoting the prolific playwright and poet Maurice Maeterlick: "Every progressive spirit is opposed by 10,000 guardians of the past." I spoke in favor of a civil rights resolution at the convention, also railing against hunger and in support of conservation.

But most of all, even though the papers failed to note it, I blatantly questioned the administration's Southeast Asian policy. "Why, why do they fear telling the American people what our foreign policy is? Even when American boys are dying in a war without a name. Tragic as is a tomb for an unknown soldier, still more tragic is the fate of the unknowing soldier, whose life may be lost in a battle, the purpose of which he has not been told—and which he is not allowed either to win or to conclude."

And it was more than just John Birchers disagreeing with me at that convention. I didn't know it but a police call came in during my speech stating a bomb lay beneath the platform from which I spoke. My friend and state police driver, Bill Newell, crawled under that platform with his flashlight, searching for bombs throughout my talk to make sure I was safe. And above him I blithely railed on against the war.

In 1965, at the National Governors' Association conference, Vietnam haunted me still. Later, many reminisced that President Kennedy would have gotten us out of the war while Lyndon B. Johnson only entrenched us further, but I doubt it. President Johnson kept all Kennedy's "whiz-kid" advisers, including MacNamara who would later declaim the war as a grave mistake. These advisers had LBJ increase the pressure, the troops, the arms, and the money we would spend. And worst of all, to increase the senseless loss of life.

But at the Governors' conference—Minneapolis in summer, humid and wet as it could be in Oregon, but without the benison of our cool rains—the session commenced and rumors flew that a Vietnam resolution would be offered. LBJ was sure to crave our support. He'd garnered resolutions from the U.S. Chamber of Commerce, the Teamsters, the AFL-CIO, and every possible group. Any time a meeting was held in Washington—whether it was the morticians or the accountants—he'd ask for a resolution backing his ill-fated plan. He was obsessed with rubber stamping whatever he deigned to do with our boys, their lives, and the lives of the "enemy." LBJ demanded any reassurance he could get, even if hollow.

Meanwhile, anti-war sentiment brewed, and Johnson wasn't about to let a conference of Governors go by without calling for support. We were a significant group in those days.

There was no escape. We began our session and Georgia Governor Carl Sanders swiftly spearheaded the charge. Eloquent, charismatic, with his southern drawl, he'd been well picked by the administration to carry the issue. Immediately, he was in command, emotionally encouraging us to back the President. But governors had no more knowledge of our national interest than the public, and Sanders gave no indication what exactly we were meant to support. As far as I could tell, we were picking up for the French. Ho Chi Minh had been our ally during World War II, but as soon as that war was over, communism became the enemy and Ho was dropped. We only courted "our kind" of commie, like Tito. Ho Chi Minh didn't make the cut.

The domino theory was prevalent too, but dominoes couldn't fall across the Pacific. Even if dominoes dropped, skipped, and jumped, the Vietnamese couldn't take up arms against us. They had no air force, no navy, and here we were, bombing the hell out of them—civilians and soldiers alike. They were peasants, pure and simple, strangled by centuries of tribal wars. Their cause was nationalism, not communism. But on the other hand, a foreign invader—French or American—that was something to rally against. They no longer wished to be dumped on, instead offering their lives for their national dignity.

The whole debate, too, occurred in the wake of Lederer's famous 1958 book, *The Ugly American*. Some in my generation had read it and came to realize that the entire world didn't want to imitate America.

Politically we might provide a model, yes, but our culture wasn't necessarily to be emulated.

I sat there in that nondescript Minneapolis conference room, like any other flourescent-lit conference room the nation over. My mind was in turmoil, a jumble of thoughts churning through. Most important was my conviction that this resolution was something I absolutely could not support. I'd simply have to oppose. It was intimidating to know I'd be in the minority, but I was surely not alone. A number of governors had agreed with me privately, mentioning in hushed tones, "This is crazy. Why should we be making a statement on foreign policy issues, we're governors!" I heard this grumbling among Democrats and Republicans alike. Republicans were especially uncomfortable, not wanting to offer a cheering section for LBJ.

Some of my colleagues even overtly agreed. "You know, Mark, this war is not going well. Why should we endorse it at a time when the people are beginning to complain about lack of progress?" After all, the U.S. had expected to take the war over and make short shrift of it. The French hadn't had their heart in it, but we were going in, winning, and getting out—short and sweet.

It hadn't exactly transpired that way but sure enough, here we were at the conference spanning a huge, rectangular table. We sat in strict hierarchy, each according to the year our state had been admitted to the union. Media milled in and out. Staff came buzzing by, pressing urgent notes into governors' hands who then stood to leave to handle state business. But the inevitable resolution came first.

I engaged in the discussion, asking what this committed us to and why we should be apt to support it. I threatened Vietnam would become quicksand for a no-win foreign policy if the people weren't given a true sense of Johnson's goals. Right then I'd shown my hand. And as soon as I spoke, an air of impatience sizzled through the room, as palpable as an electric shock. "We all know we're going to support the war, so let's not delay," was the clear attitude. "Get on the boat, Mark," came an unspoken subtext, "Let's not get bogged down with inconsequential little issues—like why we're there in the first place, or what might be our national interest." LBJ wanted his crisp, clean resolution adopted without controversy and it was our task to deliver it. Why waste time?

Governor George Romney of Michigan posed a question as to timing—Johnson was flying us all to Washington the next day for a special briefing on the issue, and Romney suggested we delay the resolution until after that. Again, resentment rose around the table. "Do it now." "Get it done," came the cries, as if the entire war effort depended upon our immediate endorsement. Connally of Texas and Sanders of Georgia, among countless others, all vocally offered unequivocal support. So the vote was taken, and the chairman called for those in favor. Like a rabid cheering section at a football game, each and every governor began shouting their "ayes," every one aiming to out-shout the next in affirmation.

Finally, the chair recalled as an afterthought to ask for opposition, bringing down the gavel swiftly before I could even respond. Undeterred, in a clear voice I called out my solid, "No!"

A media throng of journalists, shuttering cameras, and television reporters swarmed in all at once while the governors attempted to go on with their meeting. I rose, not wanting to be disruptive, and met the group in the foyer. I expressed my disenchantment, my lack of confidence that the war could be won. Into the circle rushed Governor Romney. "I voted 'no,' too!" he piped. Well the press looked at him, suspicious, their expressions clearly saying, "We sure didn't hear you!"

Soon the session adjourned and one of the southern governors (who shall remain nameless) strode into the press crowd, moving aggressively to the center. He gazed straight into the TV cameras, addressing the entire nation. "You, Mark Hatfield," he barked, "have done a grave disservice to your country."

I knew well this governor was not an enthusiast for civil rights. I was tempted to call out that his stand on civil rights was a much graver disservice to Americans than my dissent on this measly resolution. But I kept quiet. The press largely echoed his sentiment, writing that I'd brought disgrace to Oregon as well.

"Hatfield," other governors also buttonholed me, "you committed political suicide. Even though I totally agree with you, if I voted the way you did, I'd be eaten alive by my constituents."

I felt isolated, but not afraid. Not yet. I had the power of my convictions. It wasn't that I had the gift of prophecy—far from it. But with the ill-defined administration position, the growing call for more money, more men, and more blood, it could only turn out as it did. If I survived long enough, I hoped I'd find myself in the majority. Antoinette teased me. "Mark," she said, "wouldn't it be nice to be on the winning side as well as on the right side?" I laughed along with her but stuck to my convictions.

The following morning, Johnson awaited. He had been scheduled to speak at the Governors' conference itself, but days before he escalated bombing of North Vietnamese missile targets and was too busy dealing with that attack to make it. Instead, he had sent his emissary, Hubert Humphrey, to speak. Humphrey told us no more than we already knew, his words dripping the common rhetoric of ruthless Communist aggression. So dutifully we boarded Air Force One and flew to D.C.

As we arrived, Johnson ushered us into the East Room—a beautiful room highlighted with gilt and chandeliers. In the front stood the great and lofty portrait of George and Martha Washington, and placed in a semicircle before the podium were 50 velvet-covered opera chairs cozily lined up for our group. The president spotted me immediately. "Mark," he gestured warmly, "I want you to come right up into the front row where you can hear everything."

"Thank you, Mr. President," I answered. He sat beside me, offering the deluxe Johnson treatment. Laying his arm around the back of my chair, practically embracing me like a polar bear in a death grip, he moved his face into mine. He offered his undivided, friendly Texas attention, and I knew he expected the same in response. While we waited, attendants passed around Paul Revere bowls overflowing with chunks of Texas beef. LBJ was not the most well-mannered president in our history. He quickly dispensed with the requisite toothpick, reaching in with his huge hand and popping meat directly into his mouth. Clearly, he loved his beef. But even so, he barely took his eyes from my face.

The briefing began and experts spoke. Secretary of Defense Robert MacNamara, Secretary of State Dean Rusk, Vice President Humphrey; generals, national defense advisers, and the President himself. It was the right war, in the right place, at the right time, they told us. And it was our duty to fight it. Yet to my dismay, they never told us why. They offered the cold war rhetoric about our obligation to stop communism, and the threat of another leader following the path of Stalin—the madman who had murdered 18 million of his own to secure his desire to rule the world.

Yet I knew Vietnam was no threat. I had been there, I had seen it from the ground, and I had read everything about the area that I could get my hands on. Later, in the fall of 1970, Wes Michaelson, my then legislative counsel, visited South Vietnam and saw what I already well knew: The South Vietnamese would never be capable of holding their own borders, even if they had a coalition behind them. It simply was not possible.

Unlike me, though, George Romney swiftly converted at that White House visit. When question time came he stood, solemnly avowing, "I have been convinced by this session."

The President—and probably most eyes in the room—turned directly to me. "Mark," LBJ asked quickly, "do you have any questions?"

"No, Mr. President, I don't," I told him. "I'm still not convinced."

The room crackled with that familiar, tense energy I seemed particularly adept at evoking.

The session ended and we filed quietly out. Then LBJ pulled me aside. "The media is waiting for you out front, Mark," he said, his arm fastened around my shoulder with a velcro grip.

"I don't want to see them, I have nothing to say," I stated. "I've said all of it already."

He looked at me, astonished, as if it finally dawned on him I was motivated by something other than politics—I wasn't lobbying for a new interstate highway or any other Oregon project here. My convictions couldn't be bought. "You really believe in your position, don't you?" he asked, incredulous.

My face must have reflected equal surprise. "Of course I do!" I exclaimed. "Now, is there any way you can get me out of here?"

LBJ had MacNamara personally escort me out the side door. Both of them, I'm sure, were only too delighted to aid and abet my escape.

In the intervening year, tension grew. 1965 hadn't been an election year, but '66 was. And by the time of the Governors' conference at the new Century Plaza Hotel in Los Angeles, California, I'd received the GOP nomination for U.S. Senate. I still held the minority view on the war. If I hadn't opposed the war in '65 I could have ducked the issue in '66, though that was never my way. Instead, I was even more sure we shouldn't be offering LBJ a blank check for his policy, and I would say so.

There was no mistaking we were in California. Outside, protestors congregated. Men and women, young and old, flower children and long hairs, yes. But academics and middle-class, mainstream Americans as well. No President, I often thought, could conduct this war without a draft. 18-year-olds still couldn't vote then, so the President easily seized their manpower to crank up the war machine. All with the lives of the least politically influential segment of our democracy— non-voting, 18-year-old kids. If LBJ had called up the reserves instead— local merchants, teachers, lawyers, doctors, and people of influence—that would have disrupted families and careers. We would have had a decidedly different public reaction than the initial, docile response of teenagers.

As dean of students at Willamette during the Korea conflict, I had had to fill out draft deferments. On paper, we lined up each student from the 4.0s down. The upper half of the freshman class could return as sophomores; the upper third of the sophomore class, and the upper quarter of the juniors. It was utterly inequitable and didn't delineate at all between those majoring in physics or phys ed. The draft was simply a grand example of outright discrimination. So many of our ancestors had come to our shores to escape the very conscription their descendants fell prey to. If there was ever a reason to abolish the draft, Vietnam was it.

Back at the conference though, other governors approached. They asked which direction I was headed this time, and of course I said I was voting the same way—I hadn't changed. It was the war which had changed, all for the worse: We'd lost more money, more weapons, and all for naught. Most unacceptable of all, we'd lost more lives and there was no end in sight.

We sat around the formal rectangular table again, Texas Governor John Connally just two seats away in the big, cavernous room. This time, the roll call vote came state by state. The chairman called each name on the role and I felt absolutely as if I were in a barrel, all the "ayes" surrounding me, echoing back and forth. The chairman's bass voice crept closer and closer to Oregon, and I felt suspended in air, the sinister sounds moving still nearer to apprehending me, each answer coming "aye, aye, aye," in rank submission. George Romney was in support now, and still the voice crept closer. It was deathly quiet in that room and I didn't know how I could find my voice. To a man, no one dissented.

Finally, the chair's call rang out, "Oregon!" The room hushed in apprehension. I opened my lips, somehow offering "Nay" into that great void of silence.

Antoinette sat near and passed a quick note: "I'm proud of you, I love you!" I took in the glow reflected in her smile, the only bright spot in that gaping room. Then the press swarmed again, a veritable plague of wasps. Before I could even rise, Connally hissed across the table, "Why don't you go outside where your friends are!" He referred to the protesters. He was the classic, boisterous Texan, but he was absolutely right—I probably did have more friends out there. Blessedly, the meeting adjourned.

Later that afternoon, a young student studying for the Jesuit ministry sought me out at a rally. "I'm so proud of you," he gushed. "I wish my father would have had the courage to vote as you did at the Governors' Conference." It turned out that young student was Jerry Brown, California Governor Edmund Brown's son.

But aside from that single positive note, the hostile response of Connally and my colleagues left one thought seared into my mind: This is exactly what I'll face when I get home. Already, 76 percent of Oregonians polled by Bardsley supported the war, and I'd never before taken on such an unpopular stand. Colored oleo didn't even come close. Particularly now, during my first race for U.S. Senate. Had I lost the campaign before it even began?

One thing was certain: Connally's reaction would be reflected only too clearly in the faces of my constituents. When I got off that plane in the midst of an election year, it would all begin.

In fact, that's exactly what happened. Travis and Warne plead with me to talk about fishing or lumber or anything else to keep Vietnam out of my speeches on the campaign trail. "Look," they said. "We know you're against the war, but you don't need to make it a big campaign issue." They were right, I'm sure, but I didn't listen.

Vietnam was the issue that called me to the Senate, and Vietnam would haunt me for a long, long time to come.

CHAPTER EIGHT

Salem to D.C.

W HEN I RETURNED TO OREGON FOLLOWING THAT FATEFUL, 1966 L.A. Governors' conference, my race for Senate was on. All the Oregonians who favored our involvement in Vietnam surely knew their governor did not. After all, I lacked the wherewithal to stay quiet about it. Once, Richard Nixon even pulled Travis aside at a Republican rally and confidingly suggested I "modify" my position on Vietnam so as not to ruin my political future.

Several of my own campaign advisers even echoed Nixon's penchant for political expediency. "We can't get you elected unless you soft pedal this Vietnam thing," they said during a tense meeting. "And we won't be able to raise any money."

"Well," I said, "nobody has to be a United States Senator."

Modifying my convictions just wasn't possible. If I ended up without an office but with principles intact, so be it. That, to me, would still be a victory.

So whenever asked, I reminded each voter in the state exactly how I felt. Yet a collusion of background events somehow worked in my favor, foretelling a different outcome from that predicted by pundits.

For starters, the economy worked vigorously for me. In terms of per capita income during my tenure as governor, Oregon had climbed from lowest to highest of all states on the Pacific Coast. On the opposite end, unemployment had scurried from highest to lowest. About 187,000 new Oregon jobs had been created. We had built on our basis of Tektronix to increase high tech jobs in what's now Oregon's silicon forest. We began a community college network and vocational training throughout the state, founded the Oregon Graduate Institute of Science and Technology, and even further diversified the timber industry so all parts of the log were utilized—and many more jobs were created as well, including new positions at International Paper Company on the coast. We increased the potential for industrial jobs in Eastern Oregon at Boardman, helped 3M start in the southern part of the state, and expanded employment across groups and over geographic boundaries. We knew now we were a state that could thrive on many industries besides timber alone.

None of that hurt my campaign a bit. Still, many Oregonians thought I was wildly wrong on the war and they let me know it loud and clear. "He's crazy about Vietnam!" they'd holler from Grants Pass to Gresham. But they knew me, too, up front and personal. They knew who they saw was who I was. At least I hope so. It was easy to be Mark, and I couldn't fit into another suit even if I'd desperately wanted to.

Besides, voters are more intelligent than many politicians give them credit for. After all, it's voters who were smart enough to stay out of politics in the first place! They have a critical ability—often wiser than many a myopic politician—to discern truth and forge great conclusions.

So Oregonians kept their minds open even while they let it be well known how they felt about the war. But they didn't stop there. They'd argue with me on Vietnam one minute, then turn to their neighbor and add, "But look what good things he helped us do here, in our town." Even some old and powerful opponents supported me. "I don't agree with Mark on this war thing," one of the biggest political movers and shakers reportedly said, "but he's a good man and he's a good Republican. We've got to support him."

I'll never know what swayed voters most, but on the opposite end of the spectrum, I doubt the support of Oregon Senator Wayne Morse, a colleague and friend, hurt much. He was a Democrat, but bipartisanship was as much a part of my nature as ever. Morse actually endorsed me against my Democratic opponent, Congressman Bob Duncan. Duncan's mantra throughout the campaign was a resounding, "If we don't fight them in the elephant grass of Southeast Asia, we'll be fighting them in the rye grass of the Columbia River Valley." Oregon voters were much too smart for that, even if they did favor the war. Meanwhile, Morse was as strongly opposed to the war as I and he offered me his support.

Morse was a peace Democrat if ever there was one, and his endorsement cut both ways. Some probably thought I took his support simply to garner votes. That's nowhere near the truth. In fact, his endorsement would result in plenty of negative fallout. But that never changed my joining my strong anti-war sentiments with his. Sure I gained Democratic support in that race, but I lost Republican conservatives as well.

Unfortunately, two years later I'd be forced to walk a fine line between endorsing Morse's Republican opponent, Bob Packwood, and maintaining a working relationship with Morse as well. But Packwood was clearly one of the most brilliant students I'd ever had at Willamette University. He was a Republican and I knew his family. We had worked on campaigns together. I'd known him as an active state legislator while I served as governor, and I wanted to encourage younger, moderate Republicans coming along. Although I endorsed Packwood, at the same time I sent a telegram to Morse and every other dove running in that senatorial election commending them on their contribution to our country and to the cause of peace.

During my first Senate run, Bob Duncan found himself stuck in D.C. most of the campaign while I was on site. That didn't hurt, but our race was close regardless. Especially since I seem to have this lifelong aversion to fund raising. I'm delighted to ask for money for causes I love, but I have a real problem asking for money for myself. If it wasn't for my incredible staff (on their own time) and dedicated volunteers, I may not have raised a penny for any re-election, let alone the Senate.

In fact, in August those polls I love to hate announced 46 percent of voters favored Duncan and 40 percent favored me. Then the largest railroad union (and again the Teamster's), endorsed me. Still I didn't sit back. I knew this would be the toughest campaign I'd run, and I knew my stance on Vietnam wouldn't get me many votes. So when I announced, I'd said, "I shall seek to be a senator of all the people—no request of yours will be too small, no order too big." And I meant it.

I got out there, even to the point of visiting eight Tigard and Beaverton shopping centers during a well-publicized food war. I must have shaken 2,000 hands that day—do you know how physically sore your hand can get after that kind of exercise? The stores offered free bread and cottage cheese, and milk (27 cents a gallon!), bacon, and coffee at bargain basement prices. Every store I entered announced my presence on the PA system. I chatted with women in curlers and stretch pants, and eventually called Antoinette to tell her she better come on down to take advantage of the deals. I bagged up groceries, telling shoppers I was an expert—I'd done this as a kid at Fred Meyer's in Salem, after all. They had to be kind to me then. They knew I had the power to break their eggs! I was fed at every store, and I'd have drunk 50 or 60 cups of coffee if I accepted all I was proffered. This kind of campaigning could be dangerous to one's health.

In Sweet Home, Oregon, I led a burro named Josie in front of an old washtub band. I chatted with people waiting in line for the movie, went into a bakery and spoke some more, then discussed the lumber industry with men in plaid shirts.

By now, a high school student poll gave me a four- to five-point edge over Duncan. Even though those students wouldn't be voting, I took it as a good sign—my best bellweather in fact. Those students reflected what they heard at home and offered an accurate prediction of the outcome. Right after, six Democratic precinct committee members and a member of the Democratic Platform Committee publicly came out to support me.

The papers even publicized it when I rushed home to take my kids out on Halloween. I donned a red jacket with a raging bull and a sporty cap, but it was the kids' night, not mine. Yet two days before the election, Duncan still officially led the race and I was tense.

Maybe it was that Halloween jaunt with my family that hit the papers that swayed things in my favor, who knows. Most of the victory goes to Travis Cross, Warne Nunn, Gerry Frank, and thousands of volunteers who worked to assure my success every way they could. In the end, I gleaned a narrow margin with a 25,000 vote lead. If ever I needed more proof that standing by convictions—no matter how outrageous in terms of supposed "political expediency"—offered the only wise and honest course to follow, my first U.S. Senate race was it.

Soon I was on my way to Washington, D.C. to join my ally, Wayne Morse.

People often wonder about my relationship with Morse, both before and in the Senate. In that '66 race, I was no threat, so he could afford the largesse of endorsing me. But he certainly didn't have to, and that's not even close to an explanation of his deed. I'm sure his support was confusing to the public. Back in 1952, about a year after my first election to the state Legislature, the Oregon Republican delegation had to elect a representative to the Republican National Convention Platform Committee. They elected me against Morse and he didn't like that. But the media liked it fine—they created quite a public stir, in fact. Then, during my first run for governor, Morse attacked me viciously, with the worst smear tactics possible. It backfired against him in a big way. Even former Governor Charles Sprague, Oregon's chief executive during World War II, ceased neutrality and supported me, but the whole debacle proved plenty hurtful. And that's strictly personal pain I speak of here, not political trauma. If anything, voters like Sprague were so outraged by Morse's tactics that his attack only aided my candidacy. Still, deep wounds remained.

But people change, and I'm first to admit it. Change is not only fair, but worthy as well. Hopefully I've always been a big enough person to change and grow myself. My increasingly liberal views on gun control and the environment—just to name two political examples—bespeak how I hope I've evolved for the better over time.

Senator Morse was a sterling example of change. Oh, after his attack we didn't speak for quite a while. We avoided each other and had no contact whatsoever. But a man named Glenn Jackson held a close relationship with both of us. A self-named ambassador in Oregon, Jackson was an industrialist from Medford and vice chairman of Pacific Power and Light's board of directors. He stayed involved in Oregon politics and did all he could for our state. I suppose he didn't think it right that Oregon's governor and senior U.S. senator were not communicating.

Jackson was a peacemaker and made sure to bring us together. Somehow, he convinced Morse to come to my office in Salem. Jackson and my administrative assistant, Warne Nunn, sat in. The outset of the meeting was pretty tense, to say the least. And then we graduated to small talk. Morse had a hobby of raising Devon cattle, as did Jackson, who had a cattle ranch in Medford. Right there, Morse sold Jackson a Devon bull. As soon as the deal was done, Morse happened to mention the bull was back on his ranch and could be picked up there—in Maryland! That bull had to be shipped all the way across the country. Humor can leaven any meeting, however somber, and this was no exception. Wayne and I never stood and declared our hearts, but it was clear he had come and offered a gesture of reconciliation. And I like to forgive and forget.

So as soon as Wayne reached forth a hand during that first gubernatorial term, our relationship completely shifted. We worked long and hard on state and federal issues affecting the Oregon we both loved. We transferred the Boardman bombing range back from the Navy, making room for a space age, Eastern Oregon industrial park. It didn't work as we planned—Boeing backed out at the last moment because they'd lost federal bidding for the superjet they'd wanted to craft in Boardman—and the whole plan became dubbed "Hatfield's folly." But industry came to Boardman and we remandered that land from the Navy back to Oregonians, just the same.

Morse introduced bills in the Senate in Washington, we addressed joint sessions of the legislature in Oregon, and together we forged a common purpose. He offered friendship and I accepted. Why allow negative history to clutter my mind, miring and bathing brain cells in unctuous ill will? That would have proved nothing but an awful, pitiful waste of energy—not to mention a great loss to Oregon, the beneficiary—hopefully—of our sincere partnership.

Antoinette and other family and close friends never understood how I could accept Morse's support. And later they still wouldn't believe it when I accepted Morse's family's wish to offer his eulogy, both at National Cathedral and at the Capitol in Salem. Yet I was honored, simply honored, to do so.

And in 1967, when I hit Washington, Wayne served as my senior senator.

My initiation proved not only wonderful, but strange as well. The swearing in itself boded pomp and circumstance. We walked through the ornately painted halls of the Capitol, itself a symbol of freedom to this day. Both my parents and Antoinette's, along with Antoinette's Aunt Dorothy and Uncle Charlie from Los Angeles, flew out to witness my oath, all pressed together in the gallery. I looked at my folks—my mother a retired school teacher, my father a retired blacksmith for the Southern Pacific Railroad—and it hit me that I could actually stand here, a senator. I didn't have to be born into wealth or status, nor did my colleagues. What a great testimony that was to the opportunities open to all in our country.

Senior senators customarily escort junior, home-state colleagues down the aisle of the Senate chamber, moving from the very rear chamber to the vice president's podium up front. Wayne beamed as he strode me down that expanse of carpet. There couldn't possibly have been a more generous or welcoming introducer to Capitol Hill in a young senator's career.

Vice President Humphrey stood waiting down the aisle and after my swearing in, I signed the oath book. Then Humphrey offered me the pen I'd used as a souvenir. The entire scene was grandiose, sure, but it only served to heighten my sense of duty to those who had—and those who had not—elected me senator.

I was proud to be a founding member of the 90th Club—the freshmen of the 90th Congress. Some 70 freshmen entered the House that year, including my great friend, John Dellenback from Medford. Through the years, he would support and aid me any way he could. Jim McClure of Idaho and George Bush of Texas also entered the House that year and were close friends as well. In the Senate, seven new members made up my class. Five of us were Republicans, including Ed Brooke of Massachusetts, my seat mate for several years and a good friend. We'd met during his run for attorney general of Massachusetts back in 1960. As governor, I traveled to support progressive Republican candidates. Howard Baker from Tennessee (later, majority leader), Cliff ' of Wyoming (also a former governor), and Chuck Percy of Illinois (a longtime friend) all came on board with me, and our coup in winning these senate seats was well publicized. Time magazine, Newsweek, and "Meet the Press" all featured us, the young freshmen who showed that, shortly following the Goldwater debacle, the Republican party was far from dead.

There were plenty of rough parts to my transition though. We had no orientation in those days, and none of us even knew where the bathrooms hid inside the byzantine halls of senate buildings. It was completely a proposition of search and discover. Luckily, I can report I succeeded in that mission.

My greatest political mentor came easily in the form of Wendall Wyatt, the longtime First District Republican congressman from Astoria, who could have held his position as long as he chose. After he retired, his seat was occupied by Les AuCoin, Elizabeth Furse, and presently, David Wu. Countless times I sought Wendall out to discuss Oregon politics, political strategy, or any number of thorny issues, and Wyatt always offered everything he could.

Critically though, I had held a swift, daunting pace in Oregon. Our political maelstrom kept me ever moving. Positive change and progress were as natural as grass in spring. Now, from one who had pushed a button on my desk to summon anyone I needed, others were now pushing buttons to summon me. From chief executive and maker of decisions I swiftly plummeted to irrelevancy. I had to wait for 99 others before I could move forward with any decision at all. I was absolutely last in the seniority line. Number 100.

As usual, that was my own fault. I had promised Oregon voters I would finish my term as the first to complete two gubernatorial terms since the late 1800s. And as usual, I meant it. The only problem was, the end of my gubernatorial term—January 9th—overlapped the eligibility date of the new Congress—January 3rd. So I showed up at my swearing in with all my classmates, having finished out my governor's term. "Okay," we were quickly told, "you're all sworn in today, but your actual term began a week ago."

"Oh, no," I piped right up with my big mouth. "Not me. I was still governor on the 3rd. My term begins today."

"Fine," they quipped, my status plunging from a measly 95 to a disgusting 100. Scarcely a member of the lofty fraternity at all, was I. I felt it, too. I was last to get an office, instead learning to migrate into and out of more venues than I'd like to remember during my first months.

The earliest was a humble room in the Russell building basement. Only 15 percent as big as the office I'd enjoyed as governor, I was okay with taking one-sixth of the space I was accustomed to, now with twice the staff. I was just glad to be "home." Even the decor—institutional green floors cracking beneath my feet and peeling plaster adorning the walls—was something I could have put up with. Until, that is, I got word the Senate wives used that very room to fold bandages for the Red Cross. Well, bandage folding season was upon us and peremptorily, we had to yield our space.

Meanwhile, as appropriate counterpoint, Antoinette and I boasted no home either. We slept in a Bethesda motel while our new house underwent remodeling to make room for six. Elizabeth, MarkO, Theresa, and Visko had stayed behind with their grandparents in Oregon so they could finish their school term. Well, just like my first office, that didn't work as we'd planned either. After a mere two weeks, neither Antoinette nor I could stand it any longer. We missed those children way too much. Immediately we flew them out and lived cozily in two modest motel rooms. At least we were warm. It was winter in D.C., and drivers panicked in even the lightest snow. Once, it took me two hours to crawl my red Mustang 11 miles to the Capitol. No cell phones, either.

At work, I next landed in Senator Bobby Kennedy's former mail room. It was plenty spacious enough for a mail room, but not for an office. There we were, so crunched together with one of those old, corrugated plastic dividers as all that separated my secretary and me. I had only to scratch a metal ruler gently down the divider whenever I needed help.

One great blessing during my itinerant wanderings were my administrative assistants. Warne Nunn accompanied me to Washington—brave soul—but within months knew D.C. was not for him so he returned home. Sam Mallicoat followed, a wonderful assistant from 1967 on into my second term. Then he, too, wished to return to the Northwest. During my first term and after Sam left us, our friend Gerry Frank became first my special assistant, then administrative assistant.

I'd known Gerry since early in my political career when he opened the Meier & Frank store in Salem. After he left Meier & Frank, I invited him to Washington to be my "dollar a year" man. In fact that's a bit of an exaggeration. I actually paid him $96 dollars a year, the lowest amount you were allowed to pay a federal employee. Gerry offered the balance from his own funds as a gift to Oregon, the state he so loves. Later, he became my chief of staff. Constantly fielding press, publicity, staff, constituents, I still can't figure how he did it. He gave more time and resources to Oregon than most will ever know, and stayed with me well into my last senatorial term.

I was delighted when we finally secured a "permanent office"— that is, until we actually moved in. The place stood in the Dirksen office building, top floor, set back on the roof, and a third smaller than all offices below. Still, that was progress. We crushed 15 or so in there, all stifled together. I can work in most conditions—I don't expect anything huge or fancy. In fact, I loved to walk around the place checking in with staff: "What's up?" "What do the letters say?" "How are the people in Oregon feeling?" "What can I do to help?" Or, when troubled by something I'd suggest, "Let's talk about this issue and clarify our thinking," and we'd all huddle together and brainstorm solutions. But not being able to turn around without elbowing a co-worker was even a little beyond me.

Finally I complained. Gratefully, we received assignment to an additional room across the hall, number 6300. I strode by one day to peek in, but the door was locked. I practically stumbled over a tray of dirty dishes outside—as if this were room service—and tried the handle once more. Suddenly the door opened and, completely unexpected, a little old lady popped her head out.

"Good afternoon!" I quickly gained composure.

"Hello," the woman answered, her greeting belying a spark of fear in her eyes.

I was gentle as I could be, even though equally startled. "I'm Mark Hatfield," I introduced myself, reaching forth a hand. "I have the office across the way and I'm newly assigned to this room. Mind if I take a look?"

"You're getting this room?" she asked, her eyes as wide as if I'd positively spooked her.

"That's what I've been told," I said, my reconnaissance mission clouded with growing confusion.

"Well, where am I going to go?" the woman questioned.

"Gee, I don't know," I told her, by now completely bewildered.

The woman allowed my entrance, and I stepped into a room shelved with wall-to-wall files. At the back, cupboards stood ajar, overflowing with canned goods. A cot and bathroom door stood in clear view as well. This woman was a benign squatter, I could see that. But why? How? I didn't want to offend her in any way, but at the same time, I groped for a tunnel out of my predicament.

"I understand this is Senator Eastland's of the Judiciary Committee's rooms?" I pried, polite as possible.

In fact, I was only too familiar with James Eastland, a Southern Dixiecrat. I may go on and on about how I slough off ill feelings, but the truth is, James Eastland was not one of my favorite people. Much later, in the mid-70s, I'd fight him to abolish his Senate Internal Security Subcommittee, a throwback to the House UnAmerican Activities Committee. Eastland wanted to keep his committee and warned us all about "leftist" groups like the American Indian Movement and the Weather Underground. His committee was never supposed to be permanent and I thought we had infinitely better ways to spend our money. But that wasn't my first encounter with Eastland. Just about the time I was scouting his quarters, I'd sat next to him on the Senate subway.

Eastland created an air of impermeability wherever he went—plenty thick to keep others far away on the subway. It wasn't just his gruff manner or constant cigar smoke that put others off. In those days, most ranking Democrats were Dixiecrats. They never supported civil rights, pure and simple. I'd worked for civil rights since the early '50s, and his views were well known to me.

As if racism weren't enough, you could never understand Eastland's words, though he communicated his meaning quite well. That big ol' cigar always hung from one side of his mouth, and he never quite spoke, instead grumbling around the cigar like an old, crusty private eye in a Humphrey Bogart film. But Eastland was no private eye, and we both knew it. Off duty, he was a gentleman cattle farmer, a professional breeder of White Charleigh, that loftiest, elite bovine breed.

114

I figured I should at least be civil on the subway. After all, we were two grown men. "Hello," I began.

"Grumble, grumble," issued the side of his mouth. Nothing close to eye contact.

Immediately, the ride grew sharply uneasy.

Finally, I couldn't stand it and couldn't help myself, either—no more than if a wasp flew up my sleeve and I pretended to ignore it. I don't know what came upon me, but it was absolutely irresistible. I actually pride myself on civil self control, but so much for that.

"Senator," I finally turned to him, a neophyte addressing my elder statesman, "I understand you know quite a bit about cattle."

"Grumble, nod, grumble." Smoke everywhere, perfusing my clothes, my skin, my eyes.

"You breed them, do you?"

Reticent assent.

"White Charleighs, I understand. A very good breed."

Assent again. He was practically acknowledging my actual humanity.

"Well, Senator, I wonder." I paused, desperately trying to stop myself. It was no use—out it flew. "I just wonder. Have you ever thought of breeding a White Charleigh with a Black Angus?"

Grim silence. Bewilderment. More smoke clouds spewing about. Then he looked stunned, the air virtually exploding as he grasped my meaning. James Eastland grumbled, growled and all but threatened to bite.

And I? Well I had cleared my conscience. I smiled the rest of the ride to the Capitol.

Now here I was, deep within Eastland's own purlieu. And a little old woman was about to change my unidimensional view of that man.

"Oh yes, these are Senator Eastland's quarters," she emphatically assured me. "I've known him for so many years," she added, befuddling me further. "But where will I go now?"

I still had no idea what would become of her. "What are all these files?" I waved my hand, changing the subject until I could grip reality.

"They're very important," she said, territorial privilege infusing her words. "They're the Internal Security files of the Senate. All of them." And, as if I was surely too naïve to understand what that meant, she assisted me. "Senator McCarthy's files," she summed up.

Certainly it was my eyes which widened now.

"Are the files ever used?" I cleared my throat, carefully modulating my voice.

"Oh yes. A lawyer comes in every week or two to handle them," she insisted.

I didn't think I could take any more. Politely, I smiled, said my goodbyes, and let myself out.

Later we spotted that lawyer she spoke of. He matched her completely. A funny little man scrunched over a briefcase.

I never uncovered the fullness of the enigma but this: for years, Senator Eastland had benevolently cared for that woman who had no other place to go. Soon, she was taken in locally, safely housed.

And I? Well I finally gained an office, albeit one pervaded by mystery.

Just like the Senate itself.

CHAPTER NINE

The Lure of Power Politics

I DOUBT THERE'S EVER BEEN A SENATOR WHO STOOD IN FRONT OF the mirror shaving (or not shaving, as in the case of the wonderful women gaining ground in the Senate chamber) who never noticed a curious thought scurrying through their brain. "I think," the thought begins, "I could do better than that person who runs things over at 1600 Pennsylvania Avenue."

That thought flit through my mind as well. In my case, it was a one issue thought. I could do better, I felt, at getting us out of Vietnam than Johnson had, or later, than Nixon did. But I can't deny what all Americans know about politicians, either: it's heady stuff, finding yourself able to walk through swinging portals straight onto the Senate floor whenever you choose, wining and dining with leaders, being constantly involved with media, constituents, and fellow members alike.

All of that began happening to me, and pretty soon I knew ego could destroy my career. Worse than that, it could easily end anything worthy I might do for this country if I didn't catch hold of it, and fast.

Politics, it has to be admitted, has more than its share of prima donnas. It's hard to keep your head sometimes, and the rarefied atmosphere in D.C. doesn't help. I wanted to set my sites far beyond ego, to my responsibilities to the Senate itself. The goal was to play my part in the body politic of this great institution. One of my senior colleagues taught me a lot about the culture of the Senate during my maiden speech.

I had been in the Senate only three months, and from the start I had a desk of my own in the Senate chamber. Of course, since I was number 100 I had the last desk on the Republican side of the aisle, to the far right of every other senator in my party—the only time I've ever been to the far right of my party, I might add. But I sat at that desk—my desk—and opened the drawer. All the previous occupants had chiseled and scratched their names into the bottom of that drawer like schoolboys. I would be no different. I read down the list and stopped, startled as I saw the name "Hatfield-West Va." The first chance I got, I slipped into the cloakroom, opening the dictionary of Senate members. There he was, Henry Drury Hatfield, an M.D. and former governor of West Virginia, Republican senator from 1929-35. It wasn't such a great omen to be number 100, but I thought it boded pretty well to sit at ol' Henry Hatfield's desk. Later, as I rose in seniority I was assigned other desks. Yet I always took that first chair with me. When I retired, my Appropriations Committee staff bought me that chair (or rather, bought its replacement) and I have the seat still.

But back in 1967, I was quite the neophyte as I stood at Henry Hatfield's desk to offer my maiden speech—a treatise on how Johnson's timber and fiscal policies displayed indifference, at best, to the needs of Oregon and Oregonians. I had given plenty of speeches and by now I was comfortable at any podium. Yet I was in the Senate this time, no longer the leader of my home state, but lowliest member of the leaders of every state. I was anxious, no doubt about it. And I didn't want to stub my toe during my first public effort.

Luckily, few senators were even present. Maiden speeches usually followed the majority leader's—Montana's Mike Mansfield, in this case—agenda for the day. And right on schedule the chair announced, "The senator from Oregon is recognized." I was on.

On the opposite side of the aisle, Senator Richard Russell, a Democrat from Georgia, stood to leave. Russell was by then an old pillar of the Senate and one of its most influential members. He even played

LBJ's mentor when Johnson was majority leader. But at this point in his life Russell had partaken too much of his state's prime crop and now suffered the ravages of emphysema. As I rose to speak he had a coughing fit and made his way up the aisle to exit, not wishing to be a distraction. I watched all this clearly. After all, I had a prime view from my back row seat.

On his way up the aisle, Russell must have realized I was venturing on my maiden speech. He pivoted, abruptly returning to his chair. He turned that seat 180 degrees around to face me, put his head in his hand and gave me his complete attention. I was baffled at first, then delighted. It was a courtesy to listen to a freshman senator give his maiden speech, even if the new member happened to be a vocal, liberal Republican from the north. It didn't matter a bit what party I was from—a strict departure from the often strangling partisanship we witness today.

In this one small act Senator Russell gifted me with the best of Senate culture: a love for the Senate institution itself, a respect for the diversity of its members, and a respect for the binding, catalytic force of civility that glued the Senate together as the greatest legislative body in the world.

That's how the Senate ran in those days, and I took notice. Today, some call it trivial shadow boxing. Why should we maintain the antiquarian modes of communication, the "My distinguished colleague from Maine...," or "The one I hold in respect from Missouri." But that civility—yes, sometimes it's tedious—makes each member remember their colleague is human, no matter how different. Their colleague has every right to believe as strongly as they, no matter how divergent.

I made it through my maiden speech without any major faux pas, though truth be told I had to look up what I spoke about, it made so little impression on me or anyone else. I'm fairly certain it made no major impact on Richard Russell, either. But when I sat, collecting myself quietly, Russell rose (yes, one of my most distinguished colleagues) and strode right over to my lowly desk. He grasped my hand. "That was a fine speech, Senator," he said. "A fine speech."

With his words, I knew even as number 100, I was a full-fledged member in that August body.

I knew Russell wasn't so expansive about equality in general, so I took his gesture even more to heart. In 1964, years before my tenure, Russell worked as hard as he could to defeat the Civil Rights Bill. But his opponents gained enough votes to impose cloture—a halt to filibustering in order to expedite the vote. Russell, gracious as ever, spoke. "I have had my say," he told his colleagues. "Now it is time for the Senate to work its will." The Senate's will, he knew, was far more important than any desire or will of his own.

Unfortunately, Senator Russell died in the late '70s and one of his cohorts, Senator Jim Allen from Alabama, equally southern and courteous, came up with a plan to overcome cloture. With his clever mind he developed procedures to create a post-cloture filibuster. Until that moment the Senate had been a collection of ambassadors from every state, committed to the institution of the Senate in a way that transcended any individual viewpoint. Russell had known the Senate's will, as a whole, came beyond the individual will in each and every case. But Allen master-minded a vehicle to shift the entire Senate culture.

Suddenly, the Senate as an institution could no longer rise in consensus, as one body reaching a decision. No longer could the Senate so readily work its will. Instead, any individual might bend the whole body to his or her will with a post-cloture filibuster. From the old Senate culture, from love and respect for the institution of the Senate itself, a new virus sprung on the body politic. Any one of the 100 individuals could choose to put their own power above the time-honored, democratic system of allowing the consensual power of the Senate to govern.

That was a sad day for the Senate, and it taught me much. Yet it was not the fault of the Senate, or even Jim Allen alone. Americans may hesitate to hear this, but I believe it true: Legislative culture is nothing if not a reflection of American culture itself. The Senate shifts and modifies its machinations, but it does so only in concert with the subtle and not-so-subtle purling of American values.

It's easy to blame politics for society's ills—and believe me, I'm first to admit politics is culpable to many. We would rather not blame ourselves, rather not take responsibility for our own part—each and every one of us that make up this nation—for the rise of individualism over the commonwealth, the excess cravings for power, money, or raw ambition that too many give way to. The Senate is not perfect, but certainly neither are we, not any one of us. Every time we point a finger at Congress, we're pointing three fingers at ourselves. There is misuse of power, of money, of ego in every arena. But if responsible government leadership is to be exercised in our institutions of government, the seeds of change must also blossom in the hearts and minds of the people.

I knew ego was something I'd have to battle daily—if not moment by moment. I told myself if ever I drove up Constitution Avenue without a sense of spine-tingling excitement at the sight of the Capitol, it would be time to leave. This was my litmus test. Luckily, I never lost that thrill at viewing the institution that represents our freedoms. Even when I go back to Washington today and see the edifices that symbolize our nation, a fervor hits me as strongly as the day I was sworn in. This litmus test was easy to pass.

Also, I tried to internalize Russell's example. I wanted to maintain balance as a senator, to know that the power of the Senate was a strength to be honored. And I wanted to respect my colleagues whether they agreed with me or not. Diversity of the body politic was as essential as breathing itself.

After all, our very nation was founded on diversity—religious diversity—and we can still take a lesson from that. Our forebears didn't learn the lesson quickly, and we must re-learn it today. The Puritans forgot diversity, quickly imposing religious conformity on all who lived in the Massachusetts Bay Colony. That's why the Baptists, Quakers, and Jews soon fled to Rhode Island to maintain their much sought religious pluralism. Since then, inclusiveness has been threatened in our culture from countless angles—religious, racial, ethnic, economic, to name but a few. What a sickness we've imposed from struggling against pluralism. We've barely begun to come to grips with racial hatreds, not to mention other hatreds which corrupt our souls. Yet our very Constitution is built on pluralism, on inclusiveness. Cultural, ethnic, religious inclusiveness. And that applies to all of us—not simply politicians.

In addition to respecting the Senate and its pluralism, I tried to prevent merging of my ego and any issue, so I wouldn't become the issue and rupture human relations. This included even my most fervent issues—war, civil rights, assisting the poor, or educating the vulnerable. I never wanted to rupture friendships. Today's adversary was tomorrow's ally, and I always looked for common ground with colleagues. And that common ground, those bipartisan coalitions, are the heart of healthy, progressive politics. So I fought issues, not people, doing what I needed to advance any cause I believed in.

Perhaps nowhere was this more evident than with Richard Nixon and our disagreements over Vietnam. Vice President Nixon had invited me to offer his nominating speech in 1960 and I became a rumored running mate in '68. Yet once he was elected, his stance on Vietnam didn't deviate much from Johnson's. I was so passionate in my fight against the war that I soon earned myself a hallowed place on Nixon's famous enemies list. Yet when he resigned, I wrote him a note expressing my heartfelt compassion.

Colleagues came to me, dumbfounded. "How can you support Nixon now, after all he's done to our country?" Well I didn't support what he'd done, not one bit. But the man was human, and he was suffering greatly. I felt sorry for him—as I did for Bill Clinton during his impeachment travails, though I did not condone his actions any more than Nixon's. I wrote Nixon that note of compassion and never regretted it. Even though often with difficulty, I learned that our opponents even—and perhaps most especially—are human, deserving care and support as much as we.

Several other factors served to keep me balanced in the maelstrom of the Senate. A critical one was my faith. In the last years of my career especially, I was confronted with occasions of humiliation and embarrassment when my very integrity or honesty were challenged. Those times were painful, for sure, but they also offered an opportunity to reassess my life and faith.

But faith constantly helped because I tried to live my life as a man of faith. This infused me with an ability to keep perspective—most of the time. I almost hesitate even to mention faith in our present culture, as religion is so often used as justification for great abuses of power, especially in politics. But the constitutional mandate to recognize religious pluralism in our country gives every individual equal right to pursue their own spiritual faith—or to have no spiritual faith at all. We all learn from each other, diversity enriching each one of us.

For me, my spiritual role model stands in the life and teachings of Jesus, centered in his ideal of love and forgiveness. With that, I try always to remember I answer to a higher power than any human authority. Jefferson, not so much a Christian as a humanist, wrote often about the best values of democracy. He didn't always embody what his lofty writings decreed, as we now know. But his intentions were true, and according to his philosophy, democracy could only work if humans subsumed their will to a higher authority—God, spirit, higher power, what have you—rather than believe they could self-centeredly determine every result themselves.

My wife and children, and my constituents, also did their part to keep me humble, and I appreciated their contribution. I also tried never to be too busy to take a moment to check in with elevator operators or dining room staff. Every day when I saw them, I tried never to be too busy to ask how were they, their spouses, and their children. Over time, they'd share their joys with me and I could rejoice too. If they were suffering I could offer a word of encouragement and hope it might help.

My staff played a critical role as well. When I was readying for a trip home, everyone became involved. Someone scheduled meetings, another typed speeches, one briefed me on issues, and someone else created a trip book. When I returned, we all got together for staff meetings, from the receptionist to the legislative director. Each person was key to our work in their way, and I needed to let them know what I'd done. I'd go over what we accomplished, what Oregonians were concerned with, and any problems. We also held seminars in the office, bringing in mystery guest speakers, from the author of Kiplinger's newsletter to the president of American University to a columnist for Time magazine. Learning is a lifelong pursuit and we all benefited from learning together. It helped me stay balanced.

Perhaps it also helped explain why I had the lowest staff attrition rate of any senator on Capitol Hill. Staffers often commented that hiring interviews in my office never included questions about political party. My interviewees were asked about education, government's role in social programs, or the issue of the day. Which party they hailed from was of little import. But who they were? That's what mattered.

Gerry Frank, too, spent immeasurable amounts of time assuring there was unity and sense of community among staff. Not unity of ideology—never! I relied on those with views different from my own to keep me thinking. But staff were bright and diverse—two great strengths. Everyone knew they were to voice their opinions without being asked. We were a family and we advanced together, never at the expense of one another. That was, and still is, an unusual way to run a Senate office, but it worked for all of us. And it helped me maintain the same respect and open mind for my colleagues, no matter how different or how opposed. I could still calmly say, "What do you think of this?" or "My concern is that. . ." or "On the other hand. . ." and gradually, a fractious debate might become more civil, and positive change could be wrought.

Intellectual corruption is deadly, and when a lawmaker begins to let go of his or her best convictions in favor of listening to only those who agree, or to pollsters placing a wet finger in the air, one's best thinking gives way to placating the most popular position and, yes, securing the most votes. Soon one begins to feel so powerful they have no time for the person on the street who wants to stop and ask a question. Or for the factory worker who disagrees with them and demands their attention for a moment. Thus, politicians reduce their exposure, wanting instead to put a third-party buffer between themselves and their voters, becoming a manufactured product—something about as relevant as toothpaste or bleach; an advertisement designed only to boost their political capital. Then, politicians no longer serve the people with the most diligent and best of their minds, energies, and convictions. And once you deny yourself access of those you represent, intellectual corruption becomes a grave risk.

And this particular risk is a syndrome, an ailment politics can very much call its own. I've even given it a name: the political-industrial complex. It goes like this—lawmakers grow alienated from those they represent (and vice versa) as buffers grow taller and taller between representatives and the people they are meant to serve. Constituents receive less and less attention while officials spend more and more time raising funds for their war chests, trying to assure success in the next election. And worst of all, this vicious cycle creates total disenchantment on the part of the voters. A sense there is no way the individual voice might be heard pervades the public mind. (When, after all, was the last time your knowledge about politicians came not from television, radio, slick junk mail, or newspaper ads, but in the form of grassroots advocacy by the people—door-to-door volunteers wanting to earnestly discuss issues and candidates?)

Whenever organized interests wield more power than individuals, democracy is thwarted. In fact, a political system like ours—where fewer than 10 percent of citizens have even met their congressional representative—is almost a travesty. And representatives seem to care less and less. Why should they? They're about to get re-elected!

Pericles, to the Athenians, perhaps summed up the political-industrial complex best: "Our constitution is called a democracy because power is in the hands not of a minority, but of the whole people." And, "....when the whole state is on the right course it is a better thing for each separate individual than when private interests are satisfied but the state as a whole is going downhill."

Although it may sound so, turning around the political-industrial complex is not hopeless. There are simple measures to be taken. One of the first is to change our campaigns from billion dollar industries to equal ground, where having the best interests of the nation at heart are far more important than a candidate's ability to raise money. Allocating time for free- or reduced-rate broadcasting for all candidates—incumbents and challengers alike—is a good place to start. Better disclosure of campaign contributions, so voters and journalists have immediate access to information on contributors both large and small will also help. And grassroots involvement—volunteers going door to door, as I said, or citizens vocally expressing their needs and views, is critical. When growing numbers of citizens take part in government, elected officials will be forced to listen, thus offering more power where it belongs—with the people.

Each of us deserves to have our voices heard as we combat the too powerful and the too self-interested. We can fight back, and we should.

Yet elements other than my philosophy inevitably popped up in the least expected places during my own career as well. Television game shows, for instance. In 1970 I was actually invited to be a contestant on a new TV pilot fashioned after "Truth or Consequences." What bizarre twists and turns politics takes—no wonder ego accretes so quickly.

I had been picked as the first contestant on "Let's Play Politics," along with (yes, my distinguished colleague!) Senator Gale McGee, a Democrat from Wyoming. Supposedly, the papers reported, we were picked for our photogenic qualities. I don't know about that but in any case, so much for deep equity in politics. Our new job was to boggle press experts, in this case two well-known columnists. If we succeeded, the videotaped pilot would be tested out on Madison Avenue.

Everyone needs work, and TV visionaries are no exception. Their brilliant brainstorm was to take an incident from either Gale or my true lives, and have us each try to convince the columnists it was a real life anecdote, even though it was actually true for only one of us. The reporters would cross examine us under the lights and heat, then decide which of us was telling the truth, and which of us "played politics."

Assuming politics was contrary to truth should have been my first clue that I might not like this ride. Knowing Gale and I were always very straightforward made it only worse.

The pilot's first scenario spun out a humble, heart-warming tale of how one of us had begun politics at the age of 10. Well that was me, going door to door with a little red wagon loaded with Hoover hand-bills in 1932. But neither Gale nor I, the alleged truthful one, could figure out what we were to do. We droned on and on about adolescent political aspirations and deeds, both of us telling the boring truth about ourselves in unbearable detail. The columnists guessed McGee was the one who began his political career so early. So much for my persuasive honesty!

The next question centered on something our national interest surely depended upon: which of us led a dance band in high school. That was McGee, but I made sure it was well known I'd played clarinet. The truth came through no matter what I did. Of course our judges could figure if I'd played clarinet, McGee must have been the band leader—these were brilliant journalists, after all, quite adept at the wonders of the process of elimination.

Finally, they asked which of us was the caveman who had eaten raw meat. Well, that was me again—as governor I'd been initiated as an honorary member of the Grants Pass "Cavemen." Initiation involved guzzling raw beef—long before the ubiquitous E. Coli, thank goodness—and I succumbed. Gale went on and on about "caveman days under Republican administrations," but our questioners were unswayed. They guessed right: Hatfield had let blood drip from his chin with a group of savages who predated what we now glorify as "men's groups"!

Luckily, the show flopped. The TV folks must have figured all politicians were even stupider than they looked.

Afterwards one of the columnists asked, "How will this thing sit with the folks back in Oregon?" I didn't even want to think about the possibility.

Gale, though, as well known a hawk as I was a dove, piped right up. "Hatfield doesn't go until '72," he referred to the elections. "I'm wondering how this will go in Wyoming this year."

Gratefully for both of us, it was a worry we could soon dismiss— the show became history before it began.

A couple years earlier, in 1968, when my name arose as a possible vice presidential running mate to Richard Nixon, it provided a sobering contrast. In a way, I had actually supported Eugene McCarthy, a true anti-war lawmaker, in the Democratic primary in Oregon. I certainly couldn't change my registration to vote for him, but that didn't stop me from asking friends to become Democrats so they could support McCarthy in the primary. He won in Oregon, too, only to lose the Democratic Convention to Hubert Humphrey.

So Nixon became my candidate, and the press mentioned my name as a potential running mate.

Nixon had only listed three qualifications for vice president: good presidential material, good acceptability as a campaigner in every corner of the country, and sound agreement with his views. He planned to give his veep plenty of responsibility and wanted whoever it was to pilot his message around the nation.

But Nixon's qualifications didn't fit me. How popular could I have been campaigning in the South, a longtime, passionate civil rights activist, dove, and former member of the NAACP? One of my very first speeches in the Oregon State Legislature supported miscegenation and non-discrimation in hotel registration. I was a well-known supporter of several other controversial civil rights bills as well.

Meanwhile, Nixon was already deep into his "southern strategy," gaining plenty of Republican support in the South to offset the heavily Democratic North. The '64 Civil Rights Bill had passed, indicating the direction this country intended to head, but it was a fragile peace. In 1968, George Wallace also rose as a presidential contender, long before renouncing his racist views. Wallace was a grave symptom of our troubled times, and I knew we had little in common.

Moreover, how could I agree with Nixon on the war? He hadn't yet voiced his stance, and even I was hopeful his view would seriously depart from Johnson's. But I certainly didn't expect it to match mine— I was far more dovish than most of my Democratic colleagues! The war was sure to be a major part of the campaign. How could it not?

Of course I fantasized about becoming Nixon's veep, a man I had respected and supported in the past. But I swung from fantasy back to hard reality. I knew it could never happen.

Still, tension rose swiftly at the convention. I was asked to offer one of the seconding speeches for Nixon's nomination. Republican supporters had me all figured out. "Speak to the religious and the peace communities," they ordered, as if these two were natural allies at this point in history.

I was bewildered by what they wanted, so I asked John Mitchell, then Nixon's campaign manager, for another meeting. "You're going to have to help me," I said. "What, for instance, would you have me say to the religious community?"

"Well," Mitchell and his associates scrambled, "Nixon's mother is a wonderful Quaker."

"Yes," I agreed. "But she's not the candidate. If you want me to talk, I have to speak to his issues, his beliefs, his actual involvements."

They struggled on, "Like Quakers, you know, he's kind of reticent to speak about his faith."

"I know his mother," I reminded them, "and she's not at all reticent to speak about her faith. She's quite loquacious, in fact." When I had nominated her son in 1960, she had been only too eager to discuss with me many of her personal religious views.

We got nowhere. "So to the peace community, for instance," I changed the subject. "What can I say?"

There was no mention then of Nixon's "secret plan" to solve the war problem. That would come later. Meanwhile though, he was making his plans as secret as possible, and no one was certainly about to tell me about them.

"Oh," his men insisted, "he's going to make it a top priority to get us out of Vietnam."

"And how's he going to do that?" I asked.

Complete bafflement. No response.

I walked off and found my friend, Travis Cross. Travis was working the convention for Walter Cronkite, covering personalities for CBS and offering his friendship as well. We chewed on my assignment and somehow got something down on paper I could believe in. Nixon's men, still nervous over what I might expound, pestered Gerry about the content of my talk. Neither he nor I ever answered. Like everyone else, they had to wait until I made my speech.

Next, the day before the final VP announcement was to come, I got a strange call from a Mr. Knight of Knight Ridder, owner of the Miami Herald. Would I have lunch with him? he asked. With no idea what was up, I agreed.

Throughout our meal Knight talked of everything besides what was on his mind. I could tell that much, but I couldn't figure out what had brought him here. Finally, as we were finishing the meal and had exhausted the weather (after all, how much can you discuss Miami's unchanging weather?), a man ran up to Knight and handed him a rolled up newspaper. Knight held it close so only he could see, then flashed it abruptly toward me. "How does that hit you?" he grinned.

"Nixon-Hatfield Ticket" the headline veritably yelled, emblazoned across the top quarter of the paper in bright red. It was the first copy of the Herald's afternoon edition, and evidently Don Oberdorfer, a Herald reporter in the Washington Bureau, wrote this scoop as if he had some inside line. In fact, it turned out he didn't know any more than I did who Nixon would choose.

I answered Knight's question without hesitation. "It depends on what the price is," I told him.

"What do you mean?" Knight asked, ever the newsman.

"If it means I have to change my position on the war, I won't do it," I stated. Soon after, we said our goodbyes.

Well, Senator Strom Thurmond, Republican from South Carolina, caught that afternoon headline. Evidently he'd brokered a deal with Nixon: If he could deliver plenty of southern Republican delegates to the convention, as he had, he could offer all the feedback he wished on a vice presidential candidate who would please the southern states. When he saw that headline he must have been shocked, let alone furious. He and I had attended prayer breakfasts together and were friendly, sure. But it must have seemed to him he had been denied his veto power with the president. And as I said, I would never pass any southern test on civil rights, Vietnam, or many other issues, I'm proud to say.

The press soon learned the Herald was wrong, but they did get word the VP short list was down to three. Each of the major networks manned the hotel of each rumored contender, and ABC assigned Peter Jennings, a junior reporter, to the Kenilworth to scout me. Besides Travis, Warne Nunn, my loyal gubernatorial chief-of-staff, Freeman Holmer, my former budget director, and our dear friends John and Mary Jane Dellenback were there as well. They scurried around scheming over how we would handle phone calls and press relations if I were offered the pick. Travis even got press releases together and they all mulled over my acceptance. I don't think they slept a bit. It was exciting being so highly speculated over for a big post, that's heady stuff for anyone—in politics or out.

That same evening, Nixon pulled an all-nighter too. While my friends sat around figuring out details and trying to second guess what would happen next, Antoinette and I went to bed. Nixon stayed up conferring with his closest advisers—including Reverend Billy Graham, a good friend of ours—but we were dreaming away.

At 2 a.m., Graham woke us up. "Just wanted to give you an update," I filtered his voice through my sleep-befuddled brain. "We're not finished, but they asked each of us to name our three choices in rank order. I told them my first choice was Mark Hatfield, my second choice was Mark Hatfield, and my third choice was Mark Hatfield." He didn't have a sense as to what our chances were and we hung up. I rolled over and went right back to sleep.

At 5 a.m. the next call came. This time, Graham broke the news: "I'm afraid to say you're out of it, Mark."

But a few minutes later the phone rang again. This time it was Herb Klein, Nixon's press man. "I think you're not out yet. There's sort of a reassessment going on here."

At 9 a.m. we got the final call. They told me it wouldn't be me, but they didn't mention who it was.

Yes, it came that close. Yes, I was caught up in the color, the excitement of political decision making, the calls coming directly from the presidential nominee's rooms, the total focus of a moment in history. And when I was awake, my adrenaline flowed. But we had been invited to go boating with friends, and it was a new day. We rode down the elevator in Bermuda shorts and hats, spiritually calm as we faced the press. Then, we had a great time on that boat.

Sure Antoinette and I were disappointed. But not devastatingly so. "Look what our life would have turned into," we mused with our friends in the bay that day. We had four little children and I was already away from home far too often. I would have had to travel constantly, missing and worrying over each member of my family at every destination.

Antoinette and I simply knew my calling was to continue as a senator from Oregon. With that, any disappointment we felt was swiftly supplanted with sheer relief. Later I'd be asked by a small group to run as president on an anti-war platform, or as VP for Eugene McCarthy. But I would turn those offers down. That outcome in Miami—in a phrase—offered a great lesson in withstanding the lure of power politics.

Who knows if Richard Nixon made a mistake. Strom delivered those southern delegates and undoubtedly tipped the balance in Nixon's favor. As Vice President, Nixon chose Spiro Agnew instead, a decision soon to haunt him. But Nixon's troubles would go well beyond Agnew or even the war, and I still thank God I had no part in any of that.

Besides, Richard Milhous Nixon was about to make his stance on Vietnam all too clear. And with that, our political relationship would never be the same.

CHAPTER TEN

Maintaining the Fight
Against the War in Vietnam

RICHARD NIXON'S 1968 CAMPAIGN HAD JUST BEGUN AND NIXON phoned me himself. He made no reference to the vice presidential post, nor did I. In fact, Nixon never mentioned it. With this particular phone call he tapped me for something else altogether—to serve as his surrogate campaigner. I was to take his message to the people.

Nixon and I went back a long way. I'd met him at the 1952 Chicago Republican Convention when he became the vice presidential candidate. I particularly respected his geopolitical views. In 1959, Eisenhower had Nixon play emissary, visiting Oregon for our centennial. I was a newly installed governor by then, and during the campaign Nixon had proclaimed me one of the "major rays of hope for the Republican Party," and "one of the most outstanding young leaders the Republican Party produced in recent years." He phoned to offer best wishes as soon as I won the office.

Soon after, he came to celebrate the centennial and we invited him to lunch in our little apartment—Antoinette and I had barely been married a year and our house was in the process of being remodeled.

As soon as he accepted the invitation the secret service descended to inspect our abode. Antoinette was quite pregnant with Elizabeth, and one of the security men smoked a cigar in the hallway. Well, cigars made Antoinette pretty sick in the best of times, and pregnancy only heightened her revulsion. She got her message clearly across and the man stamped out his cigar.

Antoinette was about to embark on her second career as cookbook author at the time, and she had everything planned for a quintessential centennial lunch in our diminutive dinette. She created a tablecloth from yellow burlap, and placed a covered wagon atop it as centerpiece. Nixon entered in a blue serge suit, and all through the meal raved about Antoinette's Oregon string bean dish. When he rose, gold burlap flaked off all over his blue suit. Antoinette moved quickly to help him wipe it off. She likes to say she was one of the first ever to "brush off" Nixon. She surely wouldn't be the last.

Later, whenever we saw Nixon socially (less and less as the Vietnam war progressed), he would recite the same comment to Antoinette. He must have kept cards on everyone invited to his events. He scratched out a note reminding himself about the individual's distinguishing characteristics, then scanned the cards the day of the event to jog his memory. "Still cooking those great string beans?" Nixon would beam at Antoinette at every meeting, as if he'd just thought it—for the millionth time.

Secretary of State Henry Kissinger's memory was like his boss'. Much later, when we first moved from Bethesda to Georgetown, Kissinger lived on the same block as we did. Soon after we moved, he and his Bassett Hound took a walk one morning and the dog decided our place was definitively the best to do his natural duty.

Antoinette poked her head out the door. "Don't let your dog use our yard!" she yelled at Henry, knowing full well who he was. He stared at her, stunned. "Leave him there and come in for scrambled eggs," she advised. He took her up on the offer, and to this day whenever we run into Henry in Washington he turns to Antoinette. "When am I going to get more of your scrambled eggs and bacon?" he asks in his deep German baritone. He was always a friend—even when Nixon was in office and things grew strained between Nixon and me.

Soon after Oregon's centennial, I was invited to nominate Nixon at the 1960 Republican National Convention for his razor-thin loss to John F. Kennedy.

So when Nixon first won his 1968 presidential candidacy, I was still on his side. I had high hopes he would distinguish his war position from Johnson's and Kennedy's, and felt he had a capacity to evolve on the war. Besides, what was my alternative—Vice President Hubert Humphrey? Humphrey was already a partner in Johnson's architectural firm and would surely continue Johnson's policy of building up the war. At least with Nixon I thought we had a chance.

As his surrogate, I stumped for him at Rutgers University when word came about his "secret plan" regarding Vietnam. To the entire nation, he announced his policy was a big secret, and he was withdrawing not from the war itself—what a gift that would have been!—but from even discussing the war. I wrote, urging him not to keep quiet, suggesting he needed to speak out so we could all hear what he had to say. He didn't repond to my letter, and I don't know if he ever actually saw it. But suddenly I stopped hearing from his campaign. I was off his surrogate list and our genial relationship began to cool. That's okay, I thought, trying to separate myself from the personal: Nixon and I could disagree politically. It wasn't about him, and it wasn't about me.

But I felt so strongly about Vietnam—one of the main issues propelling me to the Senate in the first place—that I couldn't hide my convictions. Or at least not for long. Even shortly after Nixon was sworn in, Bill Rogers, the new secretary of state, came to see me suggesting, "Let us get our act together, Mark. Lighten up on the secret plan, will you? Give us a legitimate amount of time to get our Vietnam peace policy established."

It seemed a reasonable request, and only fair. I acquiesced.

But we hadn't discussed any timelines for lifting the gag order, so I relied on my own judgment.

By this time, my thinking had developed further since my stands in the mid-60s. To begin with, I could see the war was well on its way to eroding America as we knew and loved it. It eroded the relationship between citizens and their federal government by betraying communication and trust at the most basic levels. During the Kennedy and Johnson eras, MacNamara had become well versed in double talk and Nixon must have taken a lesson. MacNamara visited Vietnam over and over and his words never changed. Neither did the fact that he was saying absolutely nothing.

In 1962 McNamara pronounced, "Progress in the last eight to ten weeks has been great. . . . Nothing but progress and hopeful indications of further progress." In 1963: "There is a new feeling of confidence. . . . The major part of the U.S. military task can be completed by the end of 1965." 1964: "Excellent progress." 1965: "We have stopped losing the war." And in 1967, in Vietnam, he was quoted as saying more progress had been made in the last nine months than in the previous six years. Well, who needed that kind of progress?

At this rate we were peddling backwards at best, and I knew it. I was sick of double talk from administration leaders, whether under Johnson or Nixon who never really told us anything about our true national interest and how it could have a bit to do with this tiny piece of soil in Asia. There were no clear objectives, no goals, no articulated interest that anyone could see, least of all the American people. But suddenly something which had affected the French and the South Vietnamese now affected us—in a big way.

Assistant Secretary of Defense, Arthur Sylvester (under LBJ), had proved even worse than MacNamara. "It is the right of the government to lie to the people to protect national policy," he said. Well, at least his words were much clearer than MacNamara's. I could read his meaning right away—no obfuscation there.

Meanwhile, Americans were suffering. They were frustrated with the war largely because they couldn't understand it. No administration proved clear on their policy, Democratic or Republican. Sure people were perplexed. Here was this terribly insignificant country in terms of power. Why couldn't we just whip them and be done with it? Defeat them, take victory. What was going on? We'd faced the Germans and the Japanese—major war powers—and now here was this rinky-dink little country holding fast to our wrists like fly paper, clinging no matter how hard we tried to flick it off. The frustration of the public alone was erosive to America.

But then values began to play into the game. Beginning with Korea, then Vietnam, later in the Persian Gulf, and most recently Kosovo, we engaged in what was called "limited warfare." In Vietnam, LBJ got out of bed each morning and picked his North Vietnamese bombing targets. No longer were generals or admirals allowed to win a battle or a war—it was a political proposition, not a military one. How deeply unfair to those trained in warfare to be assigned political, economic, or social problems to solve and then be blamed for quagmires the politicians should have dealt with outside of warfare. Increasingly we hear the military doesn't like our policies because we lack any clearly defined military agenda. The same held true in Vietnam, and our ill-fated policy could never gain peace.

In addition to our faulty thinking of limited warfare in Vietnam, we no longer measured success in terms of land captured—if we had done it that way, it would have been only too clear we were failing miserably. Instead, we began keeping body counts. By the end of the war, we lost over 55,000 of our own men. But what of "enemy" losses? Well, the enemy was not human, they were only bodies. So we played body counts day to day as if that was some honorable measure of success. How many did we kill today? became the question in the national mind. Meanwhile, body bags seeped into our nomenclature as well. Body counts and body bags. This war was more barbaric in terms of how we thought and spoke about it, than any before. The language alone became absurd.

One well-known commanding officer stood amidst rubble in the middle of a decimated South Vietnamese village—and remember, South Vietnam was our ally. "In order to save this village," the commander noted as if it made perfect sense, "we had to destroy it." It was twisted logic, perverse judgments like these, that finally made people realize they wanted to oppose this wanton war. There was no "light at the end of the tunnel," as MacNamara once euphemized. Only more death and blood. Fresh, young blood.

Economics began to slide into the erosion of America as well. By the earliest days of the '70s, over 52 cents of every tax dollar went straight for defense. Not housing, not commerce, not transportation, hunger, health, education, veterans' programs, space, or agriculture. All those programs had to divide up the less than half dollar left. The majority dripped steadily into defense. We'd spent a trillion dollars

With my mother and father (above). Family Christmas late 1960s (from left to right), Visko, me, Teresa, Antoinette, MarkO, and Elizabeth (below).

The people I live for: (clockwise) Elizabeth, MarkO, Teresa, Visko, and Antoinette, the center of my life.

In the Navy, with my buddies, I am fourth from left, the skinny one (top).

The USS Whiteside, the ship I served on in the Pacific theatre of WW II (middle).

Dean of Students at Willamette University, circa 1953, (bottom left). Relaxing at Bohemia Grove, 1954, (bottom right).

Governors' Conference, June 1964. I am in the front row, second from right.

"Boys Town." My closest gubernatorial staff, from left to right: Travis Cross, Loren Hicks, and Warne Nunn. 1959.

Doing my part to clean up Oregon beaches, kicking off increased awareness of protecting our coast.

My relation with Richard Nixon took many turns through the years.
Welcoming Nixon to Oregon's State's Centennial in 1959 (above).
Offering my controversial prayer at the 1973 National Prayer Break-
fast urging "our President and all leaders to achieve peace in all parts
of the world." A statement that the press saw as direct slap at
Nixon's Vietnam policies.

Images from five terms as Senator. Discussing the Middle East with Abba Eban and Gerry Frank, my chief of staff (above). With Sen. Edward Kennedy, working on the Nuclear Freeze campaign (middle). With Sen. Robert Dole (below).

I arrived in Washington, DC as freshman senator, ranked last in Senate seniority, and was assigned a cramped office space (above). As chairman of Senate Appropriations, I spearheaded this restoration of the Appropriations Chamber. As my years in the Senate increased, my working environment improved significantly.

Back in Oregon. With Rep. Earl Blumenauer surveying the Willamette
River (above). Walking on the Willamette University campus with Gerry
Frank, my good friend, advisor, and former chief of staff (below).

since World War II on defense alone. And just in Oregon taxpayers had spent nearly a billion on Vietnam—$364 for each and every resident. What amazing, life enhancing things we could have accomplished with our own people, our own country, with barely a shred of that capital.

Besides, here we were spending more and more money for defense, and where was it going? Several days before he died in a helicopter accident which killed five of his colleagues, a marine captain wrote relatives that a parts shortage had grounded "about 60 percent of our choppers." What were we doing with all this money—money, money, ever more military money—when we couldn't even keep our choppers in the air and were killing our own men because of simple hardware failures?

Meanwhile hunger, housing, and education at home were all in deplorable shape. This wasn't news, and it wasn't even all the fault of our policy in Vietnam. After World War II, we still had unfulfilled weapons orders. We spiked up the military budget again for Korea, escalating and re-escalating our military budget until and through Vietnam (and needless to say, after). We took all the production skills of countless scientists and had them devote their brilliant minds primarily to life destroying activities rather than life supporting ones. We devoted them to creating newer, more deadly, ever more vicious weapons. What we could have accomplished with that brainpower!

And why did we do it? Because of the military industrial complex, of course. Unemployment figures had to be kept down at all cost, and military spending is a great way to create jobs. Jobs are good, essential even. But when you create jobs for the military industrial complex, guess what? You have to use the products you build. And to do that, you have to make war, deadly war. Even if we sell weapons abroad, which we're only too happy to do as a primary arms peddler, we still haven't rid ourselves of what we created. Those countries must make their investment worthwhile. They do so by using arms—either as threats or as weapons of destruction, selling arms, warehousing them, or eventually detoxifying them. And ever onward the arms race speeds, well past the point of redundancy, all at the expense of the hungry and the cold circling our globe. It's a far too vicious cycle.

Sometimes, during Vietnam, I was criticized for offering too many objections without solutions. Well, perhaps my solutions didn't get as much play on prime time TV, but I gave them. As early as my first few months in the Senate I fought expansion of the draft, calling for an all-volunteer military based on comparable pay instead. I lost. The draft was expanded for another four years.

Soon after, back at Nixon's 1968 convention, I sent a plank down to the floor calling for a neutral mediator at the Paris peace talks to bring both sides together and generate debate. I also advocated stopping the bombing in North Vietnam, and shifting military emphasis from search and destroy to economic development for South Vietnamese villages. After all, they'd been rice exporters until we came along. We wiped out their rice paddies so effectively they were forced to import our rice. We'd stripped them of their entire economy early on, the least we could do was try to give something back.

And finally, if this particular battle in Southeast Asia was so critical, why weren't Asians interested in fighting it themselves? Oh yes, don't forget the domino theory. Malaysia, the Phillipines, all the surrounding territory surely would fall to communism next. Well, I had a question that would not leave me: If those countries were so endangered, why weren't they on the front lines in Vietnam, pushing back the enemy before the enemy could domino onto their own shores? If Asians were willing to help the cause of their neighbors, we could have pulled out. But of course no Asian nation was anxious or capable. We, instead, announced we had to save the world for democracy. But we weren't saving anything for democracy. At best, we were watching grave challenges to democracy at home because of our misguided intervention in a civil war around the globe that had little to do with us.

After Bill Rogers came into my office however, as I said, I refrained from commenting on Nixon's peace plan. I wanted to see what his "secret plan" consisted of. But I waited, then waited longer. And all along I continued my long established criticism of defense spending and the war itself. I grew more impatient with Nixon as soon as Henry Kissinger became secretary of state. I knew him to be brilliant, persuasive, and a complete and total hawk. By then I was on the floor attacking defense costs, decrying the increasing power of the Pentagon to make war over the power of Congress to subdue it, asking for us to do our duty by diverting more money away from defense and into the coffers of domestic problems.

Sure I offered plenty of solutions, and constantly. It was just that for the first few years, most of my ideas seemed somehow mired in quicksand. I wanted us to pull out, I wanted to make the draft a volunteer proposition, I wanted to cut the purse strings. I was a lot younger then, and I suppose I knew I could change the world. But everything moved at a snail's pace in the Senate. No matter how much I spoke on the floor, it didn't seem to help. Instead, a few colleagues sniped, "What have you heard from Ho Chi Minh today, Mark?"

Usually, I ignored them. On other occasions I would smile and respond, "Oh, he sends his best regards to you!"

At one point Nixon even wanted to develop a new generation battle tank—the MBT-70. I opposed that with Senator Thomas Eagleton, the Democrat from Missouri, as I opposed B-1 bombers, new aircraft carriers, and several other questionable military proposals. Instead I wanted to wind down the war and funnel that money into a peace dividend to take care of our critical social problems.

Earlier, when I attacked Nixon's safeguard ABM missile system on the floor, warning that the greatest threat to the security of the United States was happening to our nation internally via misguided policy, not externally. My friend Senator Jack Javits, the Republican from New York, attacked me back even though we agreed on so many issues.

It's true I dissented against point after point on the Pentagon budget, and I suppose Javits got tired of my critiques. Perhaps he just wanted to shut me up. Was I, he asked, "any less loyal a Republican because you oppose the ABM?"

"My first concern is to be a loyal American," I responded. "I feel a strong loyalty to both the President and the party, but we still can have differences of opinion."

It was ever the issues that rankled me, not the players. I didn't see myself as an enemy of Nixon so much as an enemy of his Vietnam policy. I urged public dissent of the administration's penchant for war expenditures, demanding they shift priorities to developing resources. And on October 15, 1969 I even supported a day of public education on the war, billed by the press as a national day of protest. We called for anti-war demands in Congress, prayers in churches, and peaceful demonstrations on campus. We promoted nonviolence. Debate, education, discussion, human interaction was our goal. Ones who took to burning ROTC buildings were not on my support list. You can't fight violence with violence, ever.

By now the administration began struggling and had shifted the debate about the war. Nixon wanted to change focus rather than create real peace. He wanted to "de-Americanize," to increase the capacity for the South Vietnamese to fight, win, and rule on their own—a flawed policy if ever there was one. We had decimated much of what the South Vietnamese people had ever had, and now we wanted to tell them, "Here, take these weapons and cash and go take care of yourselves." Furthermore, Nixon spoke of peace as if it were completely unrelated to peace within nations, within communities, within families, and within individuals. Nixon spoke of "peace with honor," which to him meant purely an absence of military action. But the causes of war still blazed—lack of health and education, a decimated economy— all virulent seeds of conflict. Peace is more than guns not firing. Peace is fulfillment, true shalom. And peace had to begin at home.

Nixon had announced withdrawal of 25,000 troops, and after Ho Chi Minh died, Nixon announced withdrawal of 35,000 more. But the October 15th day of protest arrived and people still came out to what became one of the largest public protest in United States history. About 100,000 people marched on Washington. Senator Frank Church, Democrat from Idaho, and I took the opportunity to introduce a bill accelerating troop withdrawal. We commended Nixon for beginning the process, but calculated at his rate complete withdrawal would entail eight to ten more years of war. We had 543,000 troops in Vietnam, yet Nixon's approval rating for his conduct of the war reached 65 percent. He was bringing troops home, and that was positive. Kennedy had shipped over 17,000, LBJ 539,000. Nixon was doing something to reverse the flow. Of course Church and I lost our bill.

I said after October 15th, "No man can ignore that kind of outpouring of sincere feeling and expression, and Mr. Nixon, I'm sure, saw this and understood it. I think he already reflects that feeling."

Well, so much for encouraging Nixon to move in another direction.

In fact, here Nixon was, beginning to withdraw from the war, having already claimed Cambodia and Laos as war-free zones. He clearly stated that penetrating any further north than Vietnam might serve as invitation to China to intervene. Or, that mining Haiphong harbor may cause the Soviets to pursue the war—a proposition to be avoided at all costs. Those regions were the demilitarized zone (the DMZ) and to be kept that way.

Meanwhile, Nixon intended to veto a $19.7 billion education, health, labor, and welfare bill in Appropriations. He called it inflationary. I called it what it was—better education and health for Americans. He wanted to veto it because it would cut deeply into his military budget. I'm sure he no longer thought I was one of the major rays of hope for the Republican Party.

By the spring of 1970, Democratic Senator George McGovern of South Dakota and I had begun to talk. He was as frustrated as I, but identified as even more of a liberal than myself. We decided to draft legislation to withhold funds for future troops as of a date certain. We wanted to secure all monies needed in Indochina to sustain our troops until we could withdraw them. But we set a prospective date after which no more dollars would be sent into the vacuum of Vietnam. This was a strategy, a message. And our aim was straight at Nixon. We wanted him to take notice. And if we eliminated his ability to fund the war, maybe he would get the message that he better pull out our troops and help the South Vietnamese put their lives back together—fast.

We were "vetoing the war" by attaching our amendment to a military procurement bill. We never expected to win—not even close—but we needed to educate, to make a point, to create a positive rallying place for the country to gather momentum. We especially wanted to give youth something to focus on, something constructive and meaningful, something much more effective than burning buildings. We had barely a handful of supporters.

Yet, within 24 hours or so of announcing our legislation, Nixon and the Pentagon announced the Vietcong were using Cambodia to stash huge stockpiles of weapons with which to hammer our men. Nixon's solution? Bomb Cambodia. Suddenly, our tiny bit of far-out, rebellious legislation became the rallying cry for the entire anti-war sentiment in our land.

Funny thing. Afterwards, no evidence of weapons could be found in Cambodia. But now we had invaded. The war, instead of decreasing as promised, was expanding yet again.

And our country went wild. When the draft lottery began, young men on campuses across the country could be heard letting out blood-chilling moans across campuses as they heard their lottery numbers called. Riots grew so explosive that four innocent youths were gunned down at Kent State University. The risk of opening campuses became so great that 200 actually closed down. Four hundred more staged virulent protests.

I refused to remain silent on Nixon's supposed peace plan any longer. I went straight to the Senate floor—my bully pulpit—and spoke. "Here we have previously determined militarizing Cambodia would spread the war, and it was prohibited. Now we've reversed, and are obviously widening the war, when we were just given the signal we were winding down. It's clearer than ever that President Nixon's policies focus only on expanding the war's destructive effects." I, naturally, wanted to cut off funds for bombing Cambodia immediately.

By this point, my colleagues were as perplexed as I. Nobody, at least at first, commended the president's attack on Cambodia. Some senators became more hawkish in time, and many of the most hawkish were Democrats. There was an influential segment on both sides of the aisle who came to agree with Nixon's rationale.

But Congress was finally taking up its cudgels against the war. George McGovern's and my legislation, the McGovern-Hatfield Amendment, was supported by others. Senator Harold Hughes, the Democrat from Iowa, Senator Frank Church, and Senator Charles Goodell, a Republican from New York joined us, to name a few.

By now the student movement identified me as a friend. At a campus speech, the Oregonian reported that one student introduced me as "the grooviest senator in the nation." Anti-war protesters were in communication with my office, supporting each other, forming community. Whenever one feels a sense of minority, particularly in something as emotional as war, those of like mind draw together, sharing reactions, information, feelings. I often spoke at anti-war rallies, and one day, at the traffic circle right next to American University, I was stopped to a dead halt. I soon discovered why. Melvin Laird, then secretary of defense, stood a couple cars ahead of me in his chaffeured limosine with students blocking his passage while I witnessed the confrontation.

I stepped out of my car and immediately, a number of students recognized who I was. "Let him go!" I shouted. "Send him back to the Pentagon! The last thing we want are stories that say the secretary of defense has been attacked by anti-war protesters!" Especially in the Senate, I thought, while we were trying desperately to garner support for the McGovern-Hatfield Amendment. "For the sake of peace," I yelled. And so they let him go.

Meanwhile, the early '70s were a time of recession—how could they not be when we had sunk billions of dollars into the war? Don't people suffer enough in their daily lives? Government has no need to increase the burden. I didn't have to talk about it anymore. Americans began to feel it where it hurt most—in their pocketbooks.

Groups sprung up everywhere: Republicans against the war, lawyers against the war, teachers, doctors, mainstream professional groups. We welcomed it all. Suddenly our small amendment, created simply to make a point, became the focus for an entire movement—the Moratorium against the war.

Up until then there was always the subtle question of whether those of us opposing the war were truly American, truly patriotic. It was a not-so-subtle version of red-baiting. Now, we encouraged all these groups to organize around one single issue and move in a united direction: support for the McGovern-Hatfield amendment. We wanted a base of support at the public and private levels, in cities, counties, states—in short, everywhere. These groups spread our message, especially targeting states where legislators faced primaries and general elections. We demanded that lawmakers know we were serious and many of their constituents' votes depended on their war stance.

We also produced a commercial with senators Harold Hughes, Frank Church, and Charles Goodell, all discussing the war and appealing for support. At the end, a brief sentence asked for contributions to cover broadcast costs. Contributions flooded in and our amendment grew new names: the Peace Amendment, or the Amendment to End the War. The focus on this legislation had shifted overnight thanks to Nixon invading Cambodia. Quite literally we found ourselves in the midst of a national whirlwind.

Before we knew it, we had $500,000 in donations. We took out a full-page ad in the New York Times. We also had a top-ranked TV producer donate his time to come up with more TV commercials. One displayed a group of boys playing with toy weapons, then switched stunningly to men fighting with very real weapons in Vietnam. "Six years from now, will we still be at war?" the announcer pointedly asked, clearly implying it could only be our younger children fighting next. The commercial was powerful.

Radio ads were effective as well. Stan Freeberg, the witty, musical comic, supported the anti-war effort as well and flew into DC to record radio spots. His style was different than my own, but potent. One ad sounded as though two sportscasters sat announcing a blow-by-blow of some game, but instead they were actually reciting details of the body counts in Vietnam. Freeberg then made appointments, again with key senators up for re-election, took his tape recorder, played the spot, and nonchalantly mentioned, "Senator, we just wanted to share this with you and let you know we'll be running this ad in your home state."

Freeberg also happened to know Haldemann and Ehrlichman, and suggested they were nothing if not savvy media men who would be threatened by his work for the anti-war effort. A week or so into his stay at the Washington Hilton, he complained to Wes Michaelson, my legislative counsel, and other staff that he felt someone had broken into his hotel room. The staff rolled their eyes—after all this guy was a little eccentric, especially when he told them he'd put something behind the door so he'd know if anyone had been inside. Surely it must have been the hotel housekeeping service who slightly moved his things, Wes and the others concluded. Freeberg was just a little paranoid. Until a few years later, of course, when they heard about Haldemann and Ehrlichmann involved in a very high profile break-in.

The remainder of contributions to the anti-war effort we earmarked for public awareness. By then we were receiving bushel basketfuls of letters every day. Our legislation had become a lightning rod for all the emotion surrounding the war, good and bad. My days of receiving hate mail were at their peak—and so were the tears in my secretaries' eyes as they handed over notes dubbing me a traitor, a man against God, or much worse. I still answered those letters, and I still wrote a poignant, personal note to the family of each and every Oregon man who fell in battle.

But the tide had turned. We were absolutely deluged with letters in my office alone—the majority supportive. Volunteers came on board simply to cope with daily correspondence. I had a rule of responding to letters within days, not weeks and we set up an office across the street in the Methodist building. There we housed our Amendment to End the War staff, who worked diligently to respond to each communication.

Senator William Fulbright, then chair of the Foreign Relations Committee, however, advised us not to proceed with the Peace Amendment. He wasn't on our side yet, though he soon would be. He suggested we not run with the amendment because he knew we didn't have the votes to win. "The administration will just consider your failure as a blanket affirmation of their policy," he told us.

We knew we didn't have the votes as well as he did. But we had to begin somewhere. Even if we did win, the amendment never would have passed the House side or, if it had, the President never would have signed it. But it was Congress's constitutional right to make a declaration of war, and we certainly hadn't done so. Our constitution was designed so no president could act like a monarch. The president needed the support of Congress to declare war in Vietnam, let alone Cambodia. And he hadn't gotten it. Checks and balances were what made our democracy work, and this was clearly time to honor that.

We certainly didn't expect it to take until September for our amendment to come to vote. Nixon however, through the Senate leadership, did his best to delay the vote on the Amendment to End the War. Later still we would realize just how worried and desperate the President had become about the peace movement in general, and our amendment in particular. But we wouldn't discover that until Nixon fell on much harder times—and his indicting Watergate tapes were released.

When we did come to vote, of course, we lost. Yet we garnered 39 votes, many more than we believed possible. Hopefully, that was plenty enough to send a serious message.

By this point some in evangelical religious groups had felt alienated from me and my position, and I began to believe my stand created nothing but divisiveness in my spiritual community. I had long held my anti-war philosophy. Yet harming or dividing people of faith could hold much stronger repercussions than anything I did in the Senate. That worked against my deepest beliefs about healing with love and unity. When my sisters and brothers "in Christ" were alienated against me, when my actions created schisms in spiritual communities—divisions where there should have been none—it stung too deep. I devoted my life toward working for peace and here, where my soul resided, I conjured the opposite effect. I was ready to resign.

Things only grew increasingly contentious. For the previous 15 to 20 years I had given the Sunday school lesson at a Baptist men's camp in Oregon. A good friend and classmate from Salem High School, John Goffrier, arranged these visits and met me there. Customarily he introduced me with a few good taste barbs, then I returned his jest and went on with my remarks.

This time, though, as soon as John said hello I knew something was amiss. "Usually I introduce you and then you start," he stated. "This time, I'll give the opening prayer directly following my introduction, and then you come to the podium immediately."

I had no idea why he was so concerned with protocol, and I knew something was amok. "Come on John," I chided. "What's this all about?"

He paused a long while. "I have to tell you," he revealed, "there's an effort to organize a walkout against you because of your stance on the war."

"You've got to be kidding! I'm not here to talk about Vietnam. It's never my purpose to bring politics into a venue like this."

"I know Mark, but some of these men feel really strongly about this. They don't want to give you the recognition of speaking to them. Please, just play along with me and let me do the opening prayer. It'll be harder for them to walk out with their heads bowed, and you'll come right up to the podium as I finish."

I did, and they didn't. I suppose you can say even a walkout was organized against me, but never completed.

But by mid-1970, soon after McGovern and I introduced our

amendment, I was asked to offer a commencement address at Fuller Theological Seminary. I walked into the auditorium that day to a huge banner reading, "We're with you, Mark." I can't express what that did to my heart, to realize there were those in the religious community who supported my stand, who felt my actions were not wrong, not heinous. From there, it became a groundswell. Many more in the religious communities were coming to the conclusion that peace was the only solution. I saw that momentum, I felt it, and I persevered.

At this juncture, Nixon began inviting small groups of senators—divided alphabetically—to the East Room of the White House for persuasive briefings on Cambodia. It was deja vu, except Nixon wasn't as effusive as LBJ had been. Icy might be putting it kindly.

He stood at the entrance to the East Room, greeting us all as we walked in. It neared my turn to shake his hand, and I grew uncomfortable. What was I doing here, anyway? How was I supposed to act? I figured the nicest approach was to make light of the whole strain and stress. I neared the chief executive.

"Well, Mr. President," I dredged for humor, "I frankly don't know what I'm doing here." We shook hands perfunctorily.

"It's because," he began, his steely eyes staring at me without the slightest note of humor, "we're in the H's."

Even still, Antoinette and I received invitations to the White House on special occasions—particularly for religious offerings. Nixon had guest preachers offer church services, and I was surprised to find myself invited to the service commemorating the moon shot. I became even more shocked when asked to offer the prayer for the astronauts. By now I was speaking often at college campuses about Vietnam; both religious schools and secular. I thrived being back with students, feeling the energy of the audience, engaging in earnest discussion and questions which constantly helped me refine my positions. So I was comfortable offering a prayer, even at the White House, though completely curious as to why I was even present in the first place. As it turned out, I had only been on the guest preacher's invitation list.

That church service and the Cambodia briefing were a couple of my last visits to Nixon at the White House.

Sometimes I felt as though I was frittering away any shred of political capital I might have held with fellow Republicans. In fact, in Oregon they suggested not so quietly that I actually switch parties.

Irv Enna, the Chair of the Republican Party in Oregon, didn't let one of my statements, that "there just may not be a Nixon-Agnew ticket in 1972" slide. He stood up. "If the senator's personal views are so contrary to the Nixon administration's," he issued a statement, "he would serve the two-party system best by changing registration."

My response to the press was pretty quick. "Irv said that?" I balked. "Why, Irv's my insurance agent!" I didn't take his threat too seriously, though I knew there were plenty of Republicans only too happy to echo his sentiments. "It would have been politic to stay silent," I said of my comments. "But I think that when we see problems, we should speak out and try to correct them. If Nixon's in trouble, he should be told about it. People in politics must speak their minds. Too many make statements that can be interpreted either way." I, obviously, did not suffer from that particular affliction.

At the time one of my colleagues, Congressman Pete McCloskey, a Republican, decorated marine, and dove from California, felt quite differently than Irv. McCloskey threw my name into the ring as a presidential contender. That was exciting—for about a minute. My national name familiarity ran high at about 3 percent. I may have been idealistic or visionary about many things, but as to my career, I've always been a realist.

Irv's salvo was the type I could easily endure. The next one wasn't so harmless. Senator Mike Gravel, Democrat from Alaska, called up a dial-a-message phone number, then strode down to the Senate floor and shared with all of us what he'd heard. "McGovern, Fulbright, Hatfield, the whole rotten bunch," Dr. William Pierce, a member of the National Socialist White People's Party, announced, "need a bullet right between the eyes." This was just punishment, he went on, for our opposition to Nixon's war policy.

Gravel was a friend, and would soon be the one to release the Pentagon Papers. As he stood on the floor he spoke of the extremism and polarization currently dividing our country. And as to the National Socialist White People's Party? That was their politically correct name. The group succeeded what had formerly been the American Nazi Party.

I was actually encouraged by my colleagues' reactions. Senator Warren Magnuson, a Democrat from Washington state, and many others stood to decry the attack. What a travesty on justice to threaten the lives of our elected officials, they called. It's nothing but an invitation to mayhem and murder. Magnuson didn't even support us on the war at this time, nor did many others on both sides who spoke. But on that day, they supported us as colleagues and friends.

Yet at home in Oregon, cries came that I was too busy attacking the war to conduct Oregon's business. What if Nixon was so angry with me that he would put Oregon on his enemies list as well? reporters asked. That would only "accuse Nixon of being a petty man—which he is not," I responded. My reply was tactical as well. I hoped the message reached the president, so if he had any meandering thoughts of pettiness, he would set them aside. And in fact, he supported me on some important issues outside the war.

But support was certainly not ever present. Back in the midst of Washington's unbearably muggy and hot 1970 summer, Strom Thurmond stood up in a practically empty Senate chamber and blasted me for releasing classified Pentagon information that "threatens our national security."

Everything in the report we had submitted could be found in the *New York Times* or *Air Force* Journal. I didn't think that qualified as classified information—much less a threat to security. Besides, I made a policy of never accepting classified documents as I never wanted to be accused of leaking them. Now here I was being accused of leaking something that wasn't even classified.

Twenty-eight of us had in fact released that report, a 150-page tome on ways to save as much as $5 billion on defense that year. I clenched my teeth as I responded to Thurmond. "The senator from South Carolina knows me well enough to know I would not be putting my country in jeopardy... putting my country under the gun, so to speak. It is impugning the integrity of the senator from Oregon even to suggest such a thing," I snapped.

Turns out, Thurmond hadn't read the report, nor had he any idea what "secrets" might be contained in it. He was simply parroting a Pentagon response to our making the information more widely available. All of it already stood in the public domain.

"If the security of this country were really in jeopardy, I think they (the Pentagon) would have had somebody on my doorstep pretty fast," I went on. Strom deferred and I, well I probably felt vindicated. But I'm afraid I did not feel too humble or free from rancor that day.

Soon, the Cooper-Church Amendment passed calling for removal of U.S. forces from Cambodia. But Nixon had already withdrawn from Cambodia, so he could blatantly ignore this legislation. Still, at least an anti-war amendment had finally passed.

Next, a bill similar to ours, drafted by Senator Lawton Chiles, Democrat of florida, came up for vote in June, 1971. By this time McGovern was known as a presidential contender, and many felt he went too far to the left. Several wouldn't vote for our legislation in its second year simply because his name was identified with it. So Chiles' bill gained more support. He had the votes to just swing it, too. That is until my friend, Democratic Senator John Stennis of Mississippi, went down to the well of the Senate and convinced Senator B. Everett Jordan, the Democrat of North Carolina, to change his vote. Jordan did, and Chiles lost.

Of course we had no chance of the McGovern-Hatfield Amendment passing the President's desk because Nixon would be re-elected. Any political junkie or lay observer knew that. Watergate was all the dumber because there was no need for it—Nixon had the election in the bag. Even so, when we brought the "Amendment to End the War" up as a bill—literally 90 minutes after Chiles bill failed—McGovern and I gleaned 48 votes. We lost but we were that close, and that charred and scared the administration no end. Perhaps Nixon got the message. I like to think we finally had something to do with his withdrawal from Vietnam.

And Nixon? Well, Nixon and I began mending our scarred relationship. Just after Cooper-Church passed, he invited me for breakfast at the White House to talk with him about abolishing the draft and increasing military salaries. In 1972, I would be the one to introduce his Endangered Species Act to Congress, a proposal to save wolves and whales, among many others. Later that year, he would even aid my '72 re-election campaign. We were grown men.

In the end, Richard Nixon only—always—desperately wanted to be known as a peacemaker, as he displayed so well in creating deténte with the FSU (Former Soviet Union) and opening relations with China. He wanted a place in history as a mover and actor where his predecessors had failed.

I believe he strove to be moderately inclusive; each move a stepping stone or strategy to maintain his base of domestic support and get us out of the war. Nobody can sit in that office and not be persuaded and guided by the idea of suffering the greatest military defeat in U.S. history. That was what was happening to Richard Nixon. So he switched his policy to a political rather than military agenda, believing that would let the military retain its honor. I might even agree with that goal.

There was such a multifaceted web of horror which created Vietnam. It cannot be simplified into us or them, for or against. Yes both sides existed, but meanwhile, events contorted all we did. We had created the longest war in our history and bombed North Vietnam with more tonnage than all the Allies had dropped in every theater in Europe and Asia in World War II. What a colossal waste.

The chaos of the waning days of war only intensified. The ceasefire failed because the North Vietnamese didn't abide by it, then neither did we; we both went for a free-for-all land grab creating frenzy on both sides. The Vietcong began launching more rockets, and the FSU threatened to quadruple supplies so as to begin the war all over again.

What an ignominious defeat we suffered on every side. (As if any war is actually "won," when all that ever results is replete with loss and decimation.) What a nightmare, finally pulling our troops from Saigon with live footage of our South Vietnamese allies desperately grabbing hold of our helicopters as we lifted off the ground, crowds trying to save their lives and escape, our friends left behind. We know their woeful fate.

Everything blurs and melds together for me as I recall the war in Southeast Asia, almost as it did when I myself fought in war. Vietnam was a continuous flow of events culminating, finally, in withdrawal. No, this was not a world war, but it had a totalitarian impact on our society just the same. It had been an intractable, often hopeless fight, yet finally we were coming home.

If there was ever fundamental proof positive needed to show public opinion can change public policy, this war was it. Truly, the public voice had bubbled up from the people, linking with sympathetic voices in Congress. The work done in the hallowed halls of Washington itself was nothing compared to the ability of the people to effect Nixon's policy.

If anyone ever feels "Oh well, my opinion doesn't count," I would beg them to think again. As opinions are articulated, held firm, and mobilized, they wield tremendous power. And if they are right, I like to believe eventually they will win.

The power of the people—and not the power of any chief executive or Congress—is the power our country was founded upon.

May we always remember and use it well.

CHAPTER ELEVEN

War, Watergate, and Beyond

*T*HE WAR WAS OVER AND I WAS DELIGHTED, BUT MY WORK WAS NOT complete. Withdrawal from Vietnam had been so slow in coming and statistics showed it patently obvious we paid an awful price—even higher than I had expected. It wasn't death alone we grieved. Lost limbs, drug addiction, mental anguish, and a hostile welcome all arrived home as virulent curses accompanying our troops.

MIAs and POWs had been left to languish too, their plight unsettled and for some, unsettled still today. Rumors flew about huge POW camps. How could we bring pressure to bear on Vietnam to get questions answered about sons, brothers, fathers, husbands? How could we free these men? I had utterly distraught constituents coming into our offices begging for help. One Southern Oregon man had a son living in a cage somewhere in Vietnam and this father had nowhere to turn, no way to help. He visited our office often, needing someone to listen. We gave him succor, we reached out, we did everything we could while most had all but forgotten about these lost men. I joined my voice with others trying to encourage the government to sign off on the war and develop future relations with Vietnam. I even sent Gerry and Wes Michaelson, my top legislative aide, as observers to the Paris peace talks when they were still in session. Releasing POWs was their main focus, and they came home with a sense they had opened a critical window of establishing trust with top North Vietnamese negotiators.

At the end of the conflict, in 1973, we had passed the War Powers Act, stating no president could bring us into a war again without the approval of Congress. We lowered the voting age to 18, offering political clout to those who had only wielded power as cannon fodder. Yet aside from domestic issues I was concerned that we also respond to Vietnam as we had to Japan and Germany after World War II—helping to create recovery and stabilization. As we offered leadership in many parts of the world, in resettlement of the displaced and in refugee aid, we needed to offer leadership now.

But even as the war ended, tragedy continued. Immediately the seas became deluged with boat people, 600,000 refugees from Vietnam, Thailand, China, Malaysia, Burma, all over Asia, greatly overloading our refugee systems. Piracy had even taken hold, with refugees being slaughtered by bandits wanting to steal their few precious treasures. These were our friends, our allies, persecuted and murdered following our evacuation from the war. I still believed the entire conflict had been immoral, and we needed to at least take responsibility for our actions.

But no! legislators insisted. Don't remind us, go away. Vietnam's over, we don't want to think about it, forget the whole thing, we've already been embarrassed far too long. I understood their feelings—for or against, we were all sick of the fight—but I sure wouldn't let it rest.

With the help of Refugees International, a powerful citizen's group, I lobbied Mike Mansfield, Democrat from Montana and Majority Leader, and Hugh Scott, Republican from Pennsylvania and minority leader. By now I had visited refugee camps on the border of Vietnam and Thailand, and the facts spoke for themselves. I wanted more than to open the consciences of my fellow senators. We needed funds for refugee relief. Mansfield and Scott listened, and with them behind me pushing through an appropriations relief measure grew easier. We brought the refugees to our shores, safe, free, and ready for a new life. For our efforts, Oregon proudly boasts a large number of these refugees to this day.

In 1986 I ventured to Vietnam again, with Idaho Republican Senator Jim McClure. We became some of the first U.S. senators to visit Hanoi and we held extensive talks with Le Duc Tho. McClure and I also held a reception for the entire diplomatic corp in Hanoi, including the British, the Russians, and other major players. The diplomats—friends and competitors alike—urged us to persuade Reagan to upgrade the mission there, to become more involved.

For the first time, we were allowed to spend the night in North Vietnam. Prior to that, America had practiced shuttle diplomacy, flying in diplomats by daybreak and out by dusk. We stayed however, hosted in governmental guest quarters. On our return we offered an extensive report to Reagan and he finally increased U.S. representation in talks to release MIAs and POWs. He sent General Vessey, thus giving the talks increasing credibility. Our diplomatic men were finally established and allowed to stay in residence. For once on this issue, I had a sense of progress.

History is a great teacher. And whenever a critical, historical event transpires—and Vietnam is an excellent example—I ponder it in terms of what I might learn. What can I take away that may offer wiser action in the future? If I don't interpret events this way, I'll plow the same old furrow over and over again, as public servants often do, doomed to repeat the past with all its fatal mistakes. And then, tragically, yet again the ultimate sacrifice is made for our failed policy—in the very human lives of our sisters, wives, mothers, husbands, brothers, and fathers.

Unfortunately we're still so primitive, adhering to our tribal instincts of following the chief. If the chief says "March!" we march. If the chief says "March off the cliff!" we march off the cliff. We do this ever again because it's the patriotic thing to do. But haven't we learned, even now, that war is never a winning proposition?

Instead of war I have always yearned to dispatch international armies of doctors, nurses, engineers, technicians, and diplomatic mediators, rather than deploying troops and defining national security in terms of megatons. I'm for a military as part of our national defense, of course. I'm simply for balance—or counterbalance, if you will—of humanitarian, social, and medical "warfare," of research, education, and protection.

It's my earnest hope we will learn, and we will turn to more constructive means of problem solving than blatant bloodshed. Anyone who knows anything about human nature knows we're moving toward building alliances, working things out, listening to colleagues, even if they're opponents. Battles don't create anything except humiliation, anger, and vengefulness in our hearts. That's true at the business level, in the home, and with our dearest friends. How much truer it is amongst nations—particularly in the global web of interconnectedness we enjoy today.

Back in 1972, as the war waned, I faced re-election and battles of my own. I needed to be home and, for the first time in 20 years, I missed the Republican National Convention. I hadn't gone to the Senate and disappeared for six years. I'd been home every month, and it wasn't as if the trip was a minor one. I couldn't, like many of my colleagues, just hop a commuter to some state on the eastern seaboard. But I kept coming home throughout my term, working with people, creating policy, helping wherever I could.

But polls showed I was in serious political trouble. It was easy for opponents to rouse a perception that perhaps I wasn't doing enough for Oregon, even though I was. It simply wasn't highly profiled in the news—other than the war issue.

I often speak about the media in not so endearing terms. Both politicians and the press are fiercely independent and strong minded, causing inevitable clashes. Yet they both depend on each other; politicians to get their critical messages out, media to acquire the best stories. I struggled with the media game, noting that accuracy, fairness, and balance were sometimes missing in the products of the media, yet I always believed in the role of a free press. Their calling is essential to any just society. Around this point in time I spoke out about freedom of the press, saying it should be ensured—not restricted—by judicial means. I didn't—and don't—always agree with what the media chooses to do with those rights, but I do believe they are essential civil liberties.

In fact, sometimes the media drove me to distraction. Certain reporters seemed to burn me over and over on certain issues, and I didn't understand why, or the media in general would focus on something I thought ridiculous when there were critical stories waiting, aching to be reported. Once I actually had a reporter—one whom I'm afraid did no justice to the dignity of his profession—sit down and announce, "I'm going to ask you some questions and you're not going to like it. But if you don't answer them I'll make up the answers myself." At first I didn't even have a staff member dedicated exclusively to press relations, but in time it became essential.

I remember Jack Robertson, my press secretary after the war, coming into my office one day insisting I see a particularly unfriendly reporter about an issue.

"I don't want to talk to him," I barked.

"Senator, this is an important issue and you need to talk to him."

"Just tell him I don't want to talk to him," I stood firm.

"I can't tell him that!"

"Okay, listen," I lowered my voice, coming around the desk and laying a hand on Jack's shoulder. "This is what you tell him. Tell him to go—jump—in—a—lake!

"Go on," I shooed him away, "go tell him that."

"Okay," agreed poor Jack, who was simply doing what we hired him to do. "I'll go tell him that, Senator, but first I want to ask you one question."

I rolled my eyes. "Whatever's that?"

"Is this," he paused for effect "the Christian way to act?"

"Argh!" I slunk down in my chair, defeated. "Okay, okay, send him in."

He'd send in that reporter and I'd be as gracious as I could muster.

In 1972, my underdog status as a war opponent actually seemed to work in my favor. In my first term alone my office had dealt with around 30,000 personal requests from constituents, dealing with immigration problems, social security checks, community needs. We weren't always successful in helping, but we always tried. People felt a sense of empowerment, a bridge into the massive bureaucracy of government. To me, that was an essential part of my job, and I hope constituents felt the benefit in their lives as well. This casework turned out to be essential. As soon as polls publicized bad news about my re-election possibilities, thousands of supporters from every walk of life immediately let me know I had their support—even Abigail Van Buren, Dear Abby, a known Democrat. She gave a speech in Portland and filled a hotel with women who listened raptly to every word—and many of those words were about me!

But if opening campaign headquarters provided any omen, I might well have reconsidered the whole race. As I opened the office one opponent, an unknown speech professor, parked his camper across the street expecting to grab his limelight. Between 50 and 60 upset protesters showed up too. And if that wasn't enough fanfare, a woman stood on a street corner with a sign I was actually proud of: "Hatfield voted for forced busing." Before long, most well-wishers I'd come to greet dribbled away.

As if that scene didn't offer enough of a fight, Wayne Morse became my challenger. I'll never know Morse's inner motivations, but I suspect he wanted to stay in the public eye and keep his name in the political arena. What I suspect he wanted most was to run against Packwood again—and beat him—in 1974.

Morse and I were still friends. He ran his race and I, mine. He didn't mention my name on the stump, nor did I mention his. But if asked about his seemingly unusual turn from prior Hatfield endorser to present opponent, his reply was something to the effect that I was "too close to Nixon !" I still laugh at that. Meanwhile, Oregon Governor Tom McCall attacked me for not supporting Nixon enough. I took it flying freely from both sides.

My values are dear to me, and I work hard even to "love my enemies." I hope I meet with a modicum of success. Yet so often people think if you love everyone you must be weak. Not true. In fact, it takes an awful lot of strength to hold a philosophy of love and compassion, especially in regard to one's opponents. At least for me. I have to garner plenty of internal strength to live my beliefs.

But if I must, I can also be tough.

I don't shy from the political fray when I feel what I stand for is right. If the gauntlet is thrown and I'm the target, I will stand up for myself with great vigor, conviction, and commitment. I fight hard in political campaigns, but I like to think I do it with integrity. And I like to think I would accept any result.

Once the people have spoken, I'm not about to figure out why they spoke that way by challenging the fact they did. I'm not going to appeal or cry over the outcome. In politics in general, of course I didn't always achieve what I wished, but hopefully I succeeded in influencing the course of events in a positive direction. That was ever the goal.

In terms of winning office itself, my desire to accept the results is easy to speculate over—I never in fact lost an election for public office. But I hope I'd have the courage of my convictions; if one door closed, I trusted another would open. In fact, I always wished to win, but if I lost, I claimed I would go back to education. I must have been right. After 30 years in the Senate, I promptly flunked retirement and walked straight back into the classroom.

In a strange twist, Richard Nixon supported me in my first re-election to the Senate as well. However he might have felt about me personally, he wanted a Republican victory in Oregon to help him win his own campaign. By then, too, I had been appointed to the powerful Senate Appropriations Committee, and that helped me garner more fiscal support for Oregon projects. Citizens noticed. Word of mouth was critical. It grew easy to deflect the cry that I had ignored Oregon.

Also invaluable was the assistance of an unusual woman: Martha Mitchell, Attorney General John Mitchell's ill-fated wife. Martha liked to call us at night when she was feeling tipsy. She needed to talk to somebody and I guess she felt I would listen. In return, I frankly found her to be a very gracious person. Besides, strong, well-spoken women were certainly no strangers to me. I was married to one of the best! It was mindless conversation Martha engaged in, really. She simply rattled around in her home, lonely, needing to speak without being interviewed or judged. Her marriage to John seemed not to be an entirely happy one. She knew what would catch the media eye, knew how to perform, and relished doing so. No other cabinet wife had the colorful personality or charisma of this bleached blonde with hair piled high atop her head. While her husband led Nixon's media strategy, his wife divulged secrets or popped off about the administration. Let's say her comments were controversial at best, and not in the interest of strict Nixon/party policy at worst.

Meanwhile, I needed re-election funds. I knew Martha had a zest for challenges and would love to put on a show. I invited her to host a fundraiser for us and she immediately accepted. That was big news! Here the Republican dove was to be feted by the wife of one of Nixon's closest cabinet members. Those who said I never supported the president, or cried that I should switch parties, suddenly took notice and the fundraiser ended very successfully.

Soon John, an extremely well respected attorney in D.C., grew mired in Watergate, taking much of the rap Nixon should have taken and serving time in prison as well. The two Mitchells divorced during his incarceration. I know beneath any clever façade is a human—often a lonely, suffering human. And poor Martha soon died, a sad victim of the worst politics has to offer.

In the end, Wayne Morse lost his bid against me. He did run for Packwood's seat in '74. We'll never know what the outcome might have been. After winning his primary and gearing up for the general election, Morse suddenly died. And Packwood? He would remain undefeated until his resignation in 1995.

After re-election I was back in Washington and in 1973, much to the chagrin of my staff, I still always stood for the underdog. That proved true even of Spiro Agnew. He had attacked me as a traitor because of my stance on the war, but when he stood accused of accepting bribes as a governor of Maryland and now as vice president, I thought he was maligned; guilty before ever proven so. Agnew kept saying it was all a lie, he was being set up, it was unfair, and so on. He sounded pretty downtrodden and I listened. After all, somebody has to stand up for the rights of an individual.

Every Wednesday a group of about a dozen moderate Republicans met for lunch. It was my turn to host, and I invited Agnew to be our guest. The House was in the midst of discussing his impeachment proceedings and I set our meeting up with strict instructions it be private, no press, no leaks.

Agnew showed up with the weight of the world pressing down on

160

him. You could see the terrible shadows in his face, the fast-forward aging under his eyes. He stared at a picture in my office of Timberline Lodge on a clear, winter night, snow covering the ground and a friendly welcome light shining. "It looks very peaceful," he murmured. We ate box lunches on our laps while Agnew spoke, telling us with all the conviction he could muster that accusations against him were dirty lies, he had been set up as a terribly abused fall guy for Nixon's problems, and on and on.

Meanwhile, somebody leaked the meeting. Agnew himself, for all I knew. A media throng crammed into the hallway awaiting our exit and there was no way to avoid it. Every other senator in our group did the smart thing—they left by the side door. But I walked out with Agnew, journalists shoving mikes straight in my face. "Well what do you think about all this, Senator?" they clamored.

"I think everyone deserves his day in court," I said. "We shouldn't rush to judgement." Behind me, my staff had their head in their hands, I'm sure, woefully thinking "This is not good. How are we ever going to do damage control on the photo of Hatfield with Agnew splashed all over the papers?" All I wanted to do was let the man be listened to, but of course my staff knew they'd be spending their days getting it out of the public mind that I was somehow sympathetic to Agnew.

They let me know it too. Perhaps I had taken this siding with the underdog a bit too far in this case. In fact, a week later we discovered at the moment Agnew pled with us to believe how persecuted he was, his negotiators were meeting in the Marriott Hotel in Roslyn. As we sat, so did they—closing the final deal, pleading no contest.

At the utter opposite end of the moral compass, I also had the incredible privilege of meeting Mother Teresa, an experience which was to revive me like no other. This was long before Mother Teresa's global popularity, yet I knew of her great works through the Christian community. Antoinette and I took Elizabeth and MarkO on this journey with Gerry Frank. On my way to a World Vision board meeting in Thailand and we set off for India. Mother Teresa's compound was of ample size and she met us there, this diminutive woman with the largest flow of energy and spirituality gliding from her robes of any human I have met, large or small.

She escorted us to the orphan's area, where countless babies lay bottoms up in a huge circle on the floor, all facing inward. I suppose this was purely utilitarian—after all, Mother Teresa's attendants had much more work to do with the babies' bottoms than anywhere else on their person—but it also posed a striking image, a human circle of contented, wriggling infants. Elizabeth and MarkO each immediately wanted one of these wee ones to bring home and care for as their own.

Mother Teresa then led us to her Temple of the Dying. "We take the dying bodies off the streets of Calcutta and bring them here," she explained in her perfect, clipped English, "instead of waiting for the garbage trucks to pick them off. We clean them, we wash them, and we tell them about Jesus before they die," she finished quietly. We walked deferentially about the Temple as she murmured, "he'll be gone in two hours," or "this one will leave us in four hours," and so on. She was that intimate with the final stages of dying, the last vestiges of human life.

As we left the Temple she took us to a different part of town, underneath viaducts beneath a bridge. There people lived collecting wood and scraps and making camp as if in a hobo refuge adjacent to railroad tracks. At the sight of them we all fairly shrunk back, as this was Mother Teresa's famous leper colony. Yet when the people saw Mother Teresa they rushed straight to embrace her. And she? She reached forth her hands to gather them all in, these people so appreciative, so nourished by her love.

"It's not contagious if you have proper nutrition," she reassured us. "We all eat well so it is safe to show them our love." And so we relaxed and smiled, communicating in our non-verbal ways with these shunned, unfairly maligned human souls.

"Don't you grow discouraged," I finally asked at the end of our day, "when you see the horrible magnitude of this grinding poverty and how little you can do?"

"Oh no," she insisted emphatically. "The Lord has not called me to be successful, the Lord has called me to be faithful."

As we left her gates Mother Teresa escorted us out and a young mother waited for her there, a destitute Indian woman with a naked baby held in her arms like an offering. I will never forget this child.

Held so the skin of its little bottom hung down, empty, instead of the firm fleshed cheeks we associate with an infant. They were loose, hanging sacks of skin desperate for nourishment. Mother Teresa accepted the child warmly into her arms, into her care, and the poor mother quickly took flight.

This visit with Mother Teresa, the woman, the saint, provided me with one of the greatest highlights of my life.

And our relationship endured. She once visited our family and Visko claims she never made eye contact with him—to the point that he felt self-conscious. When it was all over and she began walking out she stopped short and pivoted, walking straight back to seek Visko out. She looked him deeply in the eyes and pronounced, "I can tell you are a very spiritual person." Needless to say, Visko has never forgotten it.

Mother Teresa also often called on me for help when she came to D.C., and I availed myself to her in any way I could. One day I received a message: "I want him to come to 7 o'clock mass." Somehow, she had found out I was on my way to Africa as part of a Congressional Delegation. I showed up for mass and afterwards she asked if I could take some medications with me on the flight and have them delivered. Certainly, I told her, surmising she referred to a box or two. As I arrived at Andrews Air Force Base to board my plane, there were several of Mother Teresa's nuns in full habits, equipped with pallets and hand trucks, scurrying around loading more boxes than I could possibly count. Luckily, the Air Force jet had a huge cargo hold and the delegation used little of it. Her medications safely reached their destination.

Whenever Mother Teresa visited our office, everyone seemed to show up to meet her, especially as she became more and more well known. On one occasion I told my staff, "Look, this time let's just make it our effort to return some energy and spiritual concern to her. She's always giving, giving, giving, and this will be our time to give back. Anybody who wishes can come into my office and join her, sharing quiet time or pray as they like."

Riki Sheehan, a key staffwoman asked, "Do you think it would be all right if I came in and offered a Jewish prayer?"

"Of course it would," I insisted. "Mother Teresa's happy to receive sustenance from anyone, not just friendly Baptists, Protestants, or Catholics!"

That day, as Mother Teresa sat in my office, staff filtered in to read biblical verses, to share thoughts, or to pray. And Riki, who had consulted her rabbi to find appropriate prayers, recited several prayers from her tradition. Naturally, Mother Teresa was absolutely delighted.

Yet the Senate did not run on spirit alone—far from it. During my second term I sat on the Appropriations, Energy and Natural Resources, and Rules committees when Watergate suddenly hit. At first, it was barely a blip on the screen. No one even paid attention.

During Nixon's 1972 election campaign, a funny thing happened at the Watergate building. We had friends living there, a couple who owned a station wagon. They always parked in the corner spot in the garage—the only spot large enough—and their car had been broken into more than once. The police advised them to put a light in the corner of the garage as a deterrent. Because of that light, on the night of the famous break-in, the night watchman could see tape on the garage door, an easy access ploy on the burglars' part. The watchman phoned the police, and the police then dispatched a patrol car with screaming sirens and blazing lights. The burglars' lookout person would surely have noticed that police car and given every culprit plenty of time to flee. But the patrol car ran out of gas. Its riders radioed an unmarked car, and that was the car which quietly proceeded to the Watergate building, its drivers' arresting each perpetrator. Operatives in Nixon's campaign had not only broken into Democratic headquarters but had been caught.

Breaking into political headquarters wasn't much news, unfortunately. That had happened before, or so we heard. But investigative reporters kept following the story, and pretty soon more and more intriguing details were exposed. A linkage fell into place between those who were arrested and people high in office in the Nixon campaign. Still, although that was interesting news—disgusting, even—it wasn't enough to topple a President.

Until links slid closer and closer to Nixon himself.

And to think, there may have been no story at all if that original police vehicle hadn't run out of gas.

Instead, the legislative process took hold. Senators Sam Irwin, a Democrat from North Carolina, and Howard Baker, Republican of Tennessee, ran the special Watergate Committee handling the investigation in the Senate. Before long it looked as though the President himself might well be impeached.

Senator Howard Cannon, Democrat of Nevada, chaired the Rules Committee while I sat as ranking Republican. Cannon called us all together, indicating we'd be responsible for handling logistics of the trial, and advising we'd best update the rules of impeachment. They'd remained untouched since Andrew Johnson's 1868 Senate trial. By now, following months and months of House Judiciary Committee proceedings—and further media exposés of intrigue and guile—we had a fairly reasonable sense of Nixon's guilt.

I wasn't welcoming a trial, but Cannon's announcement to gear up didn't stun me, either. While at first I had thought of impeachment as ludicrous, I now knew it was inevitable. Nixon haters around the Senate and in the media were fairly prevalent. They set out to prove Nixon was a crook and they succeeded. In terms of any political media antipathy, Watergate probably marked the absolute zenith. I certainly didn't excuse Nixon—in fact in 1973 I was still accusing him of arrogance in flaunting congressional laws while bombing Cambodia. I called this "flagrant disrespect. . . . The integrity of the republic is under siege."

But even when I attempted to be conciliatory it was often misinterpreted. I spoke at the National Prayer Breakfast on "healing the sin upon our nation's soul." My remarks were picked up by the press as a direct slap at Nixon and his policy. Billy Graham called me, suggesting I think pretty hard about apologizing to Nixon. But I felt all citizens had shared responsibility in this war I saw as so sinful. And where else to raise the issue than at a National Prayer Breakfast?

Soon, on the Rules Committee we set to work revising the rules of impeachment, but I'm afraid I have no great stories to tell. There wasn't any tension on our committee, partisan or otherwise. Here we were, closeted in executive session, each of us with a big, blotter-size ledger folded out before us. To the left lay columns for each possible action, rule, and procedure of impeachment, and to the right, space for notes. This all in the days long before spreadsheets and laptops. The list of procedures seemed endless, and the task of revising them nothing if not boring.

As ranking Republican, I also felt the need for a constitutional attorney as counsel. I was given the okay, and invited Orlando Hollis, dean of the University of Oregon School of Law, to join me in Washington. Hollis, a great friend and counselor on all my judicial appointments agreed to offer wise counsel.

The entire process proved sobering, for it was ours to devise vehicles for determining innocence or guilt of the President of the United States.

By this time we predicted head counts and Nixon could not have gained acquittal in a senate trial. He should have known this on the House side, when it looked like even the Judiciary Committee would lose support of a large number of its Republican members. And if convicted, Nixon would be forced to leave office. Once he grasped the inevitability of the Senate outcome, he resigned.

Naturally, I recalled all this during Clinton's impeachment. The Washington Post, CBS, and ABC, among others, phoned wanting an interview since I'd been ranking member on the Rules Committee during Nixon's debacle. But I declined to speak. I'm a private citizen now, not a senator. Let the senators and House members speak with their votes, I said, thus liberating myself from the media dance.

But unfortunately, speak the senators and House members did, and not only with their votes. All our discussions in the early '70s— and those surrounding Andrew Johnson's impeachment as well—were held without television. The proceedings never became a veritable circus, with more and more talking heads needed to fill endless hours of TV news coverage. In our most recent impeachment proceedings however, there was far more verbosity on the part of individual senators and House members, both prior to and during the trial. Legislators were only too pleased to line up before cameras, queuing up not only in the halls of Congress, but on talk shows and interview programs as well. I daresay it raised questions in the minds of citizens as to the professionalism of the impeachment process itself.

Impeachment is first a judicial, then a political proceeding. Yet it becomes as political as those conducting it. The constitutional fathers created a mixing of powers so no one ever wielded too much—not the House, the President, nor the Senate. The House was to act as a grand jury in a finding of fact, and the Senate to conduct the trial and determine innocence or guilt. Or so our constitution delineated.

And that's the utter beauty of our constitution—the heighth of its ideals.

Perhaps soon we will learn to conduct our politics befitting our constitution, thus avoiding another such national trauma.

CHAPTER TWELVE

An Exercise in
Human Relations

*T*HE FACT IS, POLITICS IS FUNDAMENTALLY AN EXERCISE IN HUMAN relations. And it's an exercise which takes skill, strength, patience, and truckloads of hard, constant work. My closest ally in a Senate battle today might turn around tomorrow and oppose me on an issue I'd stake my life on. So I wanted to build bridges and friendships every place I could, maintain respect with my colleagues, and nurture relationships even in the toughest times.

I'd seen what havoc ruptured relationships could wreak. Perhaps most poignant of all was my friendship with Tom McCall, two-term Oregon governor who filled my seat when I left for the Senate.

I met Tom as soon as I was discharged from the Navy. We fostered a strong Young Republican group in Oregon, including the two of us and many others. We represented the more progressive tradition of the Republican Party, and as we found respective professions we maintained warm friendships, often offering each other counsel, advice, or support. Tom, who entered the media and became a TV newscaster, was highly gifted, a profound wordmaster. Often he became spokesperson for our group. Many of us went on into politics. Tom was nominated for U.S. Congress, but lost to Democrat Edith Green. He served as secretary of state during my second gubernatorial term. Others among us became circuit judges or members of the state legislature.

Tom and I had individual personalities and political styles, and individual agendas as well. Whereas I tend to be more reserved amongst the media and somewhat circumspect, Tom was not. Where I was careful with the press, he was the press, and never in his element so much as when he talked to the media. He spoke so well, too, and so often. That created quite a bit of news about Tom and kept him in the public mind.

Where I might conduct meetings with staff and agency heads in my office, he was garrulous and outgoing, a barrel-up-to-the-bar kind of guy.

Over time our relationship suffered. It came to a head when Tom expected me to appoint him secretary of state as I became governor. Tom got it in his mind I had promised him the post, but I hadn't. Instead, I appointed Howell Appling. Howell filled my unexpired term as secretary of state, then was elected for a term in his own right, at the end of which he decided to return to business. Tom was elected to fill his post and we sat together on what was then Oregon's Board of Control (the governor, secretary of state, and state treasurer).

During the Vietnam war our relationship was at its worst. One of Tom's sons joined the Navy, and I understood the depth of Tom's keen and personal concern. In line with that, he was ardent in supporting Nixon and his policies. Predictably, his public comments were in stark contrast to my own. But Tom often personalized his remarks. "I'd feel safer with a Richard Nixon or a Ronald Reagan standing behind that boy," he boomed, referring to his son, "than a Wayne Morse or a Hatfield." That turned up word for word in the Oregonian.

I regretted what was happening, but I never knew what Tom might do next. Still, I was determined not to enter the fray. I didn't always succeed.

Often, Tom attacked me in public, then called contritely the next morning. "Hey Mark, I'm really sorry for having said that," he'd say, full of remorse, just after announcing to the world he slept better at night knowing Nixon—not Mark Hatfield—was in the White House.

I was sorry, too. Mostly for Tom. He was a man wrought with internal turmoil and unpredictability. I once said something on the

record to the effect of, "Tom blows hard, but he cools off quickly."
Most of the time, I said nothing. Reporters would quip, "Senator
Hatfield, McCall said such and such, how do you respond to that?" My
response was simple, if not clipped.

"No comment."

A bit later, when polls showed I was less supportive of Nixon than
any other GOP senator in Washington, D.C., Tom spoke against me
publicly once more, mentioning he'd give consideration to opposing
me in 1972 (though I had supported his gubernatorial re-election bid
two years before). Nixon deserved more support than I seemed willing
to give, Tom exclaimed. To the press I answered queries about his possible bid with, "I always say it's a free country, the water's fine, come on
in." Privately though, Tom and I discussed his candidacy and he made
it clear he was serious. "fine," I said, "but I'll give you a tough fight."

Our relationship ruptured from both sides, and I deplored the entire
fiasco. Yet when he spoke about me in the public eye, then threatened
to run against me, I was offended and hurt as well. Finally, he called
once more with one of his morning-after apologies.

"Tom," I said, "frankly, I'm tired of your public attacks and your
private apologies." I'm sure he was sorry. But all the public saw were
his verbal strikes met by my silence.

Another time Tom blustered up saying, "Well Mark, you know I'm
the most popular governor in Oregon history. We've done surveys,
and I can tell you, no other governor has been as popular as I am. I
could defeat you."

"Bully for you, Tom," I replied.

Tom was a strong Nixon supporter, and Nixon advised him to keep
his post while I kept mine. Nixon wanted to win in '72 as well,
and the last thing he wanted was a potentially ugly battle dividing the
Republican Party in Oregon, where polls showed he was already behind. Nixon's wishes probably swayed Tom. Besides, I don't think either of us had the heart for a campaign battle between us.

I'm still saddened by those years and attacks that impacted a relationship between good friends. But I learned much, too. And when
Tom, one of Oregon's great governors, died all too young of cancer, his
wife, Audrey, asked me to sit with his family at the state funeral and

stand beside her at the open casket while she stood greeting visitors.

I tell the story of Tom and me partially because I've never spoken of it. But that's a minor reason. I thought long and hard before includ-ing my relationship with Tom here at all.
In the end, I tell the story as a lesson. Long alliances can rupture all too easily over pettiness and pain. And after this schism with Tom, I reflected on whether I could have handled the war issue, for instance, in a different manner and kept our relationship intact. I would never change my position on the war, but I wondered whether I was going about the struggle in the wrong way. It wasn't just Tom who made me question my position. As I said, the Christian community, and even dear friends gave me pause. Was I too strident, too intense? Perhaps insensitive to the feelings of colleagues or friends?

It was then I contemplated leaving the Senate. I could have en-dured a lot less hassle—and possibly much more gratification—with a quiet little political science professorship at my beloved Willamette University. But in the end, I sought the deep counsel of my heart and my beliefs, and I pressed on. Yet I learned to honor everyone's feelings in the process.

To do this well I strived to keep a human face on every activity, issue, or project in the legislative arena. Whose human face? first, those I worked with. They were my colleagues, and I couldn't accomplish anything without them. Often, politicians become so interested in Sen-ate Bill X that they depersonalize the entire process. You find yourself going around calling the bill by it's number or author, "You know, SB X," as a physician making rounds might refer to "the appendectomy in Room 306." There's a person beyond that appendectomy, and many more people beyond any political bill. We can get so bogged down with process and procedures, nomenclature, mechanics, that the hu-man face disappears. I worked to keep it ever in view.

The truth is, way beyond legislators, people give these bills their ultimate human face. They're the ones whose views we represent, they're the ones who believed in us enough to elect us, they're the ones we're doing all this for, day by day, hour by hour. And they're the ones we must keep in mind each moment. Gratefully, it's on the most passion-

ate, controversial issues, like civil rights, peace and war, the environment, or even taxation, that people make their voices most heard. And
that's when the magic begins, as partisanship finally gives way to a true
human process, the best legislative method we have.

What a waste when I or any of my colleagues created enmity
amongst ourselves; a mentality of "us" and "them." For what? Something as inconsequential as a party label? We were always accountable
to our constituents. And when people note a burning need—like protecting their children from nuclear disaster, for instance, they don't
think, "This is a Democratic (or Republican) idea, I better vote my
own party." That's ridiculous. Citizens are far too bright for simplistic
thinking like that.

It's politicians who need to get away from black and white and
notice shades of gray. People didn't elect us to act like school children,
dividing a line down the playground with friends over here, enemies
there. Our legislative process will only degenerate further if we don't
pull ourselves out of this hopeless partisan rut and work together.

Beyond working to keep alive the human face and bridging the
aisle, I quickly learned never to say, "I told you so." Take Vietnam. I
began with more than 75 percent of my constituents against me and in
the end, at least that percentage on my side. People shift and change,
all of us. Even as weary as I was fighting that intractable battle, it never
would have helped if I blurted out to the newly converted, "Well, I
told you so long ago, but you just wouldn't listen, would you?" whilst
my finger wagged away.

That's no way to nourish relationships. And nourish them we must.
For if we don't, it's amazing how quickly they can degenerate. I remember two senators from the same state (who shall remain nameless). They hailed one from each party. Just as I was escorted down the
aisle to my swearing in by Wayne Morse, it's traditional for a re-elected
senator to be escorted by (in this case) his fellow senator. But for these
two, such bitter rivalry pervaded the air they breathed so much that
the sitting senator would not even deign to walk down the aisle with
his re-elected colleague.

Senators and House members often criticize their colleagues as
well, even in press conferences or public forums. On a basic level,

that's plain mindlessness—how many of your constituents also voted for your colleague? Or voted for your colleague and now consider voting for you? They won't be too delighted to hear you attack her, or him. And what possible purpose can mud slinging serve, ever? What possible good, what possible advancement of the agenda you're in office to fill? Absolutely none.

During my Senate years, my relationship with Senator Bob Packwood offered a great example of working together. Bob was brilliant in terms of political theory, practice, and organization. He can strategize issues better than anyone I know and had no peer in the Senate when it came to dissecting, analyzing, or debating certain issues, especially regarding taxes.

He and I worked as a team, though we certainly didn't always agree.

Abortion is one of the hottest issues of our time, and I can't imagine any issue more divisive and alienating among people who could accomplish so much more if they worked together for common ground. In fact, Bob was an unremitting pro-choice champion, and I just as relentless a pro-life advocate. I never felt diminishing respect or friendship because of this heart-felt distinction between us. Instead, if he was present while I offered a speech on abortion on the floor, he would offer complete courtesy, listening with full attention. I offered the same when he spoke. I can't even remember a time we personally engaged each other on the issue.

As time went on, our staffs worked together on multiple causes. He chaired the Finance Committee, where he and his staff raised money and worked on Medicaid, Social Security, trade, or taxes—issues ever present in the public mind. I worked with my staff on Appropriations. Bob helped raise the money and I helped send it where it was needed most. We deferred to each other on any issue of importance to Oregon where the other might hold greater expertise.

How strongly we differed on abortion while at the same time we advanced causes and collegiality. We respected any disagreement, working together instead on a myriad of issues we both held high. Our votes placed us in the same camp more times than not.

When Bob was forced to resign, I was disappointed in every direction and deeply saddened as well. Sad for Bob as a fellow human being, suffering, sad and sorry for all the women traumatized with shame and grief, sad for Bob's ex-wife, Georgie, and their family, and finally, sad for the institution of the Senate as it gave up one of its most effective members. What ambivalence I felt as we lost such a brilliant politician.

Today, it's almost de rigueur for politicians to have private lives we may not condone. We're human, certainly, and sometimes the ego-expanding environment of the Congress brings out the worst. But we have a standard to live up to. Our culture believes most politicians wreak a lot of mischief during their "off hours," and I disagree. That's not what I saw over 30 years. It's simply that those few we hear so much about have unorthodox private lives, while the majority of monogamy aficionados never make the news. If we hear only of errant members, rather than the vast majority of the faithful, naturally our entire perception of reality grows skewed.

In politics, I had to shift emotional gears quickly. Often times, I developed a comfort level working on issue after issue together with a colleague. Our staffs worked closely and felt allied as well. Multiple layers underlay any relationship. It becomes comfortable, stable, and you count on the alliance. Then suddenly—pop!—something divides you. That's why it's critical to keep relationships healthy. Whenever I felt strongly about an objective or goal, I could ask a colleague for a few minutes of her or his time to listen to something of consequence to me. Reciprocally, whenever they called I answered immediately.

Senator Bob Dole of Kansas and Senator Orrin Hatch of Utah and I were such allies for years. In early 1995 though, soon after I announced my retirement and while Dole was still majority leader, an issue sharply divided us.

The first Balanced Budget Amendment came up for a vote and every other Republican supported it—not to mention several Democrats. We went around and around, but I could not support the amendment because I felt it regressive. How unnecessary to amend the Constitution to force us to do what we very well should have done already. I also didn't want military spending to be exempted in any way from budget balancing. And I thought the amendment simply a political ploy to erroneously make Americans think we were actually doing something about the deficit. In fact, we knew how to truly balance the budget but lacked the political courage to do so. Instead, this amendment had a hidden escape valve, saying we could all ignore it with a three-fifths Congressional vote. And like the normal period for constitutional amendments, this one could have taken up to seven years to be adopted. We didn't have that long. (In fact, we subsequently passed a balanced budget agreement—not an amendment—and garnered Clinton's signature so it became law immediately, not seven years hence.) I wanted a balanced budget with all these kinks worked out. I've been quoted as saying, "I pray for the integrity, justice, and courage to vote the correct vote, not the political vote," and this was no time for change.

But votes were sought by arm twisting, deep persuasion, and every other means. Senator Orrin Hatch served as chairman of the Judiciary Committee and floor leader of the amendment, and he knew my commitment to my religious life was serious. One day as I worked in my Appropriations office, my receptionist advised me a Dr. Robert Schuler was in to see me. I knew Schuler, the well-known television minister who beams his Sunday morning "Hour of Power" program around the world, as far as Russia and the Far East. Naturally, I invited him and his assistant in.

"I just wanted to talk to you briefly," he began, proceeding to tell me how he started out his ministry by renting a drive-in movie theater and preaching to people who wanted drive-up Sunday services. Those were humble beginnings, he explained. "Now," he went on, "we've built our own Crystal Cathedral." As if on cue, his assistant pulled out a calendar with a glowing color photo as illustration. I simply stared. I could not in any way figure out what this had to do with me. "We built this beautiful building through gifts and contributions," Schuler added, "and when we opened our doors, we had no indebtedness." I began to see the light. "And I just came here today to tell you that I feel very strongly this is the way our government should run as well. I believe this Balanced Budget Amendment will help, and I'm anxious for you to support it."

I explained why I couldn't, then escorted Schuler out. Next, I walked up to the floor where debate on the Amendment roared. Striding by Orrin's desk I whispered, "It didn't work."

"Huh?" he looked up, dumbfounded.

"Robert Schuler," I simply replied.

"Oh," he made a face, then beamed. "I'm sending Billy Graham down next!"

"He won't come," I pronounced.

Around that time I made my way to the cloakroom. My daughter Theresa's husband, Manus Cooney, who serves as chief legal counsel for Hatch stared at me in the cloakroom. Right beside him stood a blown-up picture of my tiny granddaughter, Caitlin. "For her sake!" the placard read.

Still, I was unswerving in my belief that this amendment was not much more than a gimmick.

Yet an hour prior to rollcall Bob Dole came into my office for a tense, last minute talk. He was running for the presidential nomination and clearly inferred that passage of this amendment would have much to do with his presidential credibility and success. He's a friend, and I respect him enormously. But I did not believe in this amendment. Period.

"I'm sorry, I can't do it, I won't vote with you," I shook my head.

"Look Mark, is there any way we can make this work for you— any way at all?" Dole pled.

"No there isn't. But I'll tell you what. I don't want to be the single one to destroy this thing and impair your presidential chances. If you honestly think it all hinges on me, I'll leave now. I'll resign. So what if I leave the Senate a few months early?"

"That's not an option, Mark," he said, rising to leave.

I thought he should have gone to work on some of those Democrats who had voted for a balanced budget amendment during their re-election year. He must have known he would get nowhere with me. But moments before roll call he even tried once more. "There's still time to repent," Dole expounded from the floor, aiming his words, I'm sure, at my religious sensibilities. I took a deep breath but stood my ground. That year the Balanced Budget Amendment went down. By one vote.

Immediately, a group of younger Republican senators wanted me to resign as chairman of Appropriations. I should have stood firm with the leadership in forging this amendment through, they accused. I should have forgotten my role as an individual senator. I was nothing but a poor excuse for a Republican, they said.

I appreciated my colleague Bob Packwood's words regarding my potential removal from the Appropriations post: "If we start down that road we start eating each other and become political cannibals. I hope we haven't reached a place that when someone exercises their conscience, they feel they must offer to resign."

And as to my detractors? I made no public comment.

And retained my committee—after a few brief hours of party caucus where I remained silent.

Senator John Stennis, Democrat from Mississippi, provided another example of human relations. Conservative and hawkish, Stennis, at this time, chaired the Arm Services Committee. One day he was mugged, beaten, and shot, and Antoinette and I heard about it on our way home from a dinner party. Shocked, we detoured straight to the hospital, all a chaos of scuffling reporters, cameras, flashbulbs, and so on. Of course I couldn't see Stennis because he was in surgery, but I wanted to so something helpful—anything at all. In a small office, one staffer frantically responded to nonstop incoming calls and I sat beside her. "Let me help you," I said, and long into the night answered phones and fielded queries. When the press demanded to know who was giving them physician updates on Stennis, I simply replied, "Mark Odom." Antoinette spent her night at Mrs. Stennis' side. Though an able opponent—and often thought of as my polar opposite on defense or other issues—Stennis was my friend. And when my friend was ailing, I did the only thing I could find to help.

Later, *Washingtonian* magazine did a piece surveying all senators as to their best friend in the Senate. Unbeknownst to either of us, I listed Stennis as my best friend. At the same time, he listed me.

Senators Dole, Packwood, and I all hailed from the same party, but Senator John Stennis and Senator Ted Kennedy didn't. Still, just as with others, Kennedy and I were Senate allies as well—at least most of the time.

Back at the end of the Vietnam war, Kennedy and I disagreed on the draft. He believed the draft egalitarian, assuring all demographic groups equal representation in the military. No one minority, he stated, should take more than its share of loss.

But I abhorred the draft, and I felt Kennedy was wrong. Many minorities in the military had risen through history to positions they were barred from on the outside. More opportunities—not less—were offered to those who chose service. Even today, the military still does more work than most organizations to combat hate, racism, and sexism. You must have people who work together understand and respect each other, and you do whatever you can to make sure that happens. Your lives depend on it.

Besides, in my debate with Kennedy on the draft, numbers proved African Americans held demographic representation in the military at the same level as in the general population. The same held true for other ethnic cultures. I repeated all this on the floor, even seeking out Black and Hispanic political leaders for quotes. They vocally reviled the draft, dubbing it horrific, discriminatory, or worse.

There went Kennedy's arguments all to shreds. I won my point. We weren't belligerent, we didn't personalize the issue, and we went on to be political allies many times over.

Even Nixon and I reconciled. Directly after his resignation, as I mentioned, I wrote him. Both of us were flying simultaneously west on separate planes as soon as he resigned—he to quietly reside at San Clemente, and I to another speaking engagement, this time to dedicate the Hoover Federal Memorial at Stanford. Gerald Ford had accepted the dedication invitation while still vice president, yet suddenly found himself as President and a bit too busy for the trip. I was asked to stand in. I wrote Nixon in the air as we both sped on separate planes away from Washington. I expressed my empathy for his current circumstances and recounted the good times, the things we had shared; his 1960 nomination, my keynote in 1964, his visit for Oregon's centennial way back in 1959. If at any time he felt I could be of help or relevance, I wrote; I hoped he would feel free to call. I also knew from coverage in the papers, he was already inundated with mail gushing into San Clemente. I even suggested if he needed a top-rate organizer,

I'd be happy to share our resident organizer, Gerry Frank.

I didn't hear back. But that December as our family gathered at our home in Newport, on the coast, a call came on Christmas morning. A woman stated she was the White House operator. "Well what's this all about?" I wondered, assuming it must be my friend, Hillman Lueddemann, calling with a prank. That I would have been prepared for—but not this. "You have a call from President Nixon," the operator intoned, and I grew even more sure someone was pulling my leg. But as soon as she transferred me to the caller in California and I heard his unmistakable voice, there was no question it was Nixon himself.

"Merry Christmas, Mark," he began in that deep, vibrating tone. "I hope you and your family are having a nice time together."

"Oh yes, we certainly are," I responded.

"Please give them my warmest regards," he went on, explaining he liked to call friends and associates on Christmas day. "I got your nice letter and I appreciate it. And if you're ever in this part of the country I would certainly enjoy having a visit with you."

"Well I'd be very pleased," I told him and, after regaling him with the landscape and weather of the Oregon Coast, we signed off. I was all but shocked.

When I returned to D.C. I called Julie Nixon Eisenhower, a friend of Antoinette's. "Look," I confided, "I received this telephone call on Christmas day from your father. He invited me to come see him some time if I'm in Southern California. I was surprised to hear from him, I have to tell you, and I simply wondered whether that was an offhand, friendly remark or he meant it seriously."

"Oh," she assured me, "he would like very much to see you."

"Well, the interesting thing is, I have a meeting in San Diego in May," I explained.

I contacted Nixon's office, told his secretary that Antoinette and I would be in San Diego and that we could come up if it were convenient. She set a time and when the day came, we drove to San Clemente from San Diego, a leisurely hour-and-a-half ride. Strolling into the former president's foyer we found his secretary off duty. "Have a seat," a secret service man told us, "he'll be along shortly." We sat facing his office, the door slightly ajar, and a moment later something caught my eye. Nixon had entered his office through the back door and stood arranging himself carefully behind his desk, adjusting his suit and

179

posture, positioning himself as if to inspect a critical military brigade or welcome a head of state.

The security service man took his cue, not only escorting us in but announcing as we crossed the threshold, "The former president of the United States!"

And there he was in full view, flags flanked behind him, the desk in front, at formal attention.

After warm greetings, Nixon initiated the conversation. He knew me to be a devoted bibliophile. In fact, I have every book he ever wrote, each one nicely inscribed. So he started right off, his tone none too happy. "Did you read what Charles Hamilton said?" he asked. Of course I had. Charles Hamilton was a major autograph dealer in New York who recently pronounced he might question that Nixon actually signed his own resignation papers. It just couldn't be verified, Hamilton said.

"You know how it is, Mark," Nixon began, definitely cranked up. He abruptly swung open his drawer and yanked out a blank sheet of Richard M. Nixon letterhead. "When you're taking your time, you sign your name very carefully," he illustrated his words with a methodical signature on the page. "If you're in a hurry, you do it in one rush," he demonstrated with a flourish. "And sometimes, I just sign RN, like this" he finished his performance and blithely deposited the sheet in the wastebasket.

Well, Antoinette dove right for it, fishing the paper out and piping up, "Mr. President, would you mind dating this?" He obliged and I've held that sheet ever since, a timeless piece of presidential memorabilia.

We went on to discuss national and international politics and had a pleasant visit. Years later, when Pat Nixon succumbed to lung cancer I learned of her death while standing in the Senate cloakroom. I moved straight to the floor to pay tribute to this courageous, wonderful woman.

I had long since learned that if I could reconcile with Richard Nixon, anyone can find a way to heal any relationship. What a positive, healthy thing to do.

I want to speak of one more relationship close to my heart, this time involving a group at stake, not a single opponent. It was most of a community I lost; the Jewish community. And it hurt terribly.

Early in my career as governor, I'd been honored to receive the Eleanor Roosevelt Humanitarian Award in Portland for my work on bonds for Israel. Ironically, when they gave me the award I was cited for my "high character, tolerance, adherence to religious principles, and devotion to the principles of democracy and brotherhood." B'nai Brith, Hadassah, and other Jewish organizations asked me to speak time and again across the country as well, and I felt it a great privilege. I spoke on the role of Israel in the Mideast, of the importance of this democratic ally, and of the homeland concept. I felt deeply that Jews needed a homeland, and I was a strong advocate of Israel. In that day, I didn't think of any homeland displacing one group for another. We thought—or at least I did—of a pluralistic society, of Israelis and Palestininians co-existing peacefully, of an inclusive state. We didn't speak of a religious state, either. That concept was unknown to our nature as Americans, with our heartfelt need for separation between religion and state.

I worked for bonds for Israel to help the desert bloom, to help forge the modern-day miracle Israel created—a habitable and productive land, a strong economy, a strong people, flourishing out of mere sand.

But my relationship with the Jewish community began to unravel as soon as I went to Israel myself in 1969, just two years after the Six-Day War. I visited kibbutzim and Israeli leaders, and I visited Palestinian refugee camps as I had visited refugee camps in Hong Kong, the Philippines, and anywhere else I traveled around the globe. I wanted to witness for myself the problems of the people and their most difficult struggles. As always I wanted to represent the voice of the oppressed, the discriminated against, and those living in squalor.

What I saw in Palestinian refugee camps were refugees with hate in their eyes, enduring woeful conditions, and children dragging on my coattails. Of course they wanted money, but with a terrifying twist. "Please, please, give me money!" a little boy exclaimed, tearing at my jacket, "so I can buy a gun!"

"Well what do you want a gun for," I asked, smiling and thinking of my own children his age.

"So I can kill a Jew," he spit out, hatred infusing he words, "and get my home back!"

Right then, I knew we were in big trouble. The refugees were nothing if not an incendiary force waiting to ignite. I knew, too, that if tension turned to war in the Mideast, we'd get involved. I came home to say so. "We'll never have peace in the Mideast," I offered my report on the Senate floor and elsewhere, "until we recognize the needs of Palestinian refugees." I spoke of both Israelis and Arabs—of Israeli kibbutz dwellers living virtually underground because of constant shelling, as well as of Palestinian refugees. And I offered the critical caveat: "We won't let Israel fall militarily." I spoke with passion and perhaps naïvete, but immediately my comments were misinterpreted as nothing but venom.

Just as quickly, I was dubbed anti-Semitic. To lobbies in support of Israel and the Jewish community in those days, just mentioning Palestinians in a favorable light meant I was obviously an ardent enemy of Israel. Nothing could have been further from the truth, but I swiftly received calls from Jewish groups, all about upcoming speaking engagements. Each and every date was summarily cancelled. I received critical mail, strident visitations from Jewish delegations, and even word that one of our local politicians was strongly urged to run against me.

That politician was my good friend, Neil Goldschmidt. Back when he had been mayor of Portland, he had once called me and I never received the message. Days later Neil feared he had offended me somehow, and called my office to be sure. Of course he hadn't offended me. Instead of writing "Mayor Goldschmidt" on his message, the receptionist had written "Marigold Schmidt"!

In any case, Neil and I worked together as much as possible. While he served as mayor we met whenever he came to Washington, and when he became governor our link grew stronger still. We worked for Oregon every way we could. So when Neil was approached to run against me, he basically scolded his approachers. "You're trying to knock off Mark Hatfield," he scowled, "our best public servant in the state?" He sent them packing, later adding that though he was a Democrat, he couldn't think of a Democrat he would want to replace me with, himself included. I was honored by his great compliment.

Neil was Jewish himself, and would have voted differently, I'm sure, on arms to Israel, on abortion, on many other issues. But he followed my record on Israel, my position, my exact words. He didn't listen to hearsay, but to actions and principle. We never discussed Israel, but I knew he respected what I did. And I knew he knew I was no anti-Semite, and no enemy of Israel.

Still, Neil not withstanding, while I'd had friends across the ethnic and religious spectrum throughout my life, I felt growing tension—or worse—from the Jewish community at large. Though religious, ethnic, or any kind of discrimination was completely abhorrent to me, and my fight against it had fired my entire career, I was thought of as a bigot. A few in the Jewish community still strongly supported me, but on the whole, I felt as I did when the evangelical Christian community opposed me on Vietnam. I felt lonely and misunderstood. I knew my heart better than anyone and I knew I was not anti-semitic. And it stung, deep.

My record didn't seem to matter, either. I voted for every single piece of legislation that ever contained humanitarian aid for Israel. For money, for policy, for helping Jews escape the USSR, getting them to halfway houses in Europe and then to the U.S., for housing, food, and forestry.

But yes, I did vote against weapons for Israel, as I voted against armaments for every other nation, including my own. I simply didn't think increasing arms in a volatile area would help anything—least of all peace. I felt additional arms would only escalate the enmity and animosity that already existed, and I still do. While my support for humanitarian programs in Israel was rarely publicized, my votes against arms for Israel always were. Publicity made it sound as though I singled out Israel for special treatment when in fact, I was nothing if not consistent in my opposition to arms for every country.

When Israel bombed Lebanon in the early '80s in order to oust the Palestinian terrorists, I listened to Senate arguments in support of more arms for Israel. But just as I had condemned Palestinian terrorist attacks on Israeli children, I again spoke out. "The people of Lebanon are dying today. . . and no end to their suffering is in sight. Their bodies lie unburied and, in many families, there is no one left to mourn . . . . The tyranny of fear must be set aside and human needs met before there can be trust between people and between nations. Can Israeli children live in peace only if Lebanese children die in war?" I asked, refusing to believe it so. I knew you could not bomb an idea—any idea, let alone peace—into submission.

I opposed the offensive attack on Lebanon, as we always offered armaments to other countries with the explicit caveat that they were to be used in defense only, never in offense. In fact, shortly before Turkey invaded Cypress with our arms and we boycotted Turkey—a clear message that offensive use of weapons would not be tolerated. Now, when Israel invaded Lebanon with our armaments, including cluster bombs designed to explode into fatal pellets, this act also constituted a clear violation of U.S. law. And even in Israel itself, strong debate flourished over this invasion and its appropriateness.

I made it plain I wanted to support Israel, but I also wanted to send a clear message, as we had with Turkey. A complete boycott was acceptable then, why would no one listen now? I raised a small amendment, suggesting a purely symbolic 10 percent cut in arms to Israel. The vote was passionate, with each senator striving to yell a louder "no" than his or her colleague. During the roll call Ted Kennedy came to my seat. "Mark," he said, "I just want you to know this action on Israel's part seems way over the line. I'm a big supporter of Israel but this is too much. I'm glad someone has the courage to stand up and say so." Yet even as he spoke these words, they called out "Kennedy!" for his vote and he responded with "Nay!"

I knew no matter how good my speech, my efforts were utterly futile. Yet I could forego the rule of conscience about as easily as I could play star football in high school. It simply wasn't possible. It could just have easily been any nation I was speaking of—any aggressive action throughout the world—not just Israel. But my position on Lebanon served only to swell the fires of resentment. We gained barely a handful of votes and subsequently, it was as if someone lit a bright match to all the charges of anti-semitism leveled against me.

This went on for well over a decade and continually tore me up. Antoinette even came under attack. She worked as a realtor and virtually paid for our children's education through her efforts. Once, when she made the first million-dollar sale as a realtor in D.C., it became well publicized the buyer was an Arab ambassador. Oh that was well reported, just adding to my reputation as an anti-semite. No one happened to note that Antoinette represented the seller, not the buyer. In fact, the seller happened to be Jewish, and Antoinette made sure she got his full asking price. No one ever mentioned that.

Soon after, following an election in the mid-80s, I was so aggrieved by this rupture between myself and the Jewish community that I gave my friend Rabbi Joshua Stampfer a call. I timed my call after the election because I was extremely sensitive it not be seen as a political ploy. I knew Rabbi Stampfer—we were born the same year, in fact—and we enjoyed a long history and warm friendship. When Antoinette had been counselor for women at Portland State University, Rabbi Stampfer and his wife Goldie had five children. Goldie wanted a bit of help at home and Antoinette found them a perfect helper. They never forgot that small kindness.

Ever since, Rabbi Stampfer has been a friend forever. I spoke at Neveh Shalom, Stampfer's Conservative synagogue in Portland, and felt a personal connection with this wise scholar and sensitive person. Rabbi Stampfer thinks inclusively, shares concern for other communities beyond his own, and acts ecumenically and effectively. I think of him only with the deepest affection and respect. And although I knew he differed with me on policy, he never personalized those differences.

So naturally he was the one I called. "Can I come to your office?" I asked. He quickly agreed.

When I arrived, I immediately spoke my mind. "Rabbi," I began, "please explain to me why so much of the Jewish community seems to be against me." Still perplexed after all these years, I shared with him my experiences in that long ago refugee camp. I told him of the young boy with fire in his eyes for killing Jews. "We're building a source of terrorism in those camps," I insisted. "They're nothing but a breeding ground for hate."

I mentioned I had been invited to speak to a faculty-student group at Hebrew University in Jerusalem about Vietnam during that long ago Israeli visit. I told the group exactly how I felt, then took a risk. "Let me tell you about my feelings on Israel," I said, voicing what I later told the Senate when I returned home—my sense of the camps, my feelings about the need for a peace movement in Israel, as well as in America. The group at Hebrew University offered great support, making my rejection at home even more stunning.

But on this day Rabbi Stampfer, as always, listened quietly and intently. finally, he spoke. "Everything you say is true," he began, "but above all we're concerned with the very life of Israel. If the country is exterminated, that's categorically unacceptable. Life is the supreme value here," he stressed.

"And you have to understand," he went on, "that to a persecuted minority, guns symbolize security and defense. Yes we have a home-land, but we're surrounded by unfriendly Arab states who wish to drive us into the sea. We're threatened constantly, and weaponry offers our only security."

Rabbi Stampfer spoke of Israel as though he lived there because he had. He himself fought in Israel's 1948 War of Independence.

As I stood to leave that day, I expressed my deep appreciation for the rabbi's counsel. He helped me from my bafflement, leading me to understand why the Jewish community felt so opposed to my stance on armaments, and therefore so opposed to me.

He, in turn, thanked me for sharing my inmost thoughts, and for doing so in a way not to convince, but simply to explain why I felt misunderstood. He would later say our talk shifted him 180 degrees—from being critical of my position to completely understanding my inner convictions.

Within a few years, Rabbi Stampfer attended a conference given by the Interreligious Committee on Peace in the Mideast, and he too came to believe the needs of Palestinians were an essential part of any peace. He viewed the direction we had been taking as, in his words, "plain wrong." He was the first rabbi in Portland, and one of the first in the nation, to come out for peace with the Palestinians, and it took tremendous courage for him to do so. He stood from his pulpit and admitted, "I was wrong, and this is how I see it now." As leader of the largest conservative congregation between San Francisco and Vancouver, B.C., his words put him at grave risk. But he spoke his heart, and though his congregants were at first perplexed, they came to see his way. I admire no one so much as a man or woman who put themselves at total risk for what they believe.

During my final term, Rabbi Rose, of the Reform Temple in Port-land, invited me to his home. His wife, Lorraine, and Antoinette knew each other as realtors. Rabbi Rose met us at the door, escorting us in, and every eye in the room turned immediately upon us. Clearly, we were the few non-Jews present. Everyone was friendly, greeting us with true warmth, and I felt the invitation as a beautiful gesture on Rabbi Rose's part. I was grateful for yet another opportunity to strengthen old friendships and reacquaint myself with a community I held dear.

It may be true there are no permanent political alliances—or adversaries—in the political arena. But there are permanent friendships, and that was ever my goal, whether with colleagues, constituents, communities, or friends. When a relationship is based on compassion and respect, it will stand the toll of any political difference.

This is true in every relationship, including marriage—the ultimate relationship of all. To me, marriage offers the most inclusive, complete, intimate relationship humans can have. Even in wedlock though, a small spat can make all the wonderful elements, like love, compassion, teamwork, and humor, fly right out the window. If that happens in marriage, the highest of unions, how can it not occur among mere mortals in politics?

Of course it happens in politics. And it's the responsibility of politicians to work diligently to correct that.

For me, that diligence sometimes provided critical opportunities for deep change.

As when I attempted to keep the world from destruction.

CHAPTER THIRTEEN

Freeze!

*T*HE AGE OF ANXIETY, AS I DUBBED IT, PERVADED OUR CULTURE AND I determined to do something about it. But where was I to begin? There were plenty of choices, each one a veritable plague.

Historically, even as I served in the state legislature, children knew how to scuttle beneath desks, ducking and covering at the first blaring siren signalling an air-raid drill. In my governor days, I'd worked to garner tax exemptions for fallout shelters. The Department of Civil Defense was popular too, training countless leaders to act as block wardens and civilian organizers. I'd tried to keep that department from funding slashes. Massive evacuations were a fashionable idea then, but not to me. One accident on the freeways during evacuation would plug up the entire system, literally frying citizens in their cars. Better to find bomb shelter in public buildings, I thought.

All this elaborate planning transpired just in case.

In case of what?

In case of nuclear war, of course. A seed bed of fear bloomed within the country throughout the Cold War, and people grew increasingly aware of the devastation nuclear weapons could spew. TV movies only added to the dread and anxiety, painting a graphic portrait of waste, death, and destruction.

Even just recently, as Cold War documents aired, we found the Soviet Union was indeed intent on our destruction. Exaggeration and anti-communist rhetoric fueled the terror in our country, certainly, but our fear of Soviet nuclear attack capability was well founded. And panic simply fired American fantasies of nuclear war.

Yet from my viewpoint, the USSR would never attack us—and we would not attack them—because no consequence could ensue except mutual destruction, including annihilation of the earth itself. Even if we could survive the bombing, fallout alone would wreak havoc, poisoning our air, our water, and our very bodies. But intentional nuclear war wasn't even our main concern. Errors were. The stark possibility of fatal computer errors. Simple mistakes. How many might have been made or, worse, had been made already?

Numbers accrued, until we began reciting faulty computer chips in our computer-driven alert system. How many misfires had the system offered to date? Over 100 in a 20 month period during the early '80s, for starters. How many times had we been put on nuclear alert for no reason? Countless times. This was, remember, before the advent of a requisite PC or Mac on every desktop. Technology was antiquated by our standards today—if you could even call that antediluvian era technological at all—as much of our present technology will be antiquated by next year.

So worries brewed and bubbled. We were the most sophisticated. And if our missile alert system kept misfiring, we could only imagine what the Soviet system was doing. By mistakes—unknown, benign, technology-driven mistakes—we could blow up the entire planet, unbenownst to any of us.

During President Carter's tenure yet another plague faced us. He recommended a neutron bomb which could spare buildings but wipe out people, leaving sci-fi biological fallout and genetic effects for generations. How misdirected our science had become.

The Senate, though, was all in favor of the neutron bomb. How tidy, to have a bomb designed to kill Soviets in their tanks while leaving the landscape unharmed. Our soldiers could go right in and snuff out Soviet tanks while leaving everything else intact. You could even argue this was sound environmental policy. The logic was so attractive people actually believed this was nothing more dangerous than a conventional weapon, not really a nuclear warhead at all. But in fact the neutron bomb was definitely a nuclear weapon, and would offer Soviets the perfect entrance to escalate their armaments, possibly triggering World War III in the process.

We brought an anti-neutron bomb amendment to the floor, and so much tension and arm-twisting immediately commenced that my chief staff adviser on the issue, Jack Robertson, was called off the floor to see a physicist from Los Alamos—the inventor of this bomb. They had flown this man up in a wheelchair, rolling him into the reception area wearing a big cowboy hat and bolo tie. He patronizingly suggested we had it all wrong. If we could just understand the beauty of this weapon, we would surely realize we were making a terrible strategic mistake.

Jack reported the encounter back to me, and in fact I could see he was flustered. Perhaps we could be wrong on this thing, he suggested. The bill moved so fast, maybe his information was in error somehow. "Don't worry about it," I reassured him, "we're right." I left him, checking in at the well of the Senate as the roll clerk tallied votes, listening while others hovered around deciding which side to take. As I left the well I knew we had it won—by one vote alone.

But at the last second one senator surprised us and changed his position. We lost our bill—by his one vote.

That night in the Senate dining room with Jack, Armed Services Committee leaders Senators John Stennis and Sam Nunn approached. Both dear friends, Nunn had proved my greatest opponent on the neutron bomb that day, standing strong with the defense establishment behind him. We had fought with each other for hours, coming up with nothing but ash. Yet when Nunn and Stennis came into the dining room I greeted them both.

Jack witnessed our interchange dumbfounded. "What are you doing?" he demanded as they left. After all, this was the age when nuclear holocaust seemed evident, hair-trigger bomb alerts were commonplace, and we were still reeling from Vietnam. "This guy," Jack referred to Nunn, cranking himself up, "wants to end the world. Do you or do you not believe he's leading us, through his actions, to nuclear war? In fact, Senator, do you or do you not believe what I heard you say all day on the floor?"

"Of course I believe every word," I told him.

"Then how can you get up and shake Nunn's hand?" his voice grew higher still. "What's more important, Senator, preserving a relationship or saving the world?"

"Look," I told him, "of course saving the world is my priority. But if you can't maintain friendships you lose the entire fabric that holds any culture together. You'll deteriorate into war faster that way—nuclear war or otherwise. I don't hate Sam because of what he stands for. I hate what he stands for, absolutely, but I don't hate him."

Jack was not convinced—perhaps he is now, but not then.

And the story ended well despite my failed efforts. We didn't kill the neutron bomb that day, but soon Jimmy Carter would.

By the time Reagan took over from Carter, Star Wars quickly showed itself as the next "great plague." And there we were to oppose it—primarily Senator Ted Kennedy and I. We were determined to prevent Star Wars or whatever the next generation of nuclear weapons might be.

But step by step the arms race had already taken off, with louder calls for nuclear superiority followed by an ever more enhanced capacity for destruction. And each system or component legislators discussed—every one many times more powerful than what we had unleashed on Hiroshima or Nagasaki—was to be manufactured but hopefully never detonated.

If we went on, how many nuclear arms would we have today? Who knows? Perhaps no one, as none of us might be left to witness the result.

And why? That was my question. Politically, we were to use arms only for defensive action—never offensive—or so went the strict party line. Curious as I am, though, I couldn't quite get it straight: If arms were only for defense, why did we need enough atomic power to destroy the entire planet countless times over? This wasn't foreign policy we were discussing at all, but rather global suicide.

But in our fight against nuclear terror we were met by the same old defense arguments we had heard for years. Opponents claimed, for instance, that the Soviet Union had more missiles of x variety than we and therefore we must increase our arsenal of x. Instead, we came up with a counter-strategy of our own: It wasn't the number of missiles in our arsenal that accurately measured our capabilities, it was the number of launchers. And the United States was obviously superior in launchers. We hoped military proponents would quiet down after that. And they did, for a bit. But they came back.

"The Soviets are about to reach parity in launchers," they insisted.

So we claimed it wasn't only the number of rockets or launchers that was critical, but the number of warheads on each rocket that created superiority. Clearly, we claimed the advantage there too. That worked. The military pundits scratched their heads, thought a while, but ultimately returned.

"The Soviets will soon catch up on warheads."

Okay, we said, it's not simply the rockets, launchers, or warheads that make the critical difference, but the accuracy of our warheads....

And so on. We tried to place a qualitative analysis on what opponents saw as purely quantitative. Our efforts succeeded, but only temporarily.

One day I sat in my office discussing how to put a halt to this mindless escalation once and for all. My staff and I hit on an intriguing concept. Nuclear testing had become the fuel driving the entire arms race. Underground testing, surface testing, defenseless ocean atoll testing. If only we could cut off testing, we would hit the fundamental peg driving the entire nuclear escalation. And thus was born the nuclear freeze.

And we had plenty of support. By then leaks came from labs, testing areas, and even the military. Our arsenal was completely redundant, they told us. Some military personnel assured us they had tested more than enough nuclear weapons. They knew accuracy and safety numbers for each missile; there was no need to test another single armament. Sure this arms build-up kept unemployment rates down by creating more jobs and infinitely more weapons than any nation could possibly use, but what good would low unemployment do if we annihilated the earth and everything on it? What a morally bankrupt foreign policy we had (and unfortunately, still seem to have).

Senator Kennedy and I went out and rallied for the cause. We wrote a book, Freeze Now. We aimed to help educate and build political support. Invisible fallout cannot be measured, we said, and it rises, blanketing the entire planet until all of us die a slow, horrific death. The belief in survivability of nuclear war was nothing but legitimized insanity. This was the apocalypse we were fighting.

In 1982 we came up with a moratorium to end nuclear testing— as Russia and France already had—and actually garnered the bipartisan support to give us a veto-proof 68 to 26 majority. Even Sam Nunn supported it! The next year we went further and announced a nuclear freeze resolution, a unilateral attempt to stop growing our arsenal, and one-third of all senators co-sponsored. We had already held hearings, inviting Hiroshima survivors to testify on the living hell after that blast. They recalled streetcars charred to a crisp, full of dead passengers, helmets with only skulls left beneath, and piles and piles of innocent, broiled bodies. Their stories were not only gripping but completely persuasive. "For the first time in the history of nuclear terror, control is shifting away from the secret cult of strategists, engineers, scientists, and other so-called 'experts' who have held the globe hostage to their theories," I said as I announced the freeze resolution.

I tried to glean votes in the unlikeliest places. One day on the floor, I paged my friend, Senator Orrin Hatch, Republican of Utah, to the phones in the cloakroom, stating I was a bishop of the Mormon church and wished to speak with him directly. From my booth in the cloakroom I watched intently as he scurried in to answer his critical page. "I'm calling long distance from Salt Lake City," I threw my voice. "We've just held a council meeting of the elders of the church. And I want to report to you we're all terribly disappointed you have not yet supported Senator Hatfield's Nuclear Freeze measure."

"Well—well," Orrin stumbled, "I respect and admire Senator Hatfield greatly, but I can't begin to support this—" Hatch was at a total loss, and I am not too sad to say I loved watching his bewilderment.

"Why can't you support it?" I asked. "If you have any questions we would be happy to answer them from a doctrinal point of view," I added.

Just then, still befuddled, Hatch looked up from across the cloak-room. His eyes narrowed as he pointed, then he hung up and rushed from his booth. "You!" he accused. I smiled as we walked back to the floor, chatting. "It was worth a try," I offered in my own defense.

By now the two superpowers had the equivalent of four tons of TNT for every woman, man, and child on earth. How many times can you kill a person, after all? "Today we are cutting immunization for children in order to finance the weapons that may someday kill them," Senator Kennedy liked to say, commenting on how ridiculous the build-up had become. "It comes down to a question of how high the rubble will bounce."

President Reagan countered us of course, even hinting that Soviet agents backed our freeze movement. Senator Kennedy and I just looked at each other. He was no Soviet agent, nor was I. We kept pressing.

Now several states, the District of Columbia, and many cities passed freeze resolutions on their own ballots. Unfortunately, in retrospect I think we accomplished precious little. We didn't halt the military-industrial complex in any significant way at all. We did, hopefully, fashion the debate and help get people thinking.

Later, I helped appropriate all the money I could to help Russia identify and destroy as much of their nuclear arsenal as they were willing to liquidate. They'd built up weapons as the USSR, but as soon as the Iron Curtain fell and the Soviet Union dismantled, all the smaller former Soviet countries still held nuclear power. Russia didn't want smaller states turning on their mother nation, and so Russia had a great incentive to destroy their cache across the entire Former Soviet Union.

In the late '70s it was not only arms but a human tyrant I wanted to stop. Idi Amin splashed into the news. Remember him? The insane Ugandan military leader who snagged his post by rising from one tribal military role to the next. We tend to look at Africa in terms of its most recent, oppressed past, with the Dutch, Belgian, British, or Portuguese dividing up the continent and taking colonial rule. But Africa traditionally is a proud and time-honored tribal continent, with many tribes co-existing upon its land. Superimposed colonial boundaries never fit and never would.

Amin rose by dictatorship, conquering other tribes, committing genocide against them to maintain supremacy, and creating a blood-bath in the process. Rumors spilled over our borders: Amin was a syphilitic, a cannibal, why, it was even said he murdered his wife in front of his own children. Who knew what was true? Yet there was no question the Ugandan people were oppressed, and soon, word got out that Amin had orchestrated the murder of the archbishop of the Anglican church. The assistant to the bishop, Festo Kivingiri, went down to claim the archbishop's body and in the process learned he was next in line for killing.

He gathered his family and fled to Kenya, then to the U.S. to alert our nation of the butchery befalling the Ugandan people. He even wrote a book, I Love Idi Amin, from a religious perspective. God taught him to love his enemies, Kivingiri wrote, and Amin was an enemy to his people. But he could love him and hope for salvation and a change of heart at the same time. The message of his slim volume became quite a celebrated concept.

In Washington, Kivingiri sought me out. "We have to exert some kind of influence to bring this madman down," he and some groups appealed to me. My staff was ever sensitive to issues—particularly peace issues—on which we could be effective and offer true help. This was one of those times and we took up the cause.

During Amin's genocidal rule, the Ugandan economy had all but collapsed. The only remaining cash crop proved an excellent one: coffee. Virtually all Ugandan coffee was exported to the U.S. And Proctor and Gamble and other major companies imported Ugandan coffee here, unintentionally sustaining Amin's economy.

I introduced a resolution to boycott Ugandan coffee in 1978, and testified before a House committee. I quoted from foreign as well as African sources on the present regime in Uganda. The lead lobbiest on Proctor and Gamble's side had served as Nixon's chief of staff during Watergate. He was highly respected by both parties and pled this was not a political issue at all but a trade one—of course Proctor and Gamble did not support Amin. And this lobby was a powerful force.

About this time, Amin invited me to Uganda to witness his rule myself. I made a decidedly not-so-politically-correct comment to my staff. "I'm not going to accept his invitation because I'm not willing to become the entrée for dinner!" I demurred.

The U.S. Senate food service was one of the first to take up the boycott, sending cases of Ugandan coffee back to distributors. From there, the embargo spread. We won the coffee boycott and Amin's economy crumbled. He could no longer sell coffee to the U.S. and was deposed and then succeeded by a government of former exiles. That government restored order and began marketing coffee while we lifted sanctions, and the country went through its transition. Yes, like any transition it included suffering, but now the people of Uganda suffered with hope for a new life, and hope for the loss of human tyranny.

Sometimes—not always—a well-focused boycott works. And well.

In time the Gulf War would break, however, and victory didn't look so simple. In 1987, during the Iran-Iraq war when the U.S. offered Kuwaiti oil tankers Navy escort protection in the Gulf, I protested, stating we should invoke the War Powers Act and make Reagan admit this was a hostile escort policy. Once again, my amendment failed, as amendments usually do.

Yet in 1990, when Saddam Hussein—another autocratic madman—began making characteristically bellicose statements, no one even paid attention. We'd heard his vacant bellowing for years. This time, though, Saddam acted. He not only threatened to move troops into Kuwait, he moved them.

President Bush, his administration, and the media all likened Saddam's move to the hostile takeover of democratic Czechoslovakia. If we didn't stop Saddam in Kuwait he would move on and Saudi Arabia—our ally and major oil source—might well be next in the line of attack. If Kuwait and Saudi Arabia fell, Bahrain, the United Arab Emirates, and the entire Arab Middle East might be next. The majority of our oil supply would be threatened and we couldn't allow that. It came down to our access to oil and that's what I still believe the Gulf War was all about: an oil war. How much were we willing to pay for a gallon of gas—the lives of our own sons and daughters?

Besides, anyone could look at a map and know this madman, with his chemical weapons, could wreak plenty of destruction even if he lost. He certainly had the capacity for wanton disaster. And just as we were panicked over oil, the Israelis were anxious as well. We supported Israel, and it was no secret Saddam was a threat to his Jewish neighbor.

During the Gulf War debate I listened, trying to understand the administration's policy as described by Bush's Secretary of State James A. Baker. Bipartisan support in the Senate was powerful and I knew Bush's action would be well sustained. Bush was clear, too, never hiding his intention to move in troops, aircraft carriers, Air Force, Army, Marines, Navy, and the National Guard—all at once.

The public was completely supportive, as were dozens of our allies. There was that common sentiment of rallying around the chief, and more. People do have self-interest, and they knew what a decreased oil supply foretold. So Bush acted, submitting what came to be the Republican resolution on the war, stating that as of a date certain (January 15, 1991), if Iraq didn't withdraw from Kuwait, a full military response would take effect.

But the Democrats drafted a resolution of their own. They felt the Republican resolution came off as too threatening and wanted to offer a less aggressive alternative. They spoke of circumstances which would instigate war on our part, but only as a last resort. I voted against the Democratic resolution, though it did garner some Republican support. I voted against the Republican resolution as well—after all, both resolutions supported war. I became the sole senator to vote against the Democratic and Republican position.

"The Pentagon is now doing everything possible to give us the impression that war will come in a tidy little package," I said. "Even our words are neat and tidy—body bags are not body bags anymore. That's too messy. That conjures up all the wrong images—images of blood and pain and suffering. Now body bags are 'human remains pouches.' There, America, doesn't that make you feel better? Your sons and daughters and mothers and fathers will have their faces blown off, their limbs torn apart, their chests ripped open, but they won't come home in body bags. They'll come home in neat and tidy human remains pouches."

I wasted my breath. The Democratic resolution failed, while the Republican resolution won. In fact, the Democratic resolution contained a caveat that if Saddam's elite Republican Guard went into action, we would respond immediately. The Republican Guard actually struck prior to the Republican resolution's date certain. Days later, on January 17th, we responded in full.

In the end, though, war is war. Under the Republican resolution, war broke out in full force, and reporters hunkered down in Baghdad to record it all. Films showed how precise our patriot missiles were, with a display of one sliding deftly down a chimney, perfectly aimed. We were so great and mighty that overall, the public was thrilled.

This was an easy war to sell. We weren't running through rice paddies with no way to distinguish friend from foe. We were running along strict battle lines in crisp uniforms, overwhelming the enemy with tanks, soldiers, Marines, and aircraft. Traditional warfare.

The greatest miracle of all were the minute number of casualties on our side. They were so few and the war so completely successful.

Or so it seemed.

When we actually viewed the aftermath, it was clear the war despoiled much of the land, and clean-up would be costly. Land mines needed to be identified and eradicated, and environmental devastation meant a clean-up of major proportions and cost. To our credit we assumed the clean-up, as we'd created a goodly portion of the destruction.

The medical and psychosocial aftermath lingered as well, as it does after any war. Just as we struggle still with the unusual aftermath of Agent Orange in veterans of Vietnam, we now add the Gulf War Syndrome, an equally baffling confluence of symptoms plaguing Gulf War vets. Who knows what vague ills the war in Kosovo may yet cause, let alone the costs accrued to replace or repair buildings, infrastructure, and fractured, traumatized families. And let's not forget, long after the Gulf War, Saddam is still very much in power. The same is still true of Serbia's Milosevic.

But when Gulf troops arrived home, a D.C. welcome parade turned into a total patriotic frenzy, all flags flying to fete our heroes. No president in the history of the United States enjoyed as high an approval rating—85 percent—as George Bush following that war. In some circles it was even said Lloyd Bentsen, the nationally-known and well-respected Democratic senator from Texas (who served as Walter Mondale's vice presidential running mate in 1984) considered running against Bush in 1992. But as Bentsen considered Bush's high approval rating, he concluded winning the Democratic nomination would be nothing but futile.

Bush supporters exuded overconfidence at their own peril. Yes, the Gulf War reflected broad public support for Bush's foreign policy, but he couldn't ride that alone to victory. War sometimes offers coattails, as it did in the cases of FDR, Eisenhower, and Grant. But not always. Politicians have to look beyond the poll of the moment to determine true public sentiment. They may think policy is played out on the world stage, and support for foreign policy will automatically translate into votes at home. But voters' patterns are more often influenced by domestic policy, by how well their own lives and problems are considered. Bush's economic policy had no time to flourish on his watch, so voters couldn't see the domestic upswing he set in motion. Instead, Bush lost to Clinton and as successor, Clinton became the beneficiary of Bush's economic policy.

During George Bush's term I tried to combat war another way, by eliminating chemical weapons. More than 100 nations signed an agreement abolishing chemical weapons, yet the United States Senate failed to approve the treaty. The nations which signed on have largely followed the agreement as if it were ratified. A treaty like this is negotiated by the president—in this case, President Clinton—sent to the Senate for discussion, revision and approval, then sent back to the president for signature. Through a coalition of interested citizens, I'm still supporting its passage.

Sure, the process is a bit time consuming, but for excellent reasons. It brings to mind a signal wonder of our Republic that I've mentioned before. Our forefathers created an elaborate system where, under constititutional provisions, no one person or branch of government can ever make final determination on an issue. Separation of powers is clearly defined, thus assuring checks and balances. I am still awed as I contemplate the constitutional fathers' creation of a fail-safe undergirding for all branches of government. And they accomplished this with absolutely no model guiding their deliberations. Of course, constitutional writers couldn't guarantee against incompetents finding their way into power. But they did guarantee protection against any incompetent—or any wise being, for that matter—wielding too much power. And it's our job to uphold that lofty ideal.

The constitutional convention was made up of an intellectual and creative body of men perhaps unparalleled in human history. An unfortunate detail is the fact that this occurred at a time when only white males held power. No minorities or women were represented, as both were denied education and opportunity. At least we had Abigail Adams, second president John Adams's wife, constantly writing—letters, not e-mail!—reminding him, "Don't forget the ladies, John!"

During the Gulf War debate as in others, I'm often pegged as a pacifist. In fact, I am not. I'm not totally opposed to military force (for example World War II), yet I believe force should not be used until all other options have been exhausted. And most critically, we ought to address the causes of war—poverty, lack of education, health, racism, militarism, or conflict over raw materials (such as oil)—and work to prevent war in the first place.

In addition to prevention, we need to recognize the need for an international peacekeeping force composed of many nations, under the command of the U.N. I speak of a true international peacekeeping force, created and bestowed with worldwide leadership. I long to focus on the peace in peacekeeping—the mediation, the bringing together of peoples who can solve problems, the social agendas—rather than moving straight to invasion and war.

I'm often asked what it's like to stand alone, to vote in a lone voice, as I did during the Gulf War. What was it like to be an identified black sheep in the Senate?

Politics is like all of life, not different. Everyone is a product of their home life, their training, their social and economic identifications, and even their genes.

My father was a blacksmith in overalls, in contrast to many of my friends' fathers who dressed in suits and ties. Dad taught me never to be afraid to stand alone, and so I stood. As Lord Bryce, the great British commentator on democracy observed, the duty of an elected official is to help create public opinion rather than to merely reflect it, and I took that as my task.

Freeze!

When I first came to politics, during Hoover's lost re-election bid against FDR in 1932, I soon became accustomed to the minority role. Roosevelt went on to win three more terms. During my entire coming of age, he was my president and I unhappily accommodated. I knew I was usually on the losing side, but I survived nevertheless. I imagine it might feel similar in ethnic and religious minorities as well. Nietzsche said, "What does not kill me makes me strong," and that applies well here. I had endured, and I would stay on the side of what I believed. To their credit, my senate colleagues and the President serred respected stands of conscience, no matter how frustrating to their own designs, and understood my position.

There are some issues I have yet to see flourish to the degree I'd like. The nuclear race is certainly one, as are the social, political, and international issues our nation continues to battle. But as I matured in politics I realized events occur and evolve in cycles, finally coming to fruition even if not in one's lifetime. Many said Woodrow Wilson failed in not creating his League of Nations before his death. Yet if he hadn't brought the entire nation—the world, in fact—to an awareness of his idea, we may have never created the United Nations following World War II.

I look at politics from the advantage of longevity, versus viewing a loss as a loss, final and crushing. When failure became evident I proposed a new idea or tried again the next session. I sowed seeds, hopefully aiding others to view things in a different light and witnessing the harvest that comes in time. If my convictions were truly that—convictions—I had an obligation and desire to try again.

Yes, we may miss the realization of certain goals in our lifetime, but that doesn't portend the world must be denied culmination of our vision. We all reap the joy of seed sowing from those who came before us, and we all take risks for the benefit of those who will come after. I am aware of the world as it was given to me, aware of the opportunities I have been gifted, and aware of my obligation to assure those same opportunities are secure for the next generation, even though it may not be mine to complete the task.

I keep a wooden sculpture in my office—given to me by Antoinette—representing the Tanzanian people's rise toward democracy in the 1980s. The wood is polished to a fine lustre, portraying several genderless humans artfully rising, one above another.

Some might say this is a spurious notion—those at the top rising only by standing on the backs of those who fall below. I know better, and the sculpture was given to me with an explanation and a hope: All of us need each other, all of us must lift and pull others as we rise, all of us must rise together, powerful, free, one self-determined people.

All of us.

CHAPTER FOURTEEN

A Troubled Planet: Health and the Environment

S OME SAY ATTITUDE IS EVERYTHING, AND THEY'RE RIGHT. BUT I BE-
lieve attitude also arises from great health. So to me, health is
everything.

From those early days at the Boy Scout Jamboree I realized good
health—or illness—could impact plans of those surrounding the globe.
In the military I observed the utter devastation of hunger and disease.
Then at Stanford, one of my political science professors changed my
life.

Professor Johnson, who taught Latin American politics, made a
comment that sowed fruitful seeds forever in my mind. "Unless you
understand the health problems of a nation," he said, "you can't understand the politics. You simply cannot build stable governments on
the backs of sick people." I heard those words in the late '40s and ever
after would relate health to politics. One of the most critical corner-
stones of democracy, I realized, is a healthy, well-nourished people.

In Oregon following the Korean conflict, a Mr. and Mrs. Holt (from
a family of farmers outside Eugene) gathered up for adoption children

from Korea and brought them to Oregon to live. Amerasian children sadly left behind by American servicemen, these youngsters made up the first postwar adoption program. "One of Korea's major problems," I once heard Mrs. Holt say, "is that out there, most people are a little sick most of the time."

It wasn't major illness she spoke of, but creeping, life-depleting sickness. Undernourishment, parasites taken in through water, ill-prepared food, or the feet; little things that accrete into a country comprised of the poor and the unhealthy. I saw this as not only a health problem, but a political conundrum as well. A nation's health relates straight back to stability in its society, its community, its families.

Largely due to Holt and Professor Johnson, I was keyed into aiding the essential struggle for health throughout my career. I relied on medical experts, scientists, and my own reading and study. I listened to colleagues at governors' conferences or in the Senate, and to interested citizens who told me poignant tales of health and disease. I sought information as a basis for action.

In 1955, while a state senator, Oregon Health Sciences University (OHSU) didn't have a teaching hospital. Instead, medical students had to be educated throughout the community in smaller facilities. Dean Baird drove to Salem one day, bent on lobbying for the creation of a teaching hospital. He was a great mentor, infecting me with a vision of improving the health of all Oregonians—a vision still embodied by OHSU through the inspired leadership of former President Leonard Laster and current President Peter Kohler. I was honored to co-sponsor and battle for Baird's bill in the State Senate, and thus University Hospital was born.

In 1959, I spoke to a luncheon for the handicapped. We didn't use terms like "disabled" or, better yet, "differently-abled" in those days. But I spoke of each of us as disabled in some way, and urged people not to look at disabilities but to focus on abilities instead. I encouraged hiring the differently-abled, and used scientific sources to stress this group was perfectly able to handle many professions. I wasn't speaking the lingo of the '90s or the new millenium, but my heart was there, way back then.

In 1963, my governor's budget included items such as Oregon's first tax on cigarettes, our first fixed speed limit, blood tests for suspected drunk drivers, seat belts in new cars, stronger air and water pollution laws, expanded medical care for the aged, and stronger legislation against "dangerous drugs." (Later, I'd introduce a bill in the Senate under the premise that addiction was a medical-social problem. I wanted doctors to administer free drugs to addicts to cut down on crime and funnel addicts into medical care. Okay, so sometimes I invited controversy, but the premise was sound).

Also in 1963, I spoke before American Medical Association (AMA) delegates, urging them to focus more on the needs of our nation and to fight "hate, dependency, and materialism." It was my desire to have physicians think of the link between health and government, educating patients as to human rights, inclusiveness, and self-determination. Even then I wanted physicians to be more involved with insurance companies to better meet the nation's health needs.

The individual has responsibility for her/his health—the responsibility can't all lie in the lap of government or the medical community. I was an example. I helped introduce legislation requiring warnings on every cigarette pack, yet I was a reformed smoker myself. As a faculty member at Willamette, smoking was disallowed on campus, so students and faculty alike stood on the curb of State Street, across from the State Capitol, partaking of the evil weed. But what kind of example was I setting? I quit in 1954, before the surgeon general's warning, and even then I knew smoking was bad for my health. Now we have surgeon general's warnings and great commercials—one even portraying a woman with a smoking-induced tracheostomy, sitting there on TV holding the cigarette up to her trach hole and smoking right into her neck. Now that's pretty compelling. We all know it's a rare person today who lights up without being fully aware that smoking is deadly.

Yet education is not the only key to change. People must do some of the work. It's hard, I know, but health providers can help with support, medication, and information. Like smoking, drugs, alcohol, obesity, and a sedentary lifestyle, are all addictions. The medical world can help but the individual must play a role in their own change. The government will never be able to legislate that.

It's true prevention is preferable to any cure—for addiction or disease—and that's where I focus my efforts. I want to make incentives and disincentives available so people can work together toward health. It can't all fall on the individual, either, and some individuals will always slip through the cracks, lacking resources or access to health care. All of us must help.

At the same time, our current health insurance system is in need of a major overhaul. Basically, it's not health insurance at all, but rather sickness insurance. That's the absolute opposite of how it should be. Some progressive companies are learning to calculate patient risk before they quote premiums. There's a great incentive. If you exercise, eat well, and don't smoke, your premiums diminish. In ways like these— with people, health care providers, and insurance companies working together—we can accrue true health benefits, so everyone gains from wellness rather than suffers from disease.

Some worry incentives may backfire; that genetic DNA testing results will be available to insurance companies and individuals may be discriminated against by higher premiums or denied coverage if at risk of certain diseases. I worried about that too. And when the first human cloning talk began, I thought it sounded positively Orwellian. But at the same time I supported the Human Genome Project and the possibility that genetic engineering could help conquer disease. To make sure genetic testing didn't get out of hand, I worked to create the National Bioethics Advisory Committee—the body Clinton called upon for ethical recommendations in the wake of Dolly, the cloned sheep. Hopefully, all states will soon have laws preventing any discrimination on the basis of genetic testing.

I wish we practiced good health in our land, as well as healing of disease. Certainly there will ever be a critical role for medicine. But the highest vision of true healers is to make themselves obsolete. We need to elevate health in this country to a disease defense build-up. It's no longer "The Russians are coming." Instead, it's "The viruses are coming," and we all need to be prepared. We should approach this threat to our national security with as much passion and commitment as JFK did when he said, "We are going to put a man on the moon." Kennedy did it, too—and fast. We're all at least as powerful. We could revolutionize the health of our entire nation if we simply made a commitment to do so.

The first key to improving health is in supporting more medical research. There's so much we still don't know in medicine. We thought we'd won the war on tuberculosis, but now we're confronted with new, difficult, and deadly strains. We thought we'd conquered any and all bacterial infections with antibiotics as well—wonderful drugs. But now, bacterial infections exist that are so intractable to therapy that medical personnel must fear caring for these victims because the risk is so high. And I don't even need to mention AIDS. Of course we've made inroads there, and that's terrific. But AIDS is a virus. We have no magic pill to cope with viruses, only antibiotics to cope with bacterial infections. Antibiotics are worthless on viruses. Have you ever gone to a health practitioner for treatment of a common cold? Last I heard, we have nothing even approaching a cure, and that's for a simple cold. Viruses have us, it's not the other way around, and as yet we have no cure.

Medical research to date clearly hasn't been enough. We need to offer more foresight than a five-year plan or a campaign to fight a single virus. We need continual disease and health monitoring, a strengthening of all our defenses against illness. With the people's support the president and Congress can do just that, and do it well.

It's a funny thing about health and government. Research America—a research group which focuses solely on medical issues—conducts study after study. Over and over citizens tell them medical research is one of the finest issues government can expend energy and dollars on. In fact, medical research is overwhelmingly supported by the public—more than any other government research.

If I had to, after nearly 50 years of public service, I couldn't list many things the government does extremely well. But medical research is a critical exception. The National Institutes of Health (NIH), through national, regional, and local research and education, excel at their task. And the public is so behind NIH they've told Research America they're willing to pay a dollar more on insurance premiums if it's earmarked for medical research. They're even willing to pay higher taxes if they're earmarked for medical research. The public is ready, willing, and anxious to be warriors in this great battle against disease. There isn't a family or individual in this country that hasn't lost a loved one to a devastating fight against disability, injury, or disease. People are simply waiting for good leadership. So why isn't the government offering it? I ask that question often and I'm afraid I can't give you an answer. So please, do me a favor. Demand legislative initiative in the fight against illness. You deserve it.

As I said, every family is hit by disease and mine is no exception. Throughout my career I met others who suffered the grief of illness as well. I learned an estimated 3,000 to 5,000 orphan diseases exist alone. "Orphan" because they arise so rarely they usually lack even a disease registry to call their own. Every common disease—from cancer, multiple sclerosis and AIDS, to Lou Gehrig's, diabetes and Alzheimer's—has a registry, a listing of patients, a place to go for help, support, research. Most orphan diseases are so small they don't even know how many sufferers exist, let alone where they live.

One day my legislative director, Jim Towey, came into my office. "You have to meet this young man who's out here in a wheelchair," he told me, a command rather than a question. Cal Larson, a teen of perhaps 16, suffered from Epidermolysis Bullosa (EB), an orphan disease. EB attacks skin and connective tissue, as I soon discovered. When I walked out to meet the youth and his parents, he sat in his wheelchair, his skin lacking pigment. Blisters had erupted all over him. I learned that as the disease progresses, it strikes its victims more cruelly still. Teeth fall out, internal tissue scars (impeding digestion), facial expressions become drawn and strange, and fingers shrivel into arthritic-fisted stubs. Sufferers must be kept from light and rarely live until their 30s.

Cal had probably spent more than half his life by the time I met him. He was up on the Hill, approaching legislators, and I was head of Appropriations. He wanted research for his disease and he knew I might be sympathetic. He told me about EB and pled for help for a normal life. All he wanted was to be healthy, to get out, to be a regular teenager, to live.

And medicine could offer him nothing.

Cal was so articulate, so persuasive, that my response was instantaneous. "Look," I said gently, "we're having a hearing right now on the NIH budget. Please come. I want you to testify, to tell the committee your story." He did, and he persuaded the committee as he had me.

From there we launched a research project, gained a line item, and created a registry for EB. Cal's and other parents embodied the cause, taking their fire and love for their children and channeling it into help for all. We even had a researcher at OHSU working on EB. It was a great beginning, and we still continue the battle against this orphan disease.

Another time I co-hosted a simple hearing on medical research that transformed into one of the most magical moments of my career. I co-chaired with Senator Bill Cohen, Republican of Maine, and chair of the Council on the Aging. We gathered colleagues and friends— even well knowns like General Schwartzkopf—to testify on how disease and disabilities affected their own lives. Senator Connie Mack, Republican of Florida, created virtual silence throughout the room as he recounted his personal bout with cancer, his wife's, and his other family members' as well. Every contributor added magic, offering a rare moment in politics when a hearing becomes a sharing—everyone is caught up in the drive to better quality of life for all. Each person adds their own reason, at the same time exposing themselves, letting themselves be vulnerable. Every person choked up or cried in that hearing, and many had to pause before they could even go on with their tales.

I was no exception. I spoke of my father. Dad had a great physique, I began. His days as a blacksmith—an anvil and hammer in hand—left him with magnificent shoulders and chest. After retirement signs stood on our lawn announcing his avocations: "Saws sharpened," and "Night Crawlers." Dad was an incredible fisherman. He also jogged for miles, even into his early 80s. But one day he went off running and a neighbor phoned my mother. "Your husband is here," the woman began quietly, struggling for words. "He's lost, he doesn't know how to find his way home." Mother came to get him, and that was her first clue something was terribly wrong.

Soon Dad began asking where the bathroom was. He forgot to pull the plug in the bath, overflowing the bathtub, or he'd forget how to run water. On any day but Sunday, he was sure it was Sunday, insisting it was time to go to church, getting jumpy and disoriented. Here Mother was trying to restrain him, this huge, still zesty man. She'd wake in the night and see he wasn't in bed, terrified he was wandering again. finally it reached a point where she was physically unable to care for him. We inquired and were told the best place for Dad would be Mt. St. Joseph's Center in Portland.

Mt. St. Joseph's took excellent care of my father, but he hated it whenever they tried to bathe him. Young orderlies began undressing him and Dad hauled off and socked them. Even in his 80s, he was stronger than they.

I have to admit I dreaded going to visit. I knew I must, out of duty and out of love. But Gerry Frank had to insist I go each time I came home. "I don't want to see him," I'd hide my head in my hand.

"You have to," Gerry ordered. He was right, even though Dad didn't know who I was and every visit broke me up.

It wasn't that Dad was morose, far from it. He loved to sing, and he sang hymns to any nun who would listen—especially Sister Bernarda, his favorite. He sang to orderlies too, then turned around and punched them if they did something he didn't like.

When I visited I often asked questions about Roseburg, where Dad grew up. He'd regale me with tales as though he was recounting yesterday. But of course he couldn't remember what he had for breakfast, didn't know where he was, and didn't realize I was his son. He never called me by name, instead gazed at me with a complete blank. Mother thought he knew her, but I doubt it. His wife of 50 years? Another blank.

Towards the end we all stayed with Dad around the clock, in shifts. I spent the day with him and Baba (Antoinette's mother, bearing the Croatian name for "grandmother") relieved us in the evening. Baba and Sister Bernarda were there during Dad's peaceful, final moments. Sister Bernarda held Dad's hand and offered the Lord's prayer as he took his last breath. Baba called to relay the inevitable news.

Dad was 84 when he died. We requested no flowers, instead accepting donations to install a music system throughout Mt. St. Joseph's. Dad would have loved that.

I came away devastated, funneling my grief into passion. I knew firsthand the tremendous necessity of diverting others from Dad's path. And I knew there was only one way.

I kept fighting, and after that hearing we garnered awareness and support for Alzheimer's and other diseases. Sudden Infant Death Syndrome, Parkinson's Disease, AIDS, cancer, sleep disorders, heart disease, multiple sclerosis, and infertility, are only a few of the causes I defended.

I fought tobacco too. In Congress we often link subsidies together— milk, sugar, cheese, cotton, tobacco, soy, wheat, peanuts—all in one bill. I was interested in wheat mostly, since we produce more of it in Eastern Oregon than just about anywhere else. None of the other subsidies particularly mattered to me, except that I abhorred the tobacco subsidy. Just before my last term I walked onto the floor and there stood Jesse Helms, Republican from North Carolina, defending the tobacco subsidy against a resolution to repeal it.

Now Jesse knew I was opposed to tobacco and any tobacco subsidy whatsoever. He boomed out from his desk, in that thick southern drawl, "I see the senator from Oregon has arrived." I didn't reply. "Would the senator from Oregon yield to a question?" I won't repeat how he pronounced the name of my state. It's not only Jesse who does so— just about anyone who doesn't live here commits the same sin. (It's Ora-gen, not Ory-gone).

"Yes, I yield to a question," I answered Helms.

"The senator from Oregon has spoken so eloquently against the tobacco subsidy," Jesse drawled. "I would like to inquire how much tobacco is raised in the senator's home state of Oregon?"

"None, no tobacco whatsoever," I repeated what Helms well knew.

"But the state of Oregon raises a lot of wheat, is that so?"

"Oh yes, the finest in the country," I put my plug in for Oregon wheat—the Port of Portland exports more than any port in the nation. "We're big on wheat production."

I decided right then not to stride any further into his trap. "I would like to ask the senator from North Carolina a question as well, would he yield?"

Jesse yielded.

"I wonder," I paused, "if I offer an amendment to repeal our wheat subsidy along with the tobacco subsidy, would the senator from North Carolina accept that?"

Helms faded off into incoherence.

"I want to say this right now," I added. "If it's an avenue to repealing the tobacco subsidy, I will sacrifice my state's wheat subsidy for the good cause."

It didn't work that way in the final analysis. But as soon as the words issued from my mouth I made appointments to visit Oregon wheat farmers the second I next hit the state. I wanted to defend what I'd done and make sure they knew why I felt so strongly. And though they didn't like it, they listened.

Now I'm involved in a project to create a trust fund for medical research so NIH doesn't have to plead its case year after year before Congress. Dollars need to be available for research all the time, not simply when it's convenient. If I can't get money by other arguments, I even reach for the pocketbook nerve, showing medical research is great for the economy. For every $1 we spend on medical research about $50 are generated back into the economy via jobs, treatments, services, and greater productivity.

Some have asked what I want my legacy to be and I always offer the same response. I hope to have made some small difference in the quality of life for everyone on our planet.

But quality of life isn't comprised of health alone. Where we live, our environment, is just as critical—and just as dear. As we well know our planet ails, and my fight for the environment was ever as strong and constant as my struggle to improve health. I'm still at both tasks.

If you've never been to Oregon, I have to say I pity you. I'll paraphrase, Nathaniel Coe, the first permanent white settler in Hood River. In 1854 he saw our land and said he'd found paradise. I suspect he probably landed here in late spring—when the rains occasionally cease!

There is nothing like Oregon, and you can't know it until you witness it yourself.

Early in life I appreciated our bounty, and from the first days of my career I fought to protect it. During my run for secretary of state, a heated debate ensued between Republicans and Democrats over private versus public power companies. At that time 80 percent of Oregonians were served by private power. The debate also centered on Hell's canyon in Idaho, where a private company wanted to build the High

Mountain Sheep dam. Likewise, a public dam, the Nez Perce dam, was advocated by Democrats who desired public power. One dam was high upriver, the other lower. "Why argue over high or low dams; public or private?" I asked. "Let's have both public and private utilities, and before we build anything, let's find out the impact on the fish!"

Fortunately, neither dam was built, but I relied on science to steer us toward the most effective track. That has always been my approach. Back in the state legislature, if I was interested in legislation on utilities, agriculture, or what have you, I'd get in touch with the Public Utilities Commission or the Agriculture Department in Salem and get the best information I could—from the source.

As governor I saw a public ad calling people to visit the "Twenty Miracle Miles" along the Central Oregon Coast. Having traveled that span many times and noted junk, dilapidated housing, and other blights, I commented within earshot of the press, "This place would be more accurately referred to as the 'Twenty Miserable Miles.'" My comments made big news and a Mr. Parks, owner of the Pixie Kitchen in Lincoln City, spoke up. "He's right and we should rise to the governor's challenge." They launched a public clean-up. I went down to help spear litter and offered a public trophy for the best restoration.

In the Senate I helped legislate the majority of our wilderness areas in Oregon—over two million acres—to protect the unique terrain, beauty, and ecology of our state and its old growth. Joining with others, I worked with many of our Native American tribes in Oregon to foster and protect their treaty rights on tribal lands. (We can learn so much from time-honored, sustainable native ways of caring for our planet.) Some opposed restoring a land base for the Coquille tribe, testifying against it in a public hearing. I questioned them. "You don't want to give the land back? Whose do you think it was in the first place?"

Speaking out for Native tribes was something I'd been doing at least since I was governor. During the 1962 Seattle World's Fair, all the tribes in the Northwest dubbed me an honorary tribal chief, and I'll never forget how regal and elegant I felt when they draped me in full eagle-feather headdress and ermine tails. I have that magnificent crown still, at Willamette University's Mark O. Hatfield Library.

On the Indian Review Commission in the Senate, I also helped review all treaties and policies for tribes nationwide. Once in New York state, a Native woman approached me. "My father was the model for the Indian head nickel," she began, "and I want to give to you what they gave to me." She held out the large pewter mold for the famous coin.

"You should keep that," I implored.

"Oh no," she continued. "Don't hurt me, don't make me weep. I want it to be yours."

I still have that pewter cast with all my commemorative medals, one of my great treasures which I am currently contributing to the Portland Art Museum.

Often, I'm invited to powwows and am honored to go. More than once I have been asked to join in a ritual dance. The dance inevitably begins in single file, and I try my hardest to get the idea and rhythm of the step. But as soon as I do, everyone turns and faces into a circle. My ineptitude must be quite apparent. Before I know it a woman flanks me on either side, wedging me in close so I have no chance to move out of step. I have had so much fellowship and trust bestowed upon me by the tribal peoples of our land, it's an honor to be able to enjoy their rituals as well. Hopefully, my good intentions overtake my poor "dancemanship"!

From way back at Willamette I was also classmates with Cece Connor, a longtime friend. His daughter grew up to be an Indian princess, and we went through three generations of life cycle events together. Cece is perhaps my oldest friend in the Native communities, but I am blessed by countless others. (These relationships are one of the treasures of my political life.) I still remember her sisters and aunt teasing my grandmother Mary Alice Trent. "Now Alice," they'd cajole, "you know we have Cherokee blood in our veins." My grandmother declined to comment, but I'd be delighted to track that back. Nothing would please me more than to be a member of one of our Indian nations.

In addition to my work on the Indian Review Commission, I was also proud to protect over half the old growth forests across the state during my tenure in the Senate. As mentioned, President Nixon asked that I sponsor the Endangered Species Act, and through the years, I helped protect over two million acres of wilderness areas, including Steen's mountain, the John Day Fossil Beds and the Columbia River Gorge National Scenic Area. Working with Bob Packwood, the Hells Canyon recreational area came into being. With Representative Bob Smith, the Newberry Crater was protected. And with my friend and congressman John Dellenback, the Oregon Sand Dunes were preserved. I also co-sponsored the Wild and Scenic Rivers Act, adding more scenic and wild rivers to Oregon—43—than any other state. At the time, the next closest state listed only 11. As a co-sponsor we also passed the Clean Air and Water Act. I fought for salmon way back in the '60s and am still doing so.

Ronald Reagan was known for proudly serving Columbia River salmon at his state dinners, yet proposed cutting several million dollars in federal funds for Oregon salmon hatcheries. I worked to preserve spawning grounds for steelhead as well as salmon, and in 1990 invited states, agencies, tribes, and environmental groups to a Salmon Summit, laying the foundation for consensus building and a subsequent salmon recovery finance plan which is still in effect. We knew we might not see a benefit right away, but were determined to gather interested parties and shine the focus on salmon, the first time this issue had been brought into perspective in such a high profile way. I still see hope for our salmon today.

But as with any issue, there are extremes when it comes to the environment. Some told me in order to save fish, we should remove each and every dam. Now I'll consider looking at individual dams, but when someone confronts me saying, "take them all out!" I look them in the eye.

"Well, how will we produce energy?" I ask. After all, it's a logical question. We garner our electricity from hydropower.

"We'll use nuclear energy!" some expound. I kid you not, I have heard this answer more than once. Probably more times than I know as my hearing isn't so great.

Now I'm first to admit I supported nuclear power back in the late '60s—we thought it was a great solution to our upcoming energy shortages. What a terrific way to channel destructive energy into constructive means, I thought. But this was long before the executive branch came clean with the terrible truth about nuclear waste.

That news turned me against nuclear power forever.

I was the one who felt our Hanford Nuclear Reactor created the biggest environmental threat and waste problem our state ever confronted, the one who worked so hard with other environmentalists to close it down.

One of the most gratifying experiences in my entire career occurred in my last session of Congress when we secured the Opal Creek Wilderness, even while the Congressman in that district opposed this legislation. Opal Creek is an absolutely magnificent watershed with deep, old growth forests and water rushing and plunging over rocks—a great legacy for Oregon.

Forests were an extremely controversial issue throughout my career. Militant environmentalists often attacked me as favoring timber interests on one side, while on the other hand many lumber companies cooled on me as not supportive enough.

In 1976 though, Frank Church and I joined forces to pass the National Forestry Management Act. This Act required the Forest Service to draft plans for national forests, plans which included multiple uses like sustainability of the forest itself. By this time scientists had begun to show the way of the future, discovering our need to decrease timber yields in order to sustain wildlife, water, and other forest fundamentals. This news came in the days of very aggressive timber management practices, when our economy still primarily relied on the lumber industry. I wanted to move in the direction of wise stewardship that science recommended. Many of the nation's best forest scientists hail from Oregon State University, and I had their support. But I also took human need into account, as I'll describe. At this point the timber industry was in the midst of a devastating recession and countless Oregonians depended on timber jobs. I couldn't pull these out from under citizens all at once, that would have been unconscionable.

But many suggested I do just that. Whatever I came up with, it never seemed enough. Even worse, some on the other side of the debate never seemed to believe my sincerity, always figuring I had some ulterior motive. Indeed, I wanted to move the trend toward stewardship and sustained yield as much as they did. Long before we even had a term for it, my vision included managing wilderness well beyond artificial boundaries we drew of "wilderness" or "parks" into natural boundaries. The phrase for this is "ecosystem management," and I knew it to be a great idea before it even had a name. But the "100 percenters" and I had a fundamental disagreement as to what management and sustainability meant. In fact, we never agreed. In 1984, when I helped protect two million acres of Oregon wilderness with the Wilderness Act, it still wasn't enough. The "100 percenters" asked that more acres of unroaded Oregon be protected, without regard to economic or human repercussions whatsoever.

Of course timber interests opposed me just as strenuously, favoring a much more aggressive policy in the direction of cutting. They couldn't seem to understand what science was telling us, nor plan for the future. I knew harvest levels needed to come down and forests had to be managed progressively now, with the life of the forest in mind. Science no longer supported the lumber companies' long-held harvest levels. But timber fought strongly against the Wilderness Act and pushed for release of lands that were about to be protected nonetheless. They never came up with a proactive plan, thus allowing themselves to be portrayed as their opponents defined them, with blatant disregard for the land.

In the early '90s, when legal challenges to timber sales would have cost the Pacific Northwest around 40,000 jobs, (three of every four timber industry jobs available) I fought that too. I'm sure the lumber industry supported my stand on this one, but I certainly didn't do it for them. I did it for the families whom I could not let languish. I wanted to see far less timber harvesting, yes, but I needed to see a gradual decrease, swift enough to benefit our forests but slow enough to retrain loggers and allow their families to seek new livelihoods.

The debate over our forests was perhaps the most polarizing ever to rivet Oregon, with both sides so unrelenting in their fight for right that neither would give the other any sway. This was unfortunate because both sides held value, despite their blind spots. I tried to help by holding hearings and listening to the testimony of people and scientists—truly listening. Thus we crafted a bill or hammered out a piece of legislation by recognizing need on each side; environmental and human both. And, we never exceeded the annual allowable cut determined by the Forest Service.

I often put it this way: "Some people believe that more of our land should be set aside to protect biological diversity and to preserve our state's natural beauty. Others believe that setting aside additional land will have a devastating effect on the thousands of families and schools and communities which depend on the forest products industry. Both sides—all sides—have legitimate concerns."

However, whether or not to set additional land aside is not the only issue. The overarching issue, to me, is Gifford Pinchot's definition of conservation: wise utilization. In Oregon, in the Pacific Northwest, in other areas of the world as well, we are blessed with a huge timber supply. Some claim our true agenda should be complete non-utilization of forest lands. Historically, this is in strong contrast to Pinchot, the father of conservation during Teddy Roosevelt's era. Pinchot made us, as a country, aware of the need to preserve and protect our natural resources. His definition of conservation meant wise use. Wise use included forest and water quality, wildlife, scenic value, and timber and recreational use.

I have a problem with non-utilization (and unwise utilization, for that matter). Yes, I protected old growth and our unique geological areas: Opal Creek, wild and scenic rivers, and others I've mentioned. Yet along with that I fought for those forests that can be scientifically managed for production. Why? Because with non-utilization, you completely lock up a resource that translates into housing. Now, wood is the only renewable housing material we can have in perpetuity if we manage it well. We can use aluminum or other metals, all of which take a high amount of energy to produce. Or we could use clay, brick, or mortar, all of which are completely finite. The needs of humans for housing become lost in the timber equation, in the lock-up of non-utilization. And I want houses built. Not because I want a new one, or those of privilege need a second or third. No, I want housing because the solutions to poverty and oppression are rooted in housing. The homeless, the underhoused, have no resources with which to lift themselves up. A house offers safe refuge and self-esteem. People who need no longer worry about a roof can find a job, get an education, seek access to desperately needed health care, build their lives up out of squalor, obtain a sense of dignity and worth. Every human deserves that.

But what are we doing to bring the rights and privileges most of us enjoy to those downtrodden? I'm afraid not enough, and a great deal of it has to begin with housing. People have a tendency to procreate, I've noticed. We haven't passed a law against it. And as people reproduce, they need housing as a base from which to build their lives. Sure we have a population problem. But I believe giving everyone a fair share at a place to call home, at an education, at decent nutrition and health care, will turn procreation into a choice, not an inevitability. If, then, we no longer need to build so many homes, all the better.

Perhaps not all timber companies have the best interests of the forest at heart. But ought we abolish automobiles because we lose 50,000 people to accidents on the highways each year? No, we should work for better traffic safety. We should work for better forest health as well, and some timber interests do just that. They're responsible, using best forest management.

To me, wise use includes replenishing forests as they're found in nature, not through monoculture—one type of tree in one forest alone—which never occurs naturally. It means moving from clearcutting to selective cutting. (Selective cutting via fire—under certain conditions—has long been used by nature and Native Americans to manage forests. It aids wildlife and new growth.) Wise utilization means moving from wanton forest abuse to respect for the value and needs of our forests all the time. It means sustainable use, something we can all live with, stewardship, using only as much as we can replace in perpetuity. We must conserve the wood we cut as well. We used to use three trees for what we now produce from one. We used to have a huge screened-in structure called a Wigwam wherein we burned tons of slash. Now we conserve that slash, using it for wood products. We're all learning.

On the other hand, if we lock up too many forests for non-use, demands for wood will only increase. Okay, so let's go abroad and extract resources from other countries, some say. Keep our forests pristine. But many other countries have no forest management practices whatsoever. Take Siberia. We can devastate 1,500,000 acres in Siberia, with no plan for reforestation or wise use, or we can produce the same amount of usable timber here in the Northwest on 100,000 acres—one-fifteenth of the land. And we'll regenerate every tree we use. In Siberia we create environmental mayhem in lands which are not ours.

Is that environmentally defensible? Of course not.

In fact, the last Congressional Delegation I led was to Siberia, Central America, the Brazilian Rainforests, and Chile to be sure our global forestry policies were sustainable. With my own eyes I saw how rainforests are increasingly becoming a source of new timber as we reduce our domestic timber base. And decimating those foreign forests is one of the most egregious global environmental acts we could commit.

No one can call themselves a true environmentalist—whether they conserve our forests or not—if they blatantly ignore global forestry issues like these. It's our responsibility to wisely utilize forest resources everywhere, not just at home.

Here in Oregon today, the Bonneville Environmental Foundation, a coalition of environmental leaders, energy producers, and distributors of all kinds are working together to market and sell green power. In our first year alone, we have exceeded our ambitious goals. Through collaboration—rather than guerilla warfare—we're seeing renewable energy sources becoming available, and a new sense of positive partnership among all players.

In politics as in life, it never pays to wed oneself to one side of any issue. Doing so only contributes to our polarized politics and culture. Instead, citizen and politician alike need to focus on the center.

The center is where consensus builds, where trust and true solutions flourish. The center is where we learn our needs and desires are not mutually exclusive. And the center is where we find understanding, respect, and hope for all.

I'm still working to keep Oregon a paradise.

CHAPTER FIFTEEN

Pork and Legacies:
The Last Term and Beyond

MY LAST TERM COMMENCED WITH MY LAST CAMPAIGN WHICH WAS by far the most intense ever. Things looked great at the outset—the only enduring political news were all the Democrats who claimed no plans to run against me. In fact, there were plenty of Democrats declaring support for me. Earl Blumenauer, then city commissioner, supported me. Bob Duncan, my opponent during my first senate race, became my honorary chair. Neil Goldschmidt, Oregon's then governor, gave a tip of his hat, appearing with me at a youth rally he put together on the State Capitol lawn. The mayors of Springfield (Bill Morrisette), Eugene (Jeff Miller), Salem (Tom Neilsen), and Portland's mayor Bud Clark all added support to my candidacy. I knew my colleagues in the Democratic Party might run against me one day, but in the meantime my job was to work with them for Oregon, and we had done just that. We made a team, not adversaries.

Then came along an unknown named Harry Lonsdale.

I had met him. He owned a research lab in Bend and during a prior campaign had invited me to tour his lab and meet his staff. He visited me in Washington once as well. If we'd had a Green Party then, he would have been their candidate. He held a militant environmental perspective, especially on forestry. He advocated closing down all forests for non-utilization—no logging—and I knew we had a great difference on that issue.

For whatever reason, when Democrats said they had no candidate, Harry Lonsdale stepped up to announce he would run. He was willing to spend his own money to do so. He had a sufficient cache. His wife's father had served as a former campaign chair for me. He still supported me, as did Lonsdale's own wife. Yet we both won our primaries and faced off in the general election.

Lonsdale had a highly charged personality—frenetic, actually. The energy he exuded practically crackled in the air. Those sparks weren't necessarily well directed, but there were plenty of them. He spoke ably as well, constantly challenging me to debate. "I come home to Oregon every month," I told him, "visiting village to village and town to town. I've been doing this for 40 years. I tell people where I stand and they know me—that's my platform. I don't need a debate. You don't have a platform, or a record. Now you can go out there and tell the people where you stand as well." In fact, I'd been to 1,100 public functions in Oregon that year alone.

Frankly, I thought political debates had degenerated into political theater—a consummate farce—and Lonsdale was nothing if not theatrical. When I held a press conference at the Hilton in Portland, Lonsdale showed up. While answering questions from the press, Lonsdale indicated he had a question of his own. "No," I spoke up, "my opponent wants to ask a question but this is my press conference. If he wants a press conference of his own, he's welcome to organize one. Next question, please?" That irked Lonsdale no end.

Lonsdale served as a supreme example of the political-industrial complex. He had money, wealth, and the capacity to spend it. In fact, he spent more money on TV ads alone in September, 1990 than I had spent in all four of my prior terms. I was used to spending about the least of any senator in my campaigns. But here Lonsdale was, portraying himself as a small businessman against big government, when in fact his business had been born and bred off government funds. While fashioning himself as an environmentalist, he regularly dumped dangerous chemicals down the drain of his own lab. These chemicals killed the bacteria in his septic tank so efficiently the tank had to be drained over and over again. And guess who let us know about this? Lonsdale's former employees. They were so concerned about the situation they avoided drinking tap water at Lonsdale's lab. Incensed, they called to clue us in and Jim Towey, my legal counsel, took their sworn affidavits.

In September, Gerry Frank and Rick Rolf, my press director, came into my office looking grim. Gerry reported a poll suggesting we were in trouble. In fact, staff were already working on scripts, and I was on my way to cut commercials. Walking over to the media center I asked Rick to read the scripts to assure they were okay. He began shaking his head. Here Lonsdale positioned himself as an anti-incumbent at the same moment I was literally being positioned in a media room flanked by two flags, the Capitol in the distance, as stately and senatorial and gray-haired and incumbent-looking as possible. Assistants began applying make-up while Rick kept shaking his noggin. finally, I stood and we left the commercial before it even began.

Clearly this was the kind of campaign I hated, and now I stood in the middle of it. Antoinette and I flew to Oregon from D.C. and were immediately picked up and driven to a meeting with a full complement of savvy political advisors. Antoinette sat with her needlepoint and I beside her, watching Lonsdale's commercials for the first time. Afterward, the room fell silent. "If I believed those commercials, I wouldn't vote for me either," I finally said. Then, after another moment: "I'm ready to hit the beach and go on the counterattack."

Someone turned to Antoinette as she sat quietly with her needlepoint. "Are you ready, Mrs. Hatfield?" they asked. Loud and clear, Antoinette let us all know she was more than ready for the challenge.

By the last month of the campaign I was caught in D.C. wrangling over budget deficits and other bills. That congressional session extended longer than any since World War II and I couldn't get home to campaign until the last weeks before election day. When I finally arrived at Portland International Airport, a big man in a plaid shirt practically yelled at me. "Hatfield!" he boomed. "I want you to take the gloves off and clobber that SOB!" Somehow I mumbled my thanks then turned to search for my luggage.

The first time I spoke up against my opponent I pounded the podium in emphasis, yet felt as though I needed a shower after each
counterattack. But I stuck to the facts. I reported his stories as his
former employees had told them. I reported that Lonsdale had also
placed newpaper ads supporting Rajneeshpuram—a cultish settlement
that took over the government of the town of Antelope, then aimed to
take the Wasco County government as well. Wasco County Circuit
Judge William Hulse appeared on TV and recounted how Rajneeshees
had attempted to poison those in power, including Hulse himself. In
ways like these, we held Lonsdale accountable for his actions.

I couldn't have done it without the multi-talented people working
with us. Tom Imeson, a former staff member, came in during that last
month and devoted himself full time to our campaign. He played a
major role in organizing and nurturing our efforts, mobilizing 40,000
citizens across the state who rose to the cause. Rick Rolf was also invaluable. Gerry and Lon Fendall helped pull us through, as did the
unparalleled efforts of Paul Currcio, John Gratta, and Ed Rayhall.

One day Rick visited my house for nearly three hours to come up
with a TV ad based on my character. I'd always avoided this, always
run on the issues alone, and now I was to come up with a kernel of my
soul for public review. Personalizing a campaign was not my strong
suit. I'd seen too many do it with embarrassing results. Rick plied me
for family stories for hours, and I came up absolutely dry. finally, he
asked about my father and I offered the story of how Dad taught me
never to fear standing alone. That was it. Rick took off and wrote
through the night to get that one minute TV spot just right. He wanted
a piece of my character—a sense of why and how I stood for what I
believed—popular or not. And that ad worked.

Elaine Franklin, Bob Packwood's chief of staff, also came and devoted her vacation month to our campaign. Able and talented, she
raised money, garnered support from Packwood's constituency, and
came through in a big way. Elizabeth Furse, Oregon's first district, liberal Democratic congresswoman-to-be, spoke across the state going
straight for women's groups with her rip-roaring speeches. "Sure I don't
agree with him on abortion either," she'd say in her English lilt, "but
look how consistent he is, look at all the other things he's done for
Oregon, for women, for human rights." She knew very well who I

was—we'd created a Peace Institute together in Portland. Countless individuals deeply concerned about the outcome of the election flocked to our side, offering any support they could give, and I still appreciate each heartfelt gesture.

On the last day I was still campaigning. "I will campaign into the night to get my message out," I said, "because serving the people of Oregon in the U.S. Senate is a great privilege that I hope very much they will give me again."

On election night we gathered with family, friends, staff, and campaign officials, all with the expectation of celebrating. And celebrate we did. I was grateful to have won.

After that final campaign, I maintained my focus on benefiting my constituents as well as those across the country. Yet often, any vote a politician casts in favor of their own state is dubbed "pork." The Lawrence Welk museum in North Dakota is perennially dragged from the closet as the poorest example of pork—what in the world were our tax dollars doing creating a museum for Lawrence Welk?

In fact I hate the term "pork," but I like the idea of aiding my state. After all, that's why I went into public office. And in my last term I garnered plenty of funds for Oregon, but I didn't call it pork. I called it fervor and commitment. If I had to, I called it "beef"!

As you might imagine, the Appropriations Committee is a big place for beef. Everyone wants their pet project financed and they come to the chair to do it. I knew this committee was powerful, after all, I'd sat on it since my second term in 1972. Yet I had literally won the chairmanship—through no act of my own—overnight.

In 1980, no one even knew with surety that Reagan would take the election. So as usual on the final night, Republicans gathered in a hotel in downtown D.C. to watch returns hosted by Senator John Heinz from Pennsylvania, chairman of the Senate campaign committee. Festivities ran late of course, as polls didn't even close on the West Coast until 11p.m. Eastern Standard Time. Antoinette and I ventured downtown around 10:30 or 11:00, and Heinz ran over as soon as he spied us. "It's not happened yet," he boasted, "but I think I'll be able to call you Mr. Chairman."

I had little idea what he was referring to, or which chairmanship.

I sat as ranking Republican on the Energy and Natural Resources Committee (the old Interior Committee) and the Rules Committee, as well as Appropriations.

But I soon realized Heinz wasn't kidding.

That election created a cataclysm in politics if ever there was one. The unpredictable, unexpected, and unusual all coalesced in the election of Ronald Reagan. The outcome was an absolute coup d'etat. Blue collar Democrats sick of the misery index and double-digit inflation left their party by droves in Reagan's sweep, taking with them some of the strongest, most powerful Democrats the Senate was proud to claim. Senator Birch Bayh of Indiana lost his seat that night, as did Senator George McGovern from South Dakota, Senator Gayelord Nelson of Wisconsin, Senator John Culver of Iowa, and several others. The Republicans took the majority for the first time in several decades, but we lost some of our best friends in the process.

I went to bed that night as Chairman of Appropriations, and served from 1981-1987, and again from 1995 until I retired in 1997. But on that first morning, I woke and immediately began thinking about a 60-member committee staff and precious space—a commodity at a premium in Congress no matter how many new buildings get constructed. The Appropriations Committee space was divided between the Senate office buildings and the Capitol itself. Suddenly I had quarters in the Capitol, a Versailles-like, fantastically baroque structure complete with vaulted, arching ceilings, red carpets, and gilt everywhere. I sat in my new chair for the first time, drawing a deep breath. I had more awareness than ever of the element of power, yet I was aware of another equally mighty sensation: I had the opportunity to do greater things than I had ever dreamed of, and I was overcome with ideas of what I might now do for my constituents and the nation. Clearly, this was a defining moment.

Oregon has a history of paying more taxes than we receive in services from the federal government. We also pay more in gas taxes than are returned by the federal highway trust fund. Oregon senators before me took flack for never getting as much from the federal government as we gave. On the other end, I have taken criticism for getting too much.

My Oregon appropriations record, if you will, came in the form of appropriating billions of dollars for what I most believed in: health, education, environment, and infrastructure. I helped what we call the Hill—Oregon Health Sciences University—by appropriating funds for OHSU's Vollum Research Center, Cancer Center, Nursing school, clinical research building, and more. I voted in funds to replace the Veterans Administration Hospital and the skybridge linking it to the University campus.

There were projects off the Hill too. I helped one of our most innovative minds, Neil Goldschmidt, build his light rail system to keep countless cars off the road and fewer highways blighting our biggest city.

I joined with another essential partner in the House, Democrat Les Aucoin. What a team we made. Whether on light rail, wild and scenic rivers, the Oregon Graduate Institute, we spoke animatedly on the phone over one issue one day and another the next. When we wanted something for Oregon, Les worked on one aspect of it from his stance as a senior member on the House Appropriations Committee. I'd work on another aspect from Senate Appropriations, and once House and Senate Appropriations committees conferenced, we'd work to bring all parts together. Les calls those our salad days, when it seemed like everything we felt deeply about and worked for succeeded. Wilderness, timber contracts, what have you, we fought for Oregon. Later, I was honored to work with Congresswoman Elizabeth Furse and Governor Barbara Roberts.

Besides projects I partnered with others on, there were many individual projects I felt were vital for Oregon. Funds were appropriated for housing units, Pioneer Courthouse Square, a food innovation and processing lab, and the Oregon Coast Marine Sciences Center—the rehabilitation home to Keiko. I might add (since I've surely sounded less than enthusiastic on FDR!) I even became co-chairman, with Danny Inouye of Hawaii, of the Franklin D. Roosevelt Memorial project in Washington, D.C. I may not have always agreed with this president, but how could it be right that this man—who served our country in arguably the most devastating war in world history—not be recognized as a critical national figure? Instead, his monument stands in our nation's Capital today.

Initially I joined Appropriations because in my view a great legacy would be strengthening our infrastructures, diversifying our economy, keeping our people employed, improving our education.

And although I built buildings, they were simply tools. They increased the attraction for bright faculty and students to work in the buildings, to bring the infrastructure alive with knowledge and healing for humanity. I worked on other building blocks as well—transportation, public busing for the elderly and poor across the state, bridge building (Marion Street bridge in Salem, Ferry Street bridge in Eugene, a new bridge over the Alsea in Walport, and Portland's Terwilliger bridge), low-income housing, veterans' benefits, the arts, and community development, to name a few. We pushed to prevent cuts in federal Southeast Asian refugee aid and worked for refugee aid in general, prevented slices in national unemployment benefits, in childcare, and in legal aid. Along with Les AuCoin we helped Oregon tribes gain back their legal status, their rights, their land. To me, each dollar was a multiplier, helping the total economy of the state or nation. I couldn't have done it without the help of countless dedicated staff, public officials, and volunteers. And I am proud of every penny.

I never worried much about what people said regarding me and Appropriations. If I had, my hands would have been tied from ever doing anything. And I'd much rather be criticized for doing something than nothing. Besides, in time, criticism disappears but resources invested in the state bear fruit, improving life for all peoples. Sure some call it self-serving to channel resources to your own state. But not so with most senators I know. They're sincere, dedicated, trying to serve their constituency and their nation. That was my goal as well.

And if we should come up with a cure for Alzheimer's disease in Oregon because we now have the labs and brilliant researchers to do so, that magic will span far beyond our borders and I'll be most pleased of all. When we make great discoveries at OHSU—as we so often do—everyone brags about it as much as possible. Suddenly, no one complains it was related to "pork."

In the long run the intention of a senator makes little difference if the outcome is valuable. Even so, it's few senators that conspire every move to insure their own re-election. Rather, a politician who performs her/his task well, with accountability and integrity, is the only politician who deserves re-election.

Ultimately, it's the little things that give me my greatest rewards. My staff spent more time helping solve social security problems for the elderly, immigrant problems, and community needs. It was the case work I loved most, though nary a news story or profile came of it. Cal Larson with Epidermolysis Bullosa is an example, as is a young immigrant woman from Southeast Asia. Her visa had been rejected several times, and she wrote to us in desperation. We took her letter to then Secretary of State Schultz under Reagan and brought her to the U.S. When she came off that plane I was so glad to see her that I hugged her as if she were my own daughter, this young woman I had never met.

Or there was the time my staff and I worked to get a poor young woman home from a Turkish jail. Have you ever tried to deal with another nation's bureaucracy in addition to your own? I was dogged on this one. I went to Ankara myself and spoke to the government. I went to both ambassadors—theirs and ours—and pursued every avenue I knew. I didn't condone the woman's actions—she had been charged with drug smuggling—but nevertheless a Turkish jail is not a pleasant place for any human being. I wanted to transfer her here. I even spoke with the Turkish president, who flatly turned me down. The woman's mother lay dying in the U.S., but that held no sway, nor did the fact that her mother did pass away—I couldn't get her home for the funeral. It was a total deadlock and I kept at it. After years she finally received a reduced sentence and came home.

I also loved to make simple phone calls to move a project along. I once helped Mother Teresa create a ministry in Anacostia, one of the poorest sections in D.C., after her application became lost in the tangles of bureaucracy. I helped two Oregon men, both deported during the last gasp of McCarthyism, return to America after a decade and a half. One had lived in Fnland for years, unable to speak the language, living in a small room, abandoned by his ex-wife, completely bereft. We did what we could and both men came home.

I enjoyed personally calling high school students, wanting to be the one to tell them they'd won a Senate scholarship to travel and study abroad. I once dedicated a bridge in Astoria when an elderly, not

100 percent cogent man approached, telling me he'd lived there a lot longer than I had. I handed him my ground-breaking shovel and stood aside. In sadder times, I helped a woman who had three sons, two already in service in Vietnam. The same day they told her that her second son had been killed (as had her first), her third son received orders to report for duty. We got an extension for him initially, then kept him home for good. I love that minutiae, those tiny, helping things, as much as I love huge projects for Oregon.

We gave our time, our energy, and wept our tears. We enjoyed our joyful experiences, too. Letters we received saying the writer "didn't think anyone cared," or that their "faith in government had been restored," were the most gratifying of all. That, to me, is the soul of politics. The casework: bridging the gap between citizens and their government.

That was the heartbeat of our office. And there was never a public dedication, never a ribbon-cutting ceremony profiling any of that. No name in granite. Instead something priceless forged—true and enduring human connections.

I've spoken much about my last years, including the Balanced Budget Amendment and my private meeting with Bob Dole, but there are incidents I failed to mention. My relationship with Ronald Reagan, for example, was nothing if not intriguing. As ranking Republican on the Rules Committee, Clairborne Pell, Democrat from Rhode Island, asked that I chair Reagan's inauguration activities—the entire schedule of state affairs, right down to the details of who would sit where.

A year or so later, we invited President Reagan and Nancy to our Georgetown home for dinner. All the standard preparations and security preceded them. A command center was set up—presto!—in our basement, and police were posted on the street. Just before their visit, a snowstorm blanketed D.C. Like a military training mission, snow plows sped over to remove every car in front of our house, carry each away, and leave the street clear for the presidential entourage. Shortly before the Reagans arrived, a major power outage pulled darkness down upon our neighborhood. Antoinette cooked by candlelight with natural gas, and Reagan's chef shadowed her every action. Antoinette was cool in that darkness, in that candlelit heat. Nothing flustered her throughout almost 50 years of politics. Nothing does. Unless we're talking boa constrictors, which right now, we're not.

In any case, my relationship with Reagan wasn't always friendly, and our disputes most often centered around the federal deficit. He loved to dump on "my" Appropriations Committee as the player responsible for "his" rising deficit. Meanwhile I, finally chairman of Appropriations, had felt ebullient at the prospect of sending dollars to social programs in desperate need. To my great disappointment I soon learned working with the Reagan administration wouldn't exactly be that way. I had to fight every minute to maintain people programs at all, while he fought just as mightily against my efforts to cut his defense budget. I met with him at the White House on countless occasions, persuading him not to veto yet another Appropriations bill. There were other issues between us as well—I fought strongly to ban arms aid to Nicaragua and El Salvador's military juntas, and butted heads with Reagan over his opposition to civil rights legislation, timber management, sustainable energy issues, food for the hungry, and his efforts to sell off Bonneville Power Administration to private vendors, to name a few. But I worked hard for common ground. Once, when he and Secretary of State George Schultz kept the door open for Indochinese refugees, I quipped, "I'm happy there's an area where I can be in agreement with my president." Unfortunately, those times were too rare and the deficit and Reagan's penchant for defense spending were long-standing issues dividing us.

Sometimes meeting together even became contentious. When I went with Appropriations Staff Director Keith Kennedy to the White House for a meeting in President Reagan's cabinet room, we were to meet with Senator Howard Baker, the majority leader, Senator Bob Dole, then chair of the finance Committee, Senator John Tower, chair of the Armed Services Committee, and others. But we experienced a bit of a snafu. All staff had gathered in the reception area in the west wing of the White House, and as the meeting time arrived, staff were told this was a members-only meeting and they were to cool their heels outside. As I walked into the cabinet room I immediately noticed Keith's absence. "Where's our staff director and everyone else's staff?" I asked.

"This is a senate members-only meeting," I was told. "No staff allowed."

I pointed to the Head of Congressional Relations. "Well, you're staff," I announced, turning to Jim Baker, Reagan's chief of staff. "You're staff too. If the president can have his staff, I don't see why we can't have ours."

A courier walked back out to the reception room to graciously invite all staff members in.

Another time, Defense Secretary Cap Weinberger, Howard Baker, Tip O'Neill (then Speaker of the House), and I were present—among others—at one of our regular leadership meetings with Reagan. The president had reason to be testy with me—I was never in any particular rush to handle his arms requests. Instead, I'd reject them outright as often as I could. I called his Star Wars scenario a "terrifying proposal," and vocally dubbed programs in the Pentagon "technical nightmares, riddled with inefficiencies." I referred to Reagan's billion dollar defense budget increases as "neither sound nor fiscally responsible," and called deficit projections "a floating crap game." I played hard ball against him in his struggle to produce chemical weapons, suggested that our policy had to be so rigid so that—God forbid!—peace not get in the way of war. I even politely offered that Reagan was "about to shatter accepted notions of the impossible by attempting to save the Earth by militarizing space; eliminate nuclear weapons while producing them with abandon; and assuming that we will reduce the deficit in the process." In 1988 I was still spouting basically the same message, saying the administration's approach was to "shoot first and ask questions later."

I wasn't aiming my remarks personally at Reagan, of course. I'd fought military build-up in the budget long before Reagan ever came to power. But I suppose it must have felt like a private affront. In his eight years I led a coalition to cut his military budget by $100 billion, instead using those dollars to enrich energy, education, jobs, and all the social programs I loved. I wanted money where it belonged, for the people. And Reagan? Reagan went around "reminding" us that there were no homeless people in America. He wanted to starve, choke, and strangle those life-enhancing programs I held dear. The Departments of Energy, Education, Health and Human Services, and Housing? Eviscerate them, Reagan proposed. Abolish all their funding and request increases only for military spending. By 1990 we were still the number one country in weapons of destruction, yet 49th in literacy. That didn't sound like superpower status to me.

We sat together in Reagan's cabinet room on this particular day and Reagan launched into a typical attack against Appropriations. It was all our fault the budget was out of balance, he stated. The fact was, even then Ronald Reagan was quite a charming man. When he finished, I spoke. "Mr. President," I began, "the Appropriations Committee appropriated expenditures amounting to less than you requested. If we'd approved your proposal, the budget would be even further out of balance."

Cap Weinberger whispered into Reagan's ear and Reagan listened for his signal. "Well," he straightened up, "Cap tells me you've simply increased social spending at the expense of military spending."

"Yes, that's absolutely right," I concurred.

Reagan said something then that floored me. He offered the distinct impression he believed military spending did not contribute to the federal deficit. Military spending was somehow exempt. To Ronald Reagan, the only things getting us into trouble were those social programs that literally kept our people alive.

In my final term, one of my last accomplishments held special meaning to me. As a vigilant opponent of one person wielding too much power, I have long been a foe of the presidential line item veto. After Congress gave Clinton the line item veto, senators Patrick Moynihan and Bob Byrd and I protested the line item's constitutionality with an amicus brief to the Supreme Court. After us, a community in New York showed they had been harmed by the line item and the Supreme Court upheld their challenge. The line item became history rather than reality, a singular but critical example of the vital role an independent judiciary plays in our political system.

Long after, and now a private citizen, I'm here to report life exists after the Senate. Retirement, in fact, is not equivalent to idleness. I knew my last term was just that—my last—for several reasons. first, I knew I'd have many more opportunities for a second career at the age of 74 than 80. By 80 opportunities grow highly limited, as many already had at 74. Most corporation boards have strict age limits, and although a powerful utility and an international board asked me to join, I knew their rules. "Did you know I'm 74?" I asked. "Oh!" they backed away. It would be hard enough starting over at 74. 80 might be too late.

Secondly, I looked at Strom Thurmond in the Senate in his 90s, and knew I didn't want to be in the Senate chamber at his age—he'll be 100 by the end of his present term! I wanted to leave when hands were still clapping, rather than when hands were being used to shoo me out the door. Senator Abe Ribicoff, the Democrat from Connecticut had proven a great example of that philosophy, and a role model since I met him at my very first governors' conference in the late '50s. After several senate terms he easily could have won another six years, yet instead chose to step aside with integrity.

Finally, I wasn't about to spend the following six years raising money due to the political-industrial complex. Asking for funds was something I never enjoyed, and I wouldn't spend my last term doing so. I hated imposing myself on others, and I was told I'd have to spend three hours a day throughout my term raising funds. That's what the political-industrial complex has done to our system. Three hours a day on the next election, every day throughout a six-year term. Can you imagine how impossible it is for our two-year congressmen and women to accomplish anything but fundraising? What a gross caricature of representative government our political system has become.

So I enjoy my career now, even though I often say I have flunked retirement. I sit on a dozen boards and foundations, and am particularly passionate about those dealing with health, the environment, history, and of course, human needs of any kind. I love to spend time with friends and family, at the beach, in the city. We own a duplex at the Oregon Coast and that's our refuge, our home. We also rent a Portland condominium on the Willamette River, where last year we witnessed two bald eagles hatching and raising three eaglets.

And I maintain my great loves. My wife, my family, my friends top the list. And so does my work. I'm back in the classroom—a great joy to me before my career in politics, and a great joy now. There are many agendas a politician never completes as government change can be so intractably slow. In the classroom, however, I see fire in the minds and hearts of these young people and I know there is hope for us, as a people and as a nation.

I also still love to garden, as I did as a child alongside my parents and grandmother. Visko calls me "a regular Johnny Appleseed" for all the trees I've planted. I planted cherry trees at one home in D.C., and now they're huge. I planted a dawn redwood at the Capitol that's several stories high. I marvel at nature's wonder.

Another great love are my books. I've always been known as a bibliophile and I hope, a lover of knowledge. I read books and collect them, all kinds. Limited editions, inscribed editions, manuscript copies. I have a manuscript edition of Teddy Roosevelt's book on Winning the West. Included is an actual page of manuscript in the author's own hand. Historian Edmund Morris wrote a biography of Teddy Roosevelt and, knowing I had the former book, gave me a manuscript edition of his Roosevelt biography. I've collected many books personally autographed by 11 presidents and several world leaders, including Abba Eban, Margaret Thatcher, King Juan Carlos of Spain, and the Emperor and Empress of Japan.

And please don't even get me started on my presidential biographies. All I'll say about them is that my interest in presidential history is so well known that I was invited to write the forward for re-publication of Herbert Hoover's biography on Woodrow Wilson, and also wrote the forward for the Library of Congress' compendium of presidential writings. And, when President and Mrs. Reagan came to dinner at our house in that snowstorm, I was concerned Reagan had no plans for presidential biography. To keep conversation lively, I also invited Arthur Link, biographer of Woodrow Wilson, Frank Freidel, FDR's official biographer, George Nash, Herbert Hoover's biographer, and the man who wrote Theodore Roosevelt's biography, as I mentioned: Edmund Morris. That dinner triggered the selection of Morris as biographer by Reagan.

Because of my passion for books, I've fought against each and every administration striving to delete a modest, library construction line item. It was also exciting to help fund Oregon's Portals computer database system, linking the state's libraries with many educational and civic institutions. Library funding is one of the most important pieces of legislation we have, providing seed money for local communities to create or expand their own library and its technology. In our own state, libraries in Stayton, Philomath, Drain, Tualatin, and elsewhere have taken advantage of these monies, as well as libraries across the nation. I insisted those funds always remain. Libraries are a great equalizer of people—where else can we enjoy each and every cross section of our culture peacefully mingling together, as we always should? Libraries also provide a critical source of knowledge for all. And God knows we need knowledge—a vital link to our very survival.

My interest in books and libraries is neverending, and it began even prior to my foray into politics. Yet politics depends on nothing if not books—knowledge and history. If we lack access to information and knowledge, we can never boast a free people. When the Former Soviet Union was still the USSR, some lauded their efforts for literacy among their peoples. Sure their citizens learned to read, but they had access only to what the government wanted them to read. There's a lot of junk out there that goes by the name of literature that I don't believe in and would never buy, but I'd never take away anyone else's right to read it, either.

Most critically, reading, knowledgeable citizens create an obvious link to enhanced political representation. They choose candidates and issues wisely, wielding far more political strength. This cycles delightfully back. Representatives owe enhanced accountability to their informed and knowledgeable public. Thus we all win.

Knowledge, learning, a true sense of history. They benevolently offer doors to peace time and time again. In knowledge and history lay our greatest weapons, our greatest true power.

Even in retirement I carry my passions with me wherever I go.

Upon retirement, we decided to leave D.C., not allowing the temptations of lobbies and money to be made to capture our senses.

Primarily, Antoinette and I felt so strongly we'd been well treated by the people of Oregon that we wanted to reciprocate. I always said as soon as I no longer had a vote in the federal government I'd come home, and so we did. We wanted to re-establish our roots. Friends came to me, like James DePriest, conductor of the Oregon Symphony. He was first to ask me onto his foundation board, and I accepted. What a great opportunity to give back.

Other friends approach and I accept as often as I can. I do anything for a friend or former constituent, and hope to continue to do so as long as I draw breath. Friends never fled me even in the darkest days, nor do I flee them.

I might do things differently in my life if I had it all to do over—I suspect we all would. But I never regret a moment of my time. I treasure a satisfying sense of accomplishment. Peace of mind and a belief I did everything with the quality I respect most: integrity.

And what do I wish, finally? I wish a life full of blessings on every citizen—every mother, daughter, wife; father, son, husband.

That is my greatest wish for all of us who make up this precious land.

The Seeds of Spirituality, The Call to Revolution

"In the souls of its citizens will be found the likeness of the state which if they be unjust and tyrannical then will it reflect their vices but if they be lovers of righteousness confident in their liberties so will it be clean in justice, bold in freedom."
**Engraved outside the governor's office in the
Oregon State Capitol Rotunda**

*P*OWER CORRUPTS—OR SO I WAS RAISED IN THE ANABAPTIST TRADI-
tion. Political, ecclesiastical, economic, or social power ought all be viewed with wariness and suspicion—and we need look no further than history to see it.

I often speak of religion and politics in the classroom, and here's a bit of theocracy 101. I'll keep it brief and simple.

I speak here of Christianity, as I know its strengths and foibles best. At the turn of the last millenium, the first apostolic followers of Jesus created a counterculture. They became separatists, refusing to bow to Caesar whenever Caesar declared himself God. They paid taxes (it's true, taxes have been around nearly as long as death), but they refused military service. How could they harm any human when Jesus said to love one's enemies? Standing for their beliefs and defying government often constituted the highest price: execution.

Jumping ahead to the fourth century, Constantine built his politi-

238

cal power base and watched the Christian community grow. Soon he sought to add this emerging group to his empire. He made a deal with the Christians that, to me, has been the millstone around Christianity's neck ever since.

By now Christianity had an organized church and Constantine offered them a bargain: their own ecclesiastical court as well as the opportunity—finally—to own land. Such a deal! The church leapt at the offer and in turn, Constantine declared Rome a Christian nation. Rome marched its throngs to the river for mass baptisms, and now the church and Constantine both acquired the power they desired.

There was only one little glitch. Constantine threatened excommunication to any who abandoned their weapons. Loving one's enemies was no longer the fashion. Instead, Constantine proclaimed those who fought with him were true Christians, fighting for primacy over heathens the world over. Fighting against barbarians meant saving the world for Christianity. Thus grew Constantine's holy war—and the religiously-sanctioned war for the Christians.

Fast forwarding to the Reformation during the late Middle Ages, the Puritans became the latest renegades, protesting against the Anglican state church of Great Britain. Puritans left England to seek religious freedom on our shores, establishing the Massachusetts Bay Colony. All Puritans subscribed to the same religious ideals and soon power corrupted once again. They decided theirs was the right way. The only way. One of their great leaders, John Cotton, wanted to "make the Lord our governor," proclaiming the church was related to the commonwealth as the soul is to the body. He demanded theocracy and expected all to conform.

Soon the inevitable occurred: Puritans ran out all non-Puritans who had come to these shores for identical reasons as they—for the sake of religious freedom. Jews, Quakers, and Baptists were prominent among those banished. As with the Romans, time did not bode well for the Puritans. Things deteriorated over time in Massachusetts Bay, and witch burning is just one egregious case in point.

One of the banished ones, a pious Anglican named Roger Williams, vocally challenged the Puritans. Among other things, Williams said the King of England had no right to grant a charter to Massachusetts Bay as the King was not its rightful owner—the Native Americans were. To the Puritans, Williams was a dangerous subversive. They told him to leave, but said he could keep safe refuge through the winter as his wife was pregnant. However, he had to keep his mouth shut and he simply could not keep that end of the bargain. So they evicted him in the deep of winter and he stumbled several days through an impermeable snowstorm. Finally, he found haven among the Massasoit Indians and subsequently purchased land from them.

There, in 1636, he founded Providence, Rhode Island. He named his city after God, and began government by the will of the majority. Yet the majority ruled only in civil matters. His colony was founded on complete religious liberty.

Williams had it right. The cornerstone of all our freedoms is freedom of religion. All rights issue from this one, as spirituality—one's individual faith—is such a personal liberty that it cannot and should not ever be adjudicated, quantified, or interfered with by any government. Freedom of speech and all other civil liberties issue from freedom of religion. And freedom of religion means one has freedom to be non-religious as much as freedom to be religious, I might add.

Not much has changed today since Williams' time, and I still hold grave concerns regarding politics and religion. Joining the two as one only ends up corrupting both—usually to religion's detriment. Take the mid-70s, for example, when the CIA used missionaries for intelligence gathering around the world. Can anyone possibly think that's a reasonable, spiritual use of a religious community? Of course not. In 1976, as CIA director, George Bush responded by stopping the practice. Yet too often, as it did in this case, religion ends up as some kind of strange adjunct to government—turning faith into "civil religion" at best, and sheer idolatry at worst—rather than what religion is meant to be, a personal living out of faith teachings. Thus, religion loses its mission and fails miserably in its duty.

So today, as I look at those who believe we should have a Christian state, I know they are tragically wrong. Any conservative triumvirate of religion, the military, and the state is doomed to fail. I need look no further than the Holy Roman Empire, the Puritans, or countless other examples I didn't detail. Theocracy didn't work for them then, and anything even remotely like it certainly won't work for us now.

In my life, religion is a powerful matter. It offers peace of mind, a sense of destiny, an understanding of my role as part of humanity, all beautifully exemplified by the life of Jesus. What I find there greatly impacts me. It's my way, and it's perfect for me. I'm delighted to share its treasures with any who would ask. But I respect every other way as well. I will not judge other forms of spirituality, nor dissuade their followers. We each have the right of religious and spiritual freedom, as diverse as those religions may be.

Thus, I don't believe in prayer in the public schools, and I am as ecumenical as I can be, especially whenever a good cause beckons—civil rights, hunger, housing, or social justice. In the Senate, I often attended mass several mornings a week because the Catholic church opened its doors early enough for me to do so, whereas the Protestant church did not. There was no synagogue nearby—they have early morning services as well—or I might have been found quietly praying there.

If others wish to speak of their faith, they have that right. We all enjoy freedom of speech. I may not agree with their doctrine, but everyone has the right to influence policy—religious or political—in the direction of their choice; to advocate or to evangelize. The most vocal and vehement, however, might do well to learn that ardent advocates are often less than sensitive to the needs of listeners. Thus, they may minimize their own impact.

Even the "religious right" has every liberty to believe as they do. I may not agree with their political agenda, but so be it—I can disagree with their agenda as a fellow citizen.

I do, however, become gravely concerned about the message they communicate relating to Christianity—as if acceptance of their political agenda automatically defines a true Christian. That's simply spurious, because true Christianity means walking one's life in line with Jesus' teachings. Love, reconciliation, forgiveness are all primary. There's nothing in the Gospel that states I must accept school prayer or support war. Being pro-life, for example, does not make me a Christian. To identify any political agenda with Christianity is a miscommunication of the Gospel, plain and simple. Instead, we would all do well to infuse our personal, spiritual ethics into politics, rather than bringing more politics into our religion.

To me, spirituality means having faith and doing works. Message and mission. Reaching out to people with compassion and love, bringing the Gospel alive. This has always been my goal and my work, even if it could never be neatly pegged by any facet of the religious community.

Many ask how I came to my faith, and I suppose I was born to it. I grew up in an enculturated Christian environment, went to Sunday school, joined the church at 13. But Christianity was rote, with no particular relevance to my everyday life.

After World War II, I knew I had a greater responsibility, as one who was spared, to live out my faith in relation to God. I came home with new objectives. I felt an obligation to effect policy, to carry the message home—especially after Hiroshima—that this should never happen again.

And as dean of students at Willamette, when I noticed a Christian renewal among many students, I witnessed an unbelievable change in their lifestyles. Many became more serious about their studies and their lives, sharing with other students, showing compassion, reaching out. These young people lived their religious commitment and reflected it. They weren't self-righteous. Spirituality simply permeated their every act.

One of these students, Douglas Coe, came to my office. I had been challenging students to work out their own political philosophy, and not simply imitate one's parents or community. This student asked me to define my own religious philosophy. After stating the Golden Rule, I got nowhere. I was appalled to find I had not defined any religious philosophy, and I wanted to articulate one. I knew I needed more than a Sabbath faith, and I could say I had an awakening. I committed myself anew to the proposition that if Jesus was worthy enough to follow and acknowledge, he was worthy of emulation, of faith in action. Jesus, too, had challenged institutionalized religion in his time, by offering commentary on the Pharisees and Saducees. I liked that. Institutionalized religion has often served as an impediment to spiritual seekers rather than facilitator.

I took on my commitment, trying to live out Jesus' ideals. This offered a far more liberated life—more forgiving, loving, and inclusive—though I certainly can't say I have perfected any of these lofty traits. I miss the mark many times, yet hope my conscience—a great barometer—is sensitive enough to know I missed, demanding action to reconcile or correct my error.

And though Antoinette and I make time for our devotions each morning, I strive not to wear my religion on my sleeve. Instead I try to let my actions, attitudes, deeds, even my body language reflect those ideals that attracted me to the Gospel in the first place.

I hold a deep respect for all great religious truths, and Christianity, as I said, is simply my way. Professionally, it helped me realize the aisle was no barrier in my work, that arbitrary labels between Republican and Democrat were just that—arbitrary. Labels are never important in a spiritual context—the heart is. Labels can be divisive, particularly in politics where tension and debates over issues ensue, and labels such as conservative, moderate, liberal, or right wing are thrown about as if they were swords.

In truth, we all belong to the human race—children, adults, women, men, all cultures, the poor, the wealthy, the marginalized and the high profile. Each group has equal claim to this land. And under our clothes, our uniforms, our titles and identities, there lies one unity: a human heart fundamental to us all.

And since, thank God, you cannot legislate the hearts or minds of any people, I believe a spiritual renaissance is critical to those who make up our nation. By spiritual renaissance I mean revolution, a grassroots revolution sparking within each heart, leading us in new directions that, for instance, can lead to harmonious relationships with all those around us—rather than into repetitive bloodshed. What a culture we could create if we focused on intrinsic, loving, human values rather than consumption, selfishness, and disregard for life.

I speak of a spiritual renaissance that will probe the soul of people, affecting us socially and economically, and addressing our need to improve the quality of life for all—rather than speeding destruction of life for the entire planet. Society is decimated by hate crimes, adolescent suicides, and abuse, to name a few. Yet so much anesthetizes the human conscience and heart. When a crowd watches a poor soul on a high ledge contemplating jumping, and responds with a chant of "jump,

jump, jump!" or when an individual walks by a poverty-stricken person without a pang of conscience, we are numb, anesthetized. We're no longer outraged by crass, demeaning, dehumanizing experiences. Everything becomes sickeningly tolerable, and we rarely react with righteous indignation. We need open our hearts once more to experience outrage, to reach forth a hand to fellow humans rather than simply wringing our hands with the abject plea of terrible social problems. Undergirding all these dilemmas, I believe, lies a simple lack of spiritual sensitivity.

I'm serious about revolution, and I believe we need to activate ourselves now, using our healthy power in forging change and advancing the way—just to choose one example—that our government misguidedly expends resources.

But change must come from within—government cannot do it all. Yet gratefully, government can and will respond to a changing voice of the people. Then they, too, will begin recognizing social, educational, housing, or nutritional needs, and even begin fulfilling the human soul through expanded arts and culture.

We, the citizenry, are not a docile body. We wield more power than we know and we must activate it. The guarantee of our democracy is an alert, assertive, dynamic citizenry. That's the only key to making our nation its best, and we must do more. Sure we respond to the needs of refugees, but what of being alert and involved enough to challenge the policy that created refugees to begin with? Sure we pay taxes, but what if it means prioritizing our taxes for the poor or outcast? We must be serious enough in our own lives and behavior to reform faulty policies that have been tolerated far too long.

John Adams once said, "But what do we mean by the American revolution? Do we mean the war? The Revolution was effected before the war commenced. The Revolution was in the minds and hearts of the people." I'm often questioned as to how to create a contemporary revolution in the hearts and minds of the people, and there is no simple formula. Yet I believe we can each revive ourselves spiritually, in our hearts. Then we'll be unable to suppress the humane, right action that flows forth.

I believe there's a hunger in each human heart for knowledge and for God. This hunger manifests in as many ways as there are individuals, and this is as it should be. If a spiritual seed is to be enlivened, it must be nurtured first in the individual soul. This multiplies exponentially to our families, our groups, our associations, whereby demands for reform and change in our ailing society evolve as naturally as flowers in spring.

Slavery provides an excellent example in the last century. In the pulpits of the North, sermons grew stating enough was enough, that the North could no longer benefit from low-cost cotton picked through the anguish of slaves. Today we could do well to heed the message again, to prevent sweat shops in foreign lands which create our treasured consumer products, to stop child labor. Instead we turn away, buying objects as we choose. During slavery the voice of conscience did not quell, it kept erupting. This is evil, this is wrong, it whispered. Spirituality had its role in abolishing slavery, as it has in so many things.

In this century when orphanages were established, when the working classes were downtrodden into squalor, people became outraged by poverty of the poor and richness of the rich. Change fomented within the people, bubbling up. Public leadership arose to lead the charge. Trade unions and religious bodies took up the call.

But sometimes, institutionalized religious bodies are the last to become involved. Recall the squalid conditions in the coal mines of West Virginia, when the secular saints of trade unions addressed the outrage of conditions wherein workers toiled. The mine owners owned houses, stores, churches, and those who stood in pulpits knew who paid their bills. There were countless sermons intended to maintain the status quo, preaching on the text of "the poor we will always have among us," rather than preaching righteous indignation. But the church awakened finally, after prodding by the unions.

Religious bodies would do well to join hands more often with those who identify a righteous cause, especially if clergy are not the first to see the cause themselves.

Define your own spiritual commitment. Encourage your conscience. Use loving spirituality to infuse your personal, public, and political acts. Take advantage of spiritual stewardship when dealing with political issues such as the environment, the needs of humans, the dangers of war. Demonstrate commitment by actions which address the needs of humans, not actions which destroy. Find like-minded friends, encourage one another and build support as you would a living cell. Your spirit will multiply as naturally as the cells within us all.

In the process, you'll experience, I hope, a dethronement of ego and self, a focus on others, a realization like John Donne's, that "each man's death diminishes me." You'll feel outrage, uneasiness, all an impetus to change. These transmute to a vision for right action, a positive revolution in company with others. Not a mass movement—revolution never is. Instead a determined, well focused and articulate minority is the path to healthy change.

Historically, this is how it has always been. Any passion that's wrought positive change in the world encompasses heart and spirit, and that's why I call it spiritual revolution.

People working toward a higher good—moved by commitment, truth, and vision—will change our world for the better.

May we all activate our inner seed of spirit, each one of us. Together we will build a nation stronger than its military, mightier than its economic institutions, more powerful than its very culture. A nation—a people—exemplifying true liberty.

And in turn may we each reap the greatest gift of all: a heart free from hate and discrimination, a heart replete with love.

INDEX

Against the Grain was supported by generous support from

Oregon Health Sciences University, (Dr. Peter Kohler, President)

Oregon State University, (Dr. Paul Risser, President)

Willamette University (Dr. M. Lee Pelton, President)